BUSY at MATHS

6

Sixth Class

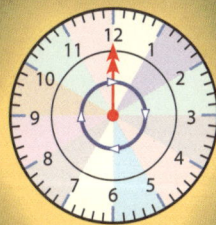

Maths for Primary Schools

Orla Murtagh • Claire Leane • Tom Roche • Martin Kennedy
General Editor: Kevin Barry

Published by

CJ Fallon
Ground Floor – Block B
Liffey Valley Office Campus
Dublin 22

First Edition April 2015
This Reprint July 2018

ISBN: 978-0-7144-2071-4

© Orla Murtagh, Claire Leane, Tom Roche, Martin Kennedy
General Editor: Kevin Barry

Printed in Ireland by
Turner Print Group
Earl Street
Longford

BUSY at MATHS 6

Sixth Class

Introduction

Busy at Maths 6 provides the most effective **problem-solving** strategies to ensure that pupils are exposed to **real-life maths** in the classroom.

The series encourages **collaborative learning** and **pair/small group work**, and is supported by excellent **digital interactives** and **tutorials** for use on the interactive whiteboard.

Busy at Maths provides the latest teaching methods for primary schools. It embodies sound **constructivist** principles and draws clear links with the Project Maths approach used in secondary schools.

Busy at Maths 6 includes the following elements:

- A Pupil's Book

- A Shadow Book

- Integrated digital classroom resources

- An Individual Pupil Profile Term Assessment Record for each pupil

- An extensive Teacher's Resource Book for each class, including:

  - Fortnightly teaching schemes
  - 100 Photocopiable Masters to consolidate learning
  - Home/School Links
  - A wide selection of activities and games to encourage the constructivist approach

Contents

Chapter 1: Look back

1. Write the numbers shown on each abacus.

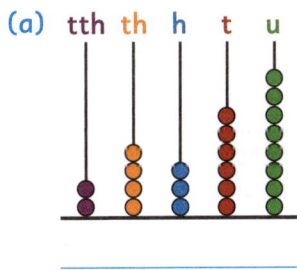

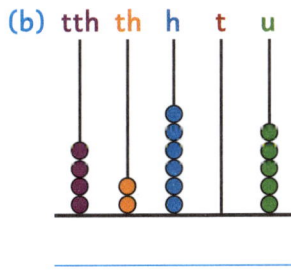

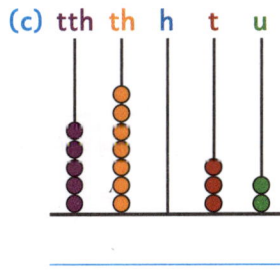

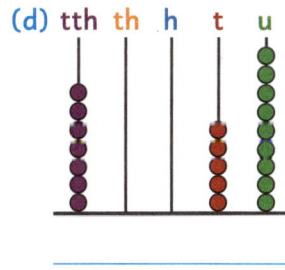

   (a) tth th h t u   (b) tth th h t u   (c) tth th h t u   (d) tth th h t u

   _____   _____   _____   _____

2. Show the following numbers on an abacus.

   (a) 12,516   (b) 19,207   (c) 27,900   (d) 40,825   (e) 85,074

3. Write the value of the <u>underlined</u> digit in each of these numbers.

   (a) 18,723   (b) 39,476   (c) 58,065   (d) 61,389   (e) 94,879

   (f) 42,365   (g) 54,186   (h) 63,007   (i) 75,306   (j) 80,609

4. Match.

   (a) Thirty-four thousand seven hundred and ten •   • 18,942

   (b) 50,000 + 4,000 + 300 + 20 + 8 •   • 13,017

   (c) 70,200 + 341 •   • 34,710

   (d)
tth	th	h	t	u
1	8	9	4	2
   •   • 48,574

   (e) Thirteen thousand and seventeen •   • 70,541

   (f) 68,574 − 20,000 •   • 54,328

5. Round these numbers to the nearest 10, 100 and 1,000.

	Number	Nearest 10	Nearest 100	Nearest 1,000
(a)	532			
(b)	1,318			
(c)	4,365			
(d)	5,894			

	Number	Nearest 10	Nearest 100	Nearest 1,000
(e)	12,086			
(f)	37,849			
(g)	42,951			
(h)	86,698			

6. Make the **largest** and **smallest** numbers using all 5 digits each time.

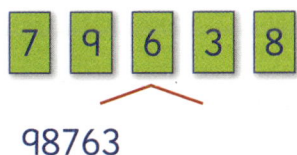

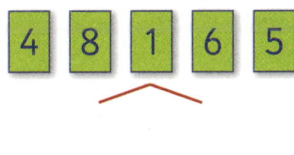

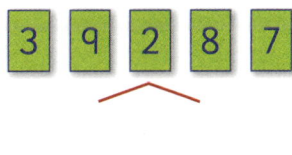

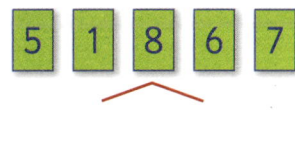

   7 9 6 3 8   4 8 1 6 5   3 9 2 8 7   5 1 8 6 7

   98763 _____   _____   _____   _____

7. Write the following number words in figures.

   (a) Nine hundred and seventeen thousand.   (b) Thirty-four thousand six hundred and seven.

Look back

1. Write the correct name of each **2-D shape**.

| trapezium | parallelogram | pentagon | octagon | hexagon | rhombus |

(a)   (b)   (c)   (d)   (e)   (f)

2.
(a)
```
  23,105
+ 45,623
```
(b)
```
  49,876
- 25,342
```
(c)
```
  32,437
+ 24,548
```
(d)
```
  78,563
- 36,427
```
(e)
```
  46,375
+ 21,463
```

3.
(a)
```
  89,428
- 37,295
```
(b)
```
  35,945
+ 52,634
```
(c)
```
  75,386
- 23,774
```
(d)
```
  46,879
+ 35,748
```
(e)
```
  92,315
- 37,659
```

4.
(a)
```
  13,246
  24,530
+ 41,213
```
(b)
```
  31,454
  24,016
+ 42,537
```
(c)
```
  32,437
  34,253
+ 10,475
```
(d)
```
  20,435
  45,812
+ 23,541
```
(e)
```
  34,564
  25,378
+ 27,853
```

5. Write the correct name of each **3-D shape**.

| cone | square pyramid | triangular prism | cylinder | octahedron | tetrahedron |

(a)   (b)   (c)   (d)   (e)   (f)

6. Calculate the **average amount** of money spent per day by each child over the weekend.

(a) Simona

Fri	Sat	Sun
€2·86	€4·65	€3·74

(b) Sofia

Fri	Sat	Sun
€5·47	€4·98	€6·53

(c) Rowan

Fri	Sat	Sun
€5·19	€8·56	€7·37

Challenge 1   Ship A carried 36,427 passengers one month. Ship B carried 14,876 passengers more than this during the same month. How many passengers did Ship B carry that month? _____

Challenge 2   56,134 copies of the Irish Globe newspaper were sold one day. 29,486 copies of the Irish Post were sold the same day. How many fewer copies of the Irish Post were sold? _____

Look back

1. Complete the following multiplication and division questions.

(a) 7 × 10   (b) 18 × 10   (c) 79 × 10   (d) 9 × 100   (e) 24 × 100

(f) 36 × 1,000   (g) 89 × 1,000   (h) 15·4 × 10   (i) 42·8 × 10   (j) 98·5 × 10

2. (a) 24 ÷ 6   (b) 64 ÷ 8   (c) 56 ÷ 7   (d) 48 ÷ 6   (e) 72 ÷ 9

(f) 90 ÷ 10   (g) 38·6 ÷ 10   (h) 240 ÷ 10   (i) 370 ÷ 100   (j) 780 ÷ 100

3. (a) €14·27 × 3   (b) €24·68 × 4   (c) €38·59 × 5   (d) €67·43 × 6   (e) €58·67 × 7

(f) 327 × 24   (g) 178 × 46   (h) 239 × 53   (i) 437 × 67   (j) 284 × 89

4. (a) 6)762   (b) 5)710   (c) 9)882   (d) 7)826   (e) 8)928

5. (a) 621 ÷ 23   (b) 928 ÷ 29   (c) 893 ÷ 47   (d) 952 ÷ 56   (e) 871 ÷ 67

Challenge 1 There are 25 rows of seats in a theatre. How many seats are there altogether if there are 58 seats in each row? _____

Challenge 2 A car travelled 952 kilometres on 28 litres of petrol. How far did the car travel, on average, per litre? _____

6. Write the following digital times using am or pm (analogue form).

(a) 07:35   (b) 14:16   (c) 20:46   (d) 04:29   (e) 23:38

7. Write the following analogue times (am or pm) in digital form.

(a) A quarter past 2 in the afternoon.   (b) 5 to 7 in the morning.

(c) A quarter to 8 in the evening.   (d) 25 past 12 in the afternoon.

(c) 25 to 1 in the morning.   (f) 4 minutes past 10 in the evening.

8. How many hours and minutes are there from:

(a) 8.15am to 11.25am   (b) 9.50am to 12.05pm   (c) 11.46am to 2.15pm

(d) 1.35pm to 4.52pm   (e) 6.24pm to 9.56pm   (f) 8.27pm to 11.03pm

9.

(a) hrs mins	(b) hrs mins	(c) hrs mins	(d) hrs mins	(e) hrs mins
3 24	4 52	6 53	7 32	3 49
+ 1 16	− 1 36	+ 2 46	− 4 58	+ 4 38

Challenge Liam was watching television one afternoon. He watched cartoons from 14:36 to 15:48 and sport from 4.45pm to 5.36pm.

How long, altogether, did he spend watching television? _____

3

Look back

1. Write the name of each of these angles.

| straight | reflex | obtuse | right | acute |

(a)

(b)

(c)

(d)

(e)

---

2. Write the values of the **unknown** angles.

(a)

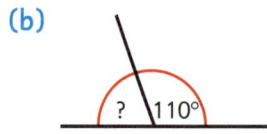

55°   45°   ?

(b)

?   110°

(c)

60°   65°   ?

(d)

120°   120°   ?

---

3. Write two equivalent fractions for each of these.

(a) $\frac{1}{2} = \frac{\square}{4} = \frac{\square}{8}$

(b) $\frac{1}{4} = \frac{\square}{8} = \frac{\square}{12}$

(c) $\frac{1}{5} = \frac{\square}{10} = \frac{\square}{15}$

(d) $\frac{1}{6} = \frac{\square}{12} = \frac{\square}{24}$

(e) $\frac{3}{4} = \frac{\square}{12} = \frac{\square}{20}$

(f) $\frac{3}{5} = \frac{\square}{15} = \frac{\square}{30}$

(g) $\frac{5}{8} = \frac{\square}{16} = \frac{\square}{24}$

(h) $\frac{5}{6} = \frac{\square}{12} = \frac{\square}{30}$

---

4. Find:

(a) $\frac{3}{4}$ of 12

(b) $\frac{2}{3}$ of 15

(c) $\frac{3}{5}$ of 20

(d) $\frac{7}{8}$ of 24

(e) $\frac{5}{7}$ of 28

---

5. Complete the following to find the **whole amount**.

(a)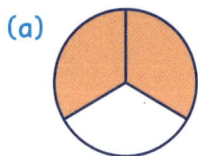

$\frac{2}{3} = 10$

$\frac{1}{3} = $ _____

$\frac{3}{3} = $ _____

(b)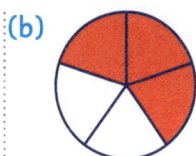

$\frac{3}{5} = 18$

$\frac{1}{5} = $ _____

$\frac{5}{5} = $ _____

(c)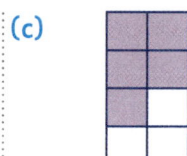

$\frac{5}{8} = 25$

$\frac{1}{8} = $ _____

$\frac{8}{8} = $ _____

(d)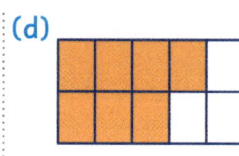

$\frac{7}{10} = 35$

$\frac{1}{10} = $ _____

$\frac{10}{10} = $ _____

(e)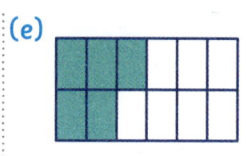

$\frac{5}{12} = 40$

$\frac{1}{12} = $ _____

$\frac{12}{12} = $ _____

---

6. Complete these **addition** and **subtraction** questions involving mixed numbers.

(a)
$$2\frac{2}{3}$$
$$+\ 3\frac{1}{6}$$

(b)
$$4\frac{3}{4}$$
$$-\ 1\frac{1}{2}$$

(c)
$$3\frac{3}{5}$$
$$+\ 2\frac{1}{10}$$

(d)
$$5\frac{9}{10}$$
$$-\ 3\frac{1}{2}$$

(e)
$$3\frac{4}{9}$$
$$+\ 2\frac{1}{3}$$

(f)
$$7\frac{8}{9}$$
$$-\ 3\frac{2}{3}$$

Challenge   Two angles of a triangle measure 47° and 62°.

What is the measure of the third angle? ☐

Look back

1. Write these **fractions** as **decimal fractions**.

   (a) $\frac{7}{10}$ = _____
   (b) $\frac{16}{100}$ = _____
   (c) $\frac{98}{100}$ = _____
   (d) $\frac{374}{1000}$ = _____
   (e) $\frac{958}{1000}$ = _____

   (f) $\frac{3}{100}$ = _____
   (g) $\frac{17}{1000}$ = _____
   (h) $\frac{306}{1000}$ = _____
   (i) $\frac{100}{1000}$ = _____
   (j) $\frac{4}{1000}$ = _____

2. Complete the following.

   (a) 2·76 + 3·07 + 4·59
   (b) 3·48 + 5·9 + 2·08
   (c) 7·8 – 2·76

   (d) 3·05 + 2·78 + 0·96
   (e) 5·83 + 0·29 + 3·09
   (f) 8 – 3·472

3. Write the following **millimetres** (mm) as **centimetres** (cm) and **millimetres**.

   (a) 24mm = _____ cm _____ mm
   (b) 38mm = _____ cm _____ mm
   (c) 47mm = _____ cm _____ mm

4. Write the following **centimetres** as **metres** in fraction form and in decimal form.

   136cm = $1\frac{36}{100}$ m = 1·36m
   (a) 43cm = _____ m = _____ m
   (b) 72cm = _____ m = _____ m

   (c) 3cm = _____ m = _____ m
   (d) 115cm = _____ m = _____ m
   (e) 295cm = _____ m = _____ m

Complete the following.

5. (a) 2·136km = _____ m
   (b) 5·065km = _____ m
   (c) 3·004km = _____ m

   (d) 0·34km = _____ m
   (e) 2·063km = _____ m
   (f) 4·3km = _____ m

6. (a) 156g = _____ kg
   (b) 2,348g = _____ kg
   (c) 7,053g = _____ kg

   (d) 3·793kg = _____ g
   (e) 5·086kg = _____ g
   (f) 3·005kg = _____ g

7. (a)   2·739 l
     + 3·485 l
     _____

   (b)   7·869 l
     – 2·587 l
     _____

   (c)   5·036 l
     + 2·987 l
     _____

   (d)   8·009 l
     – 4·563 l
     _____

   (e)   4·307 l
     + 4·998 l
     _____

8. (a) (2·85l + 376ml + 2l 375ml) × 6
   (b) $(3\frac{1}{4}$ kg + 4kg 78g + 1·732kg) × 7

   (c) $(3·042km + 2\frac{386}{1000}$ km + $4\frac{1}{4}$ km) ÷ 6
   (d) $(2\frac{3}{4}$ l + $3\frac{873}{1000}$ l + 1·985l) ÷ 8

9. Complete the following number sentences.

   (a) 6 × (3 + 5) = _____
   (b) (63 ÷ 9) × 8 = _____
   (c) 12 + (21 ÷ 3) = _____

   (d) 48 – (4 × 6) = _____
   (e) 18 + (56 ÷ 7) = _____
   (f) 8 × 9 – 30 = _____

10. Put the correct sign (<, = or >) in each oval.

   (a) 42% ◯ $\frac{4}{10} + \frac{2}{100}$
   (b) 37% ◯ $\frac{3}{100} + \frac{7}{100}$
   (c) 63% ◯ $\frac{65}{100} - \frac{3}{100}$

11. Write these **percentages** as **fractions** in their lowest terms.

   (a) 10% = _____
   (b) 20% = _____
   (c) 25% = _____
   (d) 30% = _____
   (e) 50% = _____

   (f) 15% = _____
   (g) 45% = _____
   (h) 65% = _____
   (i) 75% = _____
   (j) 85% = _____

Challenge   Tim bought his vegetables at the market. He bought $5\frac{1}{2}$ kg of potatoes, 0·37kg of cabbage and $3\frac{18}{100}$ kg of turnips. What was the total weight of his vegetables? _____ kg

A quick look back 1

1. Write the number that is 3,000 greater than 45,384. _____

2.

   €30   €20   €40

   What is the average cost of a coat?

   € _____

3. The average cost of 4 items is €9. Three of the items cost €7, €5 and €14. What is the cost of the 4th item? € _____

4. Pearse Stadium had an attendance of 25,387 for a football match. Round this number to the nearest 100. _____

5. Sarah spent 20% of her €35 buying the ball. The ball cost € _____ .

6. Write 7m 8cm as metres using the decimal point. _____ m

7. A rectangle has an area of 72cm². If one side is 8cm long, find the perimeter. _____ cm

8. Simplify this fraction:

   $\frac{8}{12} = \frac{\square}{\square}$

9. Ring the fraction that has the same value as $\frac{3}{8}$:

   $\frac{3}{4}$ $\frac{6}{16}$ $\frac{7}{24}$ $\frac{2}{3}$ $\frac{9}{10}$

10. $\frac{5}{6} \times 3 = \square\frac{\square}{\square}$

11. $\frac{4}{5}$ of a number is 12. What is 20% of the number? _____

12. Ring the digit that is in the **hundredths** place.

    $28 \cdot 579$

13. This is an _____ angle.

14. Rowan spent 25% of his €16. Cian spent 50% of his €18. Who spent more money and how much more?

    _____ by € _____

15. A hat usually sells for €16. During a sale it was reduced by 25%. What was the sale price?

    € _____

16. Ring the largest amount.

    7.34% 74% $\frac{3}{5}$ 0.734

17. Write the correct number in the frame to complete this number sentence.

    $72 \div 8 = 3 \times \square$

18. This pie chart shows the favourite sport of 36 children. How many children preferred hurling? _____

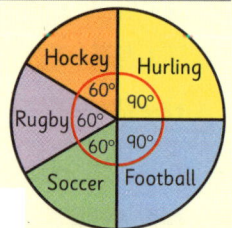

    Hockey 60°   Hurling 90°   Rugby 60°   Soccer 60°   Football 90°

19. What are the chances of throwing an even number on a die? _____ in _____ .

20. Write the next term in this sequence.

    2.4, 3.1, 3.8, 4.5, _____ .

6

Chapter 2: Place value

473,485 people visited Zooland last year. Let's record this number on the abacus and notation board.

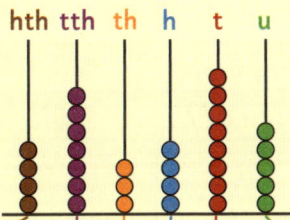

hth	tth	th	h	t	u
4	7	3	4	8	5

four + seven + three + four + eight + five
hundred thousands   ten thousands   thousands   hundreds   tens   units → (number words)

400,000 + 70,000 + 3,000 + 400 + 80 + 5 → (expanded form)

---

1. Write the numbers shown on each abacus.

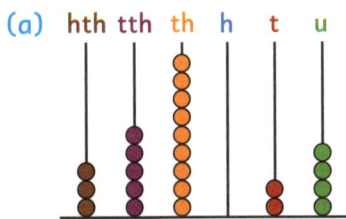

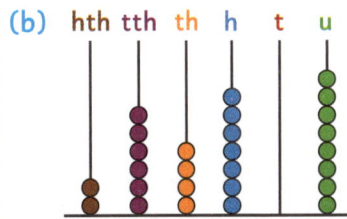

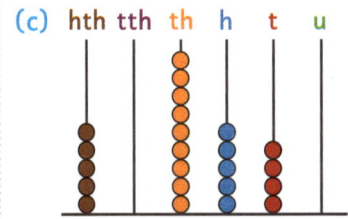

(a) hth tth th h t u

(b) hth tth th h t u

(c) hth tth th h t u

---

2. These numbers show the populations of ten towns. Show each number on an abacus.

(a) 134,268   (b) 237,591   (c) 518,462   (d) 626,419   (e) 923,056

(f) 340,263   (g) 712,304   (h) 806,102   (i) 490,380   (j) 600,594

---

3. Now write the following in (i) number words and (ii) expanded form.

(a)

hth	tth	th	h	t	u
2	3	5	6	4	1

(b)

hth	tth	th	h	t	u
8	7	9	0	1	2

(c)

hth	tth	th	h	t	u
6	4	2	7	0	2

(d) 341,095   (e) 610,204   (f) 413,007   (g) 700,514   (h) 666,666

---

4. These amounts were collected for five different charities. Write the total in each case.

(a) €300,000 + €50,000 + €4,000 + €500 + 40 + €6

(b) €500,000 + €20,000 + €300 + €60 + €5   (c) €800,000 + €2,000 + €400 + €70 + €6

(d) €600,000 + €800 + €3   (e) €700,000 + €70 + €7

---

5. Write the following number words in figures.

(a) Three hundred and forty-six thousand two hundred and fifty-three.

(b) Six hundred and twelve thousand five hundred and twenty-seven.

(c) Nine hundred and sixteen thousand.   (d) Eight hundred thousand and three.

(e) One hundred and one thousand and one.   (f) Four hundred and seven thousand.

(g) Two hundred and seventy-five thousand and eight.   (h) Five hundred and sixteen thousand.

(i) Seven hundred and one thousand.   (j) Seven hundred and eighteen thousand.

(k) Nine hundred and ninety-nine thousand and ninety-nine.   (l) Nine hundred and ninety thousand.

STRAND **Number**   STRAND UNIT/ELEMENT *Place value*
LANGUAGE *Tens, hundreds, thousands, ten thousands, hundred thousands, number words, expanded form, notation board, abacus, underlined digits, amounts, million, Roman numerals, letters*

Place value

These rugby players earned the following amounts one year.

Timmy Booth	Paul O'Donnell	Harry Bowes	Rory Goode	Simon Tabo	Bob Barney
€257,003	€330,249	€224,877	€385,505	€375,224	€289,128

Timmy Booth earned €257,003 (two hundred and fifty-seven thousand and three euro).

2 hundred thousands	5 ten thousands	7 thousands	0 hundreds	0 tens	3 units
200,000	50,000	7,000	0	0	3

1. (a) Write the salary of each of the other players (i) in words and (ii) in expanded form as above.

   (b) If the players' salaries were reduced or increased by the following amounts, calculate their yearly salaries by completing this table.

€11,000 less	€10,000 less	€1,000 less	Player	€1,000 more	€10,000 more	€10,200 more
	€247,003	€256,003	Timmy Booth	€258,003	€267,003	
			Paul O'Donnell			
			Harry Bowes			
			Rory Goode			
			Simon Tabo			
			Bob Barney			

2.
Hillcrest River Valley Ballyville Tumbleton Seaville Laketown

Town	Hillcrest	River Valley	Ballyville	Tumbleton	Seaville	Laketown
Population	246,913	631,942	924,613	462,931	329,614	629,431

(a) Write the population of each town in words.

(b) Write the value of the underlined digit in each population number.

(c) Write the towns in order starting with the town that has the largest population.

3. Match.

   (a) Six hundred and thirty-one thousand and nineteen •   • 246,913

   (b) 600,000 + 20,000 + 9,000 + 400 + 30 + 1 •   • 631,019

   (c) 2hth + 4tth + 6th + 9h + 1t + 3u •   • 462,931

   (d)
hth	tth	th	h	t	u
4	6	2	9	3	1
   •   • 629,431

   (e) 329,000 + 600 + 10 + 4 •   • 329,614

Place value – Millions

This Lotto jackpot of €4,362,758 was won last year.

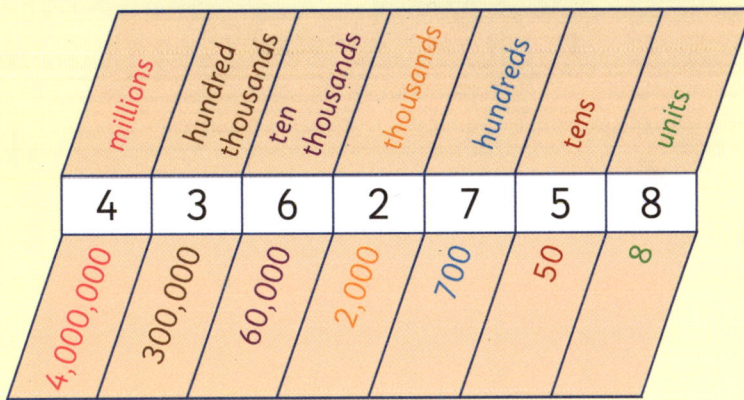

millions	hundred thousands	ten thousands	thousands	hundreds	tens	units
4	3	6	2	7	5	8
4,000,000	300,000	60,000	2,000	700	50	8

m	hth	tth	th	h	t	u
4	3	6	2	7	5	8

= 4,362,758

1. Write the amounts that are **missing** from each Lotto jackpot.

(a) **€1,249,638**

9,000   40,000
600   30
____   8
1,000,000

(b) **€3,562,325**

3,000,000   2,000
300   5
20   ____
60,000

(c) **€6,899,868**

60   6,000,000
9,000   8
90,000   ____
____

2. Write the value of the **underlined digits** in the following numbers.

(a) 2,376,5<u>8</u>4   (b) 3,9<u>7</u>2,859   (c) <u>6</u>,109,325   (d) 8,010,9<u>3</u>7
(e) 3,<u>8</u>94,2<u>5</u>6   (f) 9,4<u>3</u>8,4<u>2</u>0   (g) 5,3<u>8</u>7,94<u>8</u>   (h) 9,<u>999</u>,9<u>99</u>

3. These top sports professionals earned the following amounts in one year!

Name	Anne	Peter	Liam	Jackie	Conor	Bernie	Amar
Amount	€2,643,817	€5,629,310	€4,963,110	€8,100,623	€1,904,603	€3,612,546	€9,612,548

Anne: 2,000,000 + 600,000 + 40,000 + 3,000 + 800 + 10 + 7

Anne: Two million six hundred and forty-three thousand eight hundred and seventeen

(a) Write the amount earned by each of the others in (i) expanded form and (ii) words.

(b) Order the amounts earned from the **lowest** to the **highest** amount.

(c) If each sports professional gave €100,000 to charity, how much would each have left?

4. Write the following number words in figures.

(a) Three million four hundred and twenty-five thousand eight hundred and twenty-seven.

(b) Seven million and fifty-three thousand.   (c) Six million and seventeen.

(d) Nine million and seventeen thousand.   (e) Four million two hundred and eight thousand.

(f) Eight million eight hundred and eight thousand and eighty-eight.

Place value: Roman numerals

The Ancient Romans used letters instead of numerals to show numbers.

1	5	10	50	100	500	1,000
I	V	X	L	C	D	M

Rule 1: If a letter is placed after a letter with a larger value, you add the two amounts.

XI → 10 + 1 = 11	CLXXX → 100 + 50 + 10 + 10 + 10 = 180

Rule 2: If a letter is placed before a letter with a larger value, you subtract the two amounts.

IX → 10 – 1 = 9	CM → 1,000 – 100 = 900

MCDIV → 1,000 + (500 – 100) + (5 – 1) → 1,000 + 400 + 4 = 1,404

1. Write Roman numerals for our numerical system.
   Follow the pattern in these grids.

Hint: The Romans never used the same letter more than three times in a row.

(a)

1	2	3	4	5	6	7	8	9	10
I	II	III	IV	V	VI	VII		IX	

(b)

11	12	13	14	15	16	17	18	19	20
XI			XIV						XX

(c)

21	24	25	29	30	40	50	60	70	80
					XL		LX		

(d)

90	91	94	95	98	99	100	101	110	190
XC								CX	

(e)

199	200	300	400	500	600	700	800	900	1,000
	CC				DC				M

2. The **years** on these birth certificates are shown in Roman numerals.
   Write them using our numerical system.

(a)
BIRTH CERTIFICATE
First name: _____
Surname: _____
Gender: _____
Date of birth: MM

(b)
BIRTH CERTIFICATE
First name: _____
Surname: _____
Gender: _____
Date of birth: MMV

(c)
BIRTH CERTIFICATE
First name: _____
Surname: _____
Gender: _____
Date of birth: MMXIX

(d)
BIRTH CERTIFICATE
First name: _____
Surname: _____
Gender: _____
Date of birth: MMVI

(e)
BIRTH CERTIFICATE
First name: _____
Surname: _____
Gender: _____
Date of birth: MCMXLIII

(f)
BIRTH CERTIFICATE
First name: _____
Surname: _____
Gender: _____
Date of birth: MCMXXII

(g)
BIRTH CERTIFICATE
First name: _____
Surname: _____
Gender: _____
Date of birth: MCMLIX

(h)
BIRTH CERTIFICATE
First name: _____
Surname: _____
Gender: _____
Date of birth: MCMLXXXIV

Chapter 3: Mental strategies

Strategy A: Adding by splitting the numbers.

$2,341 + 4,526 = $ ☆

	th	h	t	u
Step 1: Add the units → 1 + 6 →				7
Step 2: Add the tens → 40 + 20 →			6	0
Step 3: Add the hundreds → 300 + 500 →		8	0	0
Step 4: Add the thousands → 2,000 + 4,000 →	6	0	0	0
	6	8 ·	6	7

1. Now do these using **strategy A**.

(a) 1,235 + 2,413 (b) 3,815 + 3,142 (c) 4,234 + 2,513 (d) 5,103 + 2,631

(e) 4,617 + 2,251 (f) 3,246 + 2,632 (g) 1,842 + 2,036 (h) 3,672 + 2,115

Strategy B: Adding by splitting the second number.

$2,431 + 3,248 = $ ☆

2,431 + 3,000 + 200 + 40 + 8

2,431 + 3,000 → 5,431

5,431 + 200 → 5,631

5,631 + 40 → 5,671

5,671 + 8 → 5,679

2. Now do these using **strategy B**.

(a) 1,632 + 4,251 (b) 2,381 + 5,416

(c) 3,624 + 1,352 (d) 4,317 + 2,562

(e) 3,192 + 4,605 (f) 2,312 + 3,135

(g) 4,125 + 3,713 (h) 3,268 + 4,511

(i) 5,365 + 2,424 (j) 4,172 + 5,317

(k) 3,246 + 4,631 (l) 7,009 + 2,760

Strategy C: Subtracting by splitting the numbers.

$6,479 - 2,346 = $ ☆

	th	h	t	u
Step 1: Subtract the units → 9 − 6 →				3
Step 2: Subtract the tens → 70 − 40 →			3	0
Step 3: Subtract the hundreds → 400 − 300 →		1	0	0
Step 4: Subtract the thousands → 6,000 − 2,000 →	4	0	0	0
	4	1	3	3

3. Now do these using **strategy C**.

(a) 6,486 − 2,134 (b) 3,687 − 1,452 (c) 5,796 − 3,562 (d) 8,874 − 3,621

(e) 4,885 − 1,563 (f) 9,956 − 4,514 (g) 7,964 − 2,431 (h) 8,793 − 4,251

Strategy D: Count up like a shopkeeper.

$4,236 - 2,564 = $ ☆

2,564 to 2,570 →		6
2,570 to 2,600 →		30
2,600 to 3,000 →		400
3,000 to 4,000 →		1,000
4,000 to 4,236 →	+	236
		1,672

Strategy E: Split the second number.

$5,486 - 3,245 = $ ☆

5,486 − 3,000 − 200 − 40 − 5

5,486 − 3,000 → 2,486

2,486 − 200 → 2,286

2,286 − 40 → 2,246

2,246 − 5 → 2,241

5,486 − 3,245 = 2,241

4. Use mental **strategy D** or **E** to do the following.

(a) 2,488 − 1,367 (b) 3,647 − 1,234 (c) 5,589 − 3,125 (d) 6,827 − 4,314

(e) 4,998 − 2,534 (f) 7,176 − 4,135 (g) 8,839 − 4,518 (h) 6,666 − 3,333

STRAND Number   STRAND UNIT/ELEMENT Operations
LANGUAGE Mental strategies, split the numbers, estimation, rounding, front-end estimation, fractions, decimals

Estimation strategy – Rounding

A: Round **254,687** to the nearest **ten**:
(i) Box the **tens** digit. → 2 5 4,6 **8** 7
(ii) Look **right** next door → 2 5 4,6 8 **7**
    at the units.
(iii) Round up if 5 or more.
    Round down if 4 or less. → **2 5 4,6 9 0**

B: Round **387,234** to the nearest **hundred**:
(i) Box the **hundreds** digit. → 3 8 7,**2** 3 4
(ii) Look **right** next door → 3 8 7,2 **3** 4
    at the tens.
(iii) Round up if 5 or more.
    Round down if 4 or less. → **3 8 7,2 0 0**

C: Round **785,639** to the nearest **thousand**:
(i) Box the **thousands** digit. → 7 8 **5**,6 3 9
(ii) Look **right** next door → 7 8 5,**6** 3 9
    at the hundreds.
(iii) Round up if 5 or more.
    Round down if 4 or less. → **7 8 6,0 0 0**

D: Round **843,989** to the nearest
ten thousand:
(i) Box the
    ten thousands digit. → 8 **4** 3,9 8 9
(ii) Look **right** next door → 8 4 **3**,9 8 9
    at the thousands.
(iii) Round up if 5 or more.
    Round down if 4 or less. → **8 4 0,0 0 0**

---

1. Round these numbers.

	Number	Nearest 10	Nearest 100	Nearest 1,000	Nearest 10,000
(a)	426				
(b)	587				
(c)	5,872				
(d)	8,739				
(e)	23,891				
(f)	48,972				
(g)	378,291				
(h)	783,926				

---

2. (i) Round the asking prices for these properties.

	Asking price €	Nearest €10	Nearest €100	Nearest €1,000	Nearest €10,000
(a)	€76,324				
(b)	€87,598				
(c)	€81,647				
(d)	€278,439				
(e)	€714,821				
(f)	€239,873				

(a) €76,324
(b) €87,598
(c) €81,647
(d) €278,439
(e) €714,821
(f) €239,873

(ii) Order the asking prices of the properties from **highest** to **lowest**.

(iii) What is the value of the **7** in each asking price?

(iv) Which house price has a **9** in the thousands place?

Estimation – Front-end strategy

In the **front-end strategy** we look at the first digit and change the others to zero. 4,678 → 4,000.

A:

h	t	u
4	3	8
+ 2	1	9

→

h	t	u
4	0	0
+ 2	0	0
Estimate → 6	0	0

B:

th	h	t	u
9	6	2	7
− 4	2	7	8

→

th	h	t	u
9	0	0	0
− 4	0	0	0
Estimate → 5	0	0	0

C:

th	h	t	u
		6	8
×		3	2

→

th	h	t	u
		6	0
×		3	0
Estimate → 1	8	0	0

D: $878 \div 43 = \star$

th	h	t	u
40)		8	0	0
		2	0

→ 40) 800 = 20

1. Use the **front-end** strategy to estimate the answers to these.

(a) 69 + 37   (b) 346 + 521   (c) 8,914 + 4,364   (d) 1,756 + 7,293

(e) 73 − 26   (f) 517 − 469   (g) 6,493 − 3,871   (h) 9,276 − 3,814

(i) 46 × 3   (j) 75 × 48   (k) 638 × 49   (l) 538 × 63

(m) 608 ÷ 32   (n) 432 ÷ 27   (o) 851 ÷ 23   (p) 952 ÷ 34

Fractions and decimals. When using the **front-end strategy** we focus only on the **whole numbers**.

E: The distance Sam ran each day.

Mon	Tue	Wed	Thur	Fri
$4\frac{1}{4}$km	$6\frac{1}{2}$km	$3\frac{3}{8}$km	$7\frac{5}{8}$km	$9\frac{1}{3}$km

4km + 6km + 3km + 7km + 9km = 29km

F: The amount Marie spent each day.

Mon	Tue	Wed	Thur	Fri
€4·36	€8·72	€1·63	€9·56	€0·75

€4 + €8 + €1 + €9 + €0 = €22

2. (i) Estimate the answers to the following using the **front-end estimation** strategy. Combine all five days.

(ii) Then work out the actual answer and compare it with your estimate.

(a) The distance run by Sophia each day.

Mon	Tue	Wed	Thur	Fri
$7\frac{3}{4}$km	$6\frac{1}{8}$km	$4\frac{1}{2}$km	$9\frac{1}{5}$km	$5\frac{1}{4}$km

(b) The amount of water consumed by Liz each day.

Mon	Tue	Wed	Thur	Fri
5l 270ml	6·34l	$9\frac{1}{2}$l	$8\frac{31}{1000}$l	$5\frac{3}{4}$l

(c) The amount Simon spent each day.

Mon	Tue	Wed	Thur	Fri
€6·37	€4·89	€3·10	€3·09	€5·93

(d) The weight lifted by Tim each day.

Mon	Tue	Wed	Thur	Fri
$2\frac{1}{4}$kg	8·963kg	$7\frac{1}{5}$kg	$4\frac{7}{10}$kg	$6\frac{1}{2}$kg

Challenge 9,385 people attended an art exhibition. 1,576 attended in the morning and 3,486 attended in the afternoon. Use the front-end estimation strategy to estimate (i) how many attended the evening session?, and (ii) if 6,124 were female, about how many males attended that day?

Chapter 4 – Addition and subtraction

Do the following. Match the answer to the correct letter. Write the words to complete the poem.

a = 59,833	
c = 927	
d = 5,216	
e = 57,417	
f = 8,155	
g = 69,099	
h = 29,431	
l = 6,337	
n = 64,535	
o = 65,212	
p = 83,057	
r = 43,128	
s = 3,751	
t = 12,412	
w = 3,289	
z = 5,054	

Louder than a Clap of Thunder!

Louder than a **A**_____ of thunder,
louder than an eagle screams,
louder than a **B**_____ blunders,
or a **C**_____ football teams,
louder than a fire-alarm,
or a rushing waterfall,
louder than a knight in armour
jumping from a ten-foot **D**_____.
Louder than an earthquake rumbles,
louder than a tidal wave,
louder than an **E**_____ grumbles
as he stumbles through his cave,
louder than stampeding cattle,
louder than a cannon roars,
louder than a giant's rattle,
that's how loud my **F**_____
G_____!

By Jack Prelutsky

A

243	3,428	24,368	39,241
+ 684	+ 2,909	+ 35,465	+ 43,816
927			
C	☐	☐	☐

B

$297 + 1,248 + 3,671 =$ _____ ☐

$4,216 + 8,912 + 30,000 =$ _____ ☐

$21,243 + 12,368 + 26,222 =$ _____ ☐

$68,492 + 38 + 569 =$ _____ ☐

$38,462 + 14,378 + 12,372 =$ _____ ☐

$56,318 + 1,394 + 6,823 =$ _____ ☐

C

5,261	84,374	7,000
− 45	− 19,162	− 1,946
☐	☐	☐
60,000	68,043	
− 2,583	− 3,508	
☐	☐	

D

$(6,248 − 2,362) − 597 =$ _____ ☐

$(72,345 − 6,541) − 5,971 =$ _____ ☐

$(27,942 − 12,546) − 9,059 =$ _____ ☐

$(46,317 − 24,973) − 15,007 =$ _____ ☐

E

$(29,542 − 14,761) + 50,431 =$ _____ ☐

$(47,321 + 26,512) − 4,734 =$ _____ ☐

$(70,000 − 34,316) + 7,444 =$ _____ ☐

$(82,312 − 4,609) − 20,286 =$ _____ ☐

F

Find the sum of 3,624 and 4,531. _____ ☐

Increase 26,349 by 33,484. _____ ☐

Decrease 16,241 by 3,829. _____ ☐

63,712 minus 34,281 = _____ ☐

What must be added to 2,583 to get 60,000? _____ ☐

From the sum of 43,287 and 36,319, subtract 36,478. _____ ☐

G

How much greater is 12,000 than 8,249? _____ ☐

How much less than 70,000 is 5,465? _____ ☐

Find the difference between 72,416 and 7,204. _____ ☐

Increase 24,356 by 18,772. _____ ☐

What is the sum of 43,826 and 13,591? _____ ☐

Subtract 4,632 from 8,383 _____ ☐

STRAND **Number**   STRAND UNIT/ELEMENT *Operations*
LANGUAGE *Addition, subtraction, bigger, smaller, more/less than, greater, increase, decrease, how much?, units, tens, hundreds, thousands, hundred/ten thousands, millions*

Addition and subtraction: Addition to 999,999

This table shows the amounts raised for three charities.
Find the total amount raised. Round to estimate.

	Jack & Jill	Barnardos	Yoobyoo
	€384,264	€516,848	€16,789

Total amount raised: €384,264 + €516,848 + €16,789 = ☆

Estimate: €400,000 + €500,000 + €20,000 = €920,000

Step 4
Add the thousands:

$4 + 6 + 6 + 1 = 17$

Regroup as 1 ten thousand and 7 thousands and move the 1 ten thousand to the ten thousands house.

Step 3
Add the hundreds:

$2 + 8 + 7 + 2 = 19$

Regroup as 1 thousand and 9 hundreds and move the 1 thousand to the thousands house.

Step 2
Add the tens:

$6 + 4 + 8 + 2 = 20$

Regroup as 2 hundreds and move to the hundreds house.

Step 5
Add the ten thousands:

$8 + 1 + 1 + 1 = 11$

Regroup as 1 hundred thousand and 1 ten thousand and move the 1 hundred thousand to the hundred thousands house.

	hth	tth	th	h	t	u
€	3	8	4	2	6	4
€	5	1	6	8	4	8
+ €	1	1_1	6_1	7_2	8_2	9
€	9	1	7	9	0	1

START

Step 1
Add the units:

$4 + 8 + 9 = 21$

Regroup as 2 tens and 1 unit. Place the 2 tens in the tens house.

Step 6
Add the hundred thousands: $3 + 5 + 1 = 9$

Add. Estimate first by rounding to the nearest **hundred thousand**.

1. (a) 136,456
      323,321
    + 420,122
    _____

   (b) 235,674
       366,328
     + 373,554
     _____

   (c) 364,857
       236,449
     + 293,875
     _____

   (d) 457,683
       248,946
     + 61,585
     _____

2. (a) 325,764 + 461,325 + 86,565
   (b) 463,815 + 234,271 + 62,319
   (c) 534,291 + 46,857 + 293,142
   (d) 68,259 + 376,984 + 269,879

3. The following table shows the cost of five helicopters.

A	B	C	D	E
€165,487	€386,921	€276,599	€98,658	€87,462

(a) Find the total cost of helicopters A, B, and C.
(b) Find the total cost of helicopters B, C and D.
(c) Which two helicopters together cost exactly €474,383?
(d) Which three helicopters together cost exactly €529,548?
(e) How much change would you have from €99,000, if you bought helicopter E?
(f) Increase the cost of helicopter D by 50%.

Subtraction

There were 354,243 cars produced in Romania one year. There were 188,969 cars produced in Sweden that same year. How many fewer cars were produced in Sweden?

354,243 − 188,969 = ☆

Estimate 400,000 − 200,000 = 200,000

Step 4
Rename 1 ten thousand as 10 thousands.
Subtract the thousands:
13 − 8 = 5 thousands

Step 3
Rename 1 thousand as 10 hundreds.
Subtract the hundreds:
11 − 9 = 2 hundreds

Step 2
Rename 1 hundred as 10 tens.
Subtract the tens:
13 − 6 = 7 tens

Step 5
Rename 1 hundred thousand as 10 ten thousands.
Subtract the ten thousands:
14 − 8 = 6 ten thousands

hth	tth	th	h	t	u
2	¹4	¹3	¹1	¹3	¹3
3̶	5̶	4̶	2̶	4̶	3̶
1	8	8	9	6	9
1	6	5	2	7	4

Step 1
Rename 1 ten as 10 units.
Subtract the units:
13 − 9 = 4 units

Step 6
Subtract the hundred thousands:
2 − 1 = 1 hundred thousand

START

354,243 − 188,969 = 165,274

---

1. Subtract. Estimate first by rounding to the nearest **hundred thousand**.

   (a) 413,256
        − 246,578

   (b) 536,724
        − 348,897

   (c) 622,533
        − 157,312

   (d) 811,429
        − 568,273

2. (a) 324,190 − 168,342
   (b) 761,492 − 423,628
   (c) (243,681 + 159,648) − 162,897
   (d) (504,587 − 342,816) + 26,947

3. This table shows the number of households in each country.

Latvia	Cyprus	Montenegro	Slovenia	Albania	Bermuda
802,848	223,790	180,517	684,847	791,830	25,148

   (a) Find the difference between the number of households in Latvia and Slovenia.
   (b) How many fewer households are there in Bermuda than in Albania?
   (c) Which two countries' number of households when subtracted give a total of 43,273?
   (d) How many more households must Slovenia acquire to equal the number of households in Albania?
   (e) Order the countries from highest to lowest, based on the number of households.
   (f) Find the difference between the highest and the lowest number of households.

Challenge From the sum of the number of households in Montenegro and Albania, take the total number of households in Cyprus and Bermuda. _____

Subtraction – Overcoming the zeros

A football club sold 800,000 official jerseys one year.
If 367,875 were sold by June, how many jerseys were still left to sell?

800,000 – 367,875 = ☆   Estimate: 800,000 – 300,000 = 500,000 (front end)

START ▶ Step 1
Rename 1 hundred thousand as 10 ten thousands =

7hth + 10tth + 0th + 0h + 0t + 0u.

Step 2
Rename 1 ten thousand as 10 thousands =

7hth + 9tth + 10th + 0h + 0t + 0u.

Step 3
Rename 1 thousand as 10 hundreds =

7hth + 9tth + 9th + 10h + 0t + 0u.

Step 4
Rename 1 hundred as 10 tens =

7hth + 9tth + 9th + 9h + 10t + 0u.

Step 5
Rename 1 ten as 10 units =

7hth + 9tth + 9th + 9h + 9t + 10u.

Step 6
Now I can subtract!

hth	tth	th	h	t	u
7	9 10 0	9 10 0	9 10 0	9 10 0	1 0
8	0	0	0	0	0
– 3	6	7	8	7	5
4	3	2	1	2	5

1. Complete this table, which shows the bike sales of 6 companies.

Bicycle Company	Pedal Pushers	Bikelicious	Chaingang	Geared Up	Cyclomania
Amount produced	200,000	300,000	500,000	800,000	900,000
Amount sold	164,382	169,748	368,045		
Amount left				499,817	677,418

Subtraction is the opposite of addition. When we subtract, we can always check by adding the answer to the number we subtracted to find the top line.

hth	tth	th	h	t	u
8	3	8	2	9	5
– 3	6	4	7	2	6
4	7	3	5	6	9

2. Now work out the missing top line in each of these.

(a)
hth	tth	th	h	t	u
– 2	4	6	0	3	7
3	5	2	1	7	4

(b)
hth	tth	th	h	t	u
– 3	8	3	2	6	4
5	5	6	8	1	5

(c)
hth	tth	th	h	t	u
– 3	7	7	6	0	8
4	8	9	9	0	6

3. Check if your answers to question 1 above are correct by using the method in question 2.

Challenge
Orange App Store had 700,000 apps available in July.
Blueberry App store had 168,005 less apps available.
How many apps had Blueberry App store available in July? _____

Real-life problems – Strawberry App Store

These are a number of different apps downloaded from the **Strawberry App Store** in the following categories.

Category	Games	Education	Music	Books	Travel	Sports
Number of apps (this year)	573,291	438,791	394,102	600,000	91,003	43,826

1. Which category has the least amount of apps downloaded?

2. Which category has the greatest amount of apps downloaded?

3. Order the number of apps from lowest to highest.

4. Round the number of apps in each category to the nearest thousand.

5. Find the sum of the number of Education and Music apps.

6. Find the total sum of apps in the Games, Travel and Sports categories.

7. Find the difference between the number of Education apps and the number of Music apps.

8. Find the difference between the sum of the Music and Sports apps together and the Books apps.

9. What must be added to the number of Education apps to equal the number of Books apps?

10. How many fewer Education apps are there than Games apps?

11. How many fewer Travel apps are there than Books apps?

12. What is the difference between the number of Music and Education apps together and the number of Games and Travel apps together?

13. Add the sum of Music and Education apps to the Sports apps.

14. Next year Strawberry App Store plans on developing the number of apps in each category as shown below. Find the total number of apps that will be available next year in each category.

Category	Games	Education	Music	Books	Travel	Sports
Number of apps (this year)	573,291	438,791	394,102	600,000	91,003	43,826
Number of extra apps (next year)	134,685	231,679	45,389	247,819	673,290	124,976
Total						

15. Strawberry App Store aims to have 900,000 apps available in each category over the next five years. How many more apps must they develop in each category to achieve this? Complete the table.

Category	Games	Education	Music	Books	Travel	Sports
Number of apps (this year)	573,291	438,791	394,102	600,000	91,003	43,826
Apps to be developed (over five years)						
Target number	900,000	900,000	900,000	900,000	900,000	900,000

Chapter 5: Data 1 – Averages

Each child below was given a number of presents. The presents were not shared equally.

If the presents had been shared equally, each child would have received 5 presents. 5 is the **average** amount.

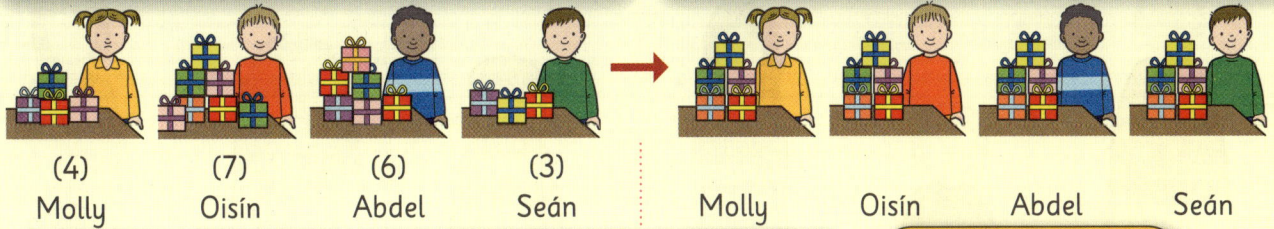

(4) Molly   (7) Oisín   (6) Abdel   (3) Seán   Molly   Oisín   Abdel   Seán

Finding the average!

Step 1: Find the total amount: $4 + 7 + 6 + 3 = 20$ presents

Step 2: Divide the total by the number of children: $20 ÷ 4 = 5$

Remember, the average lies somewhere in the middle, between the smallest and largest numbers.

1. (a) Which child received: (i) most? (ii) least presents?

   (b) Which children received less than the average number of presents?

   (c) How many presents more than the average did Abdel receive?

2. **Find the average weight of each group of animals.**

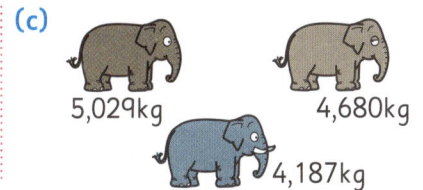

   (a) 26kg   34kg   25kg   27kg

   (b) 421g   401g   294g   365g   359g

   (c) 5,029kg   4,680kg   4,187kg

3. **Find the average percentage each of these children received in their last four exams.**

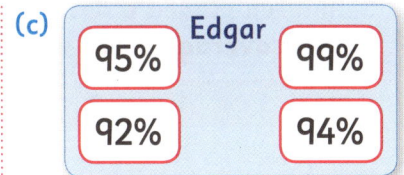

   (a) Lisa
   | 89% | 91% |
   | 63% | 81% |

   (b) Bobby
   | 62% | 68% |
   | 74% | 80% |

   (c) Edgar
   | 95% | 99% |
   | 92% | 94% |

4. Clare and her family ran a 5km race for charity. The following bar-line graph shows how long it took each family member to complete the 5km.

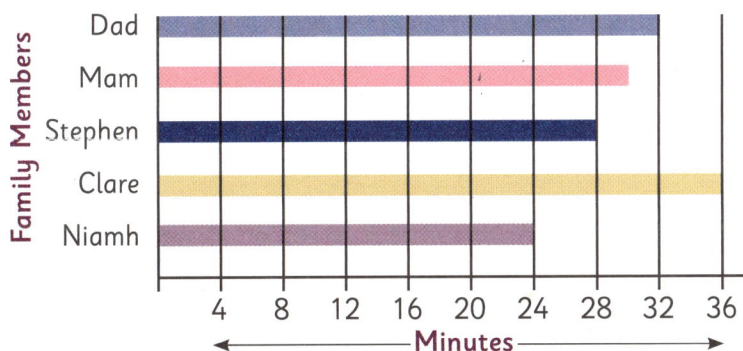

   Family Members: Dad, Mam, Stephen, Clare, Niamh

   Minutes: 4 8 12 16 20 24 28 32 36

   (a) Who ran (i) fastest? (ii) slowest?

   (b) By how many minutes did Niamh beat Clare's time?

   (c) What was the average time taken by the family to complete the race?

   (d) Who ran faster: Mam or Dad?

Challenge If each family member raised an average of €93·24 for charity, how much did the family raise in total? € _____

STRAND Data   STRAND UNIT/ELEMENT *Representing and interpreting data*
LANGUAGE *Averages, average score, smallest, largest, middle, bar-line graph, bar chart, missing numbers*

Data 1 – Averages

John Age 17	Lisa Age 7	Vicky Age 26	Jason Age 12	Ryan Age 39	Sara Age 25
184cm	118cm	152cm	141cm	191cm	168cm
71kg	26kg	62kg	43kg	79kg	73kg

1. (a) Which person is: (i) tallest? (ii) shortest? (iii) lightest? (iv) heaviest? (v) youngest? (vi) oldest?

   (b) Calculate the average height of the girls.

   (c) Calculate the average weight of the six people.

   (d) How many kilogrammes lighter than the average is the lightest person?

   (e) What is the average age of the group?

   (f) How many years younger than the average age of this group are you?

2. Working in groups of five or six children, calculate the average age, weight and height of the group.

   Use measures to the nearest year, kg and cm!

3. **5 children played a darts game. They each had 8 throws of the dart. The person with the highest average score was the winner. Sometimes the dart missed the target.**

	1	2	3	4	5	6	7	8
Billy	8	1	20	11	–	16	9	7
Aoife	60	58	32	60	60	8	30	60
Ciara	–	–	7	2	–	14	17	–
Bronagh	11	19	5	40	18	14	50	19
Spencer	60	60	36	60	60	60	60	36

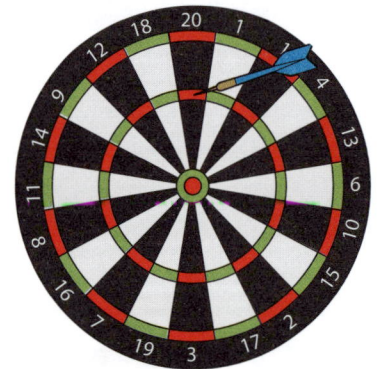

   (a) Calculate each child's total score.

   (b) Calculate each child's average score.

Challenge Billy and Ciara played a practice game later that evening.

If Ciara's average score was **11** and Billy's average score was **7** , calculate and write their missing scores.

Ciara	8	19		7	5	20	3	11
Billy	3	9	4	–	20		1	13

Data 1 – Averages

1. (a)
> The average of six numbers is 4. What is the total of the numbers?

(b)
> The average of seven numbers is 38. What is the total of the numbers?

(c)
> The average of four amounts is €5. What is the total of the amounts?

2. (a) The average of five numbers is 9. What's the missing number?

10	6	8	16	

(c) The average of seven numbers is 13. What's the missing number?

13		16	8	5	14	9

(b) The average of four numbers is 7·3. What's the missing number?

	6·9	8·4	4·8

(d) The average of six numbers is 32·6. What's the missing number?

39·4	45·2		19·6	50·8	23·7

3. The average number of kilometres travelled by each car is 83,069km. How many kilometres should the blue car show?

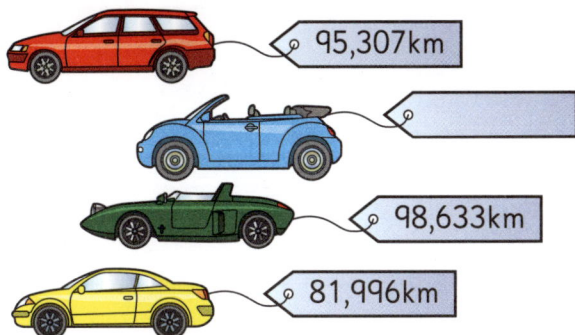

95,307km

98,633km

81,996km

4. (a) If the family showered for an average of 203 seconds per person last Monday, calculate the time spent by Jayden in the shower.

Mam:	185 sec
Dad:	173 sec
Jayden:	
Ella:	259 sec

(b) Calculate the total time spent showering by the family, in minutes and seconds.

5. This bar chart shows the number of texts sent by each of seven children one day. If the average number of texts sent was 9, how many texts did **Síona** send? Complete the bar chart.

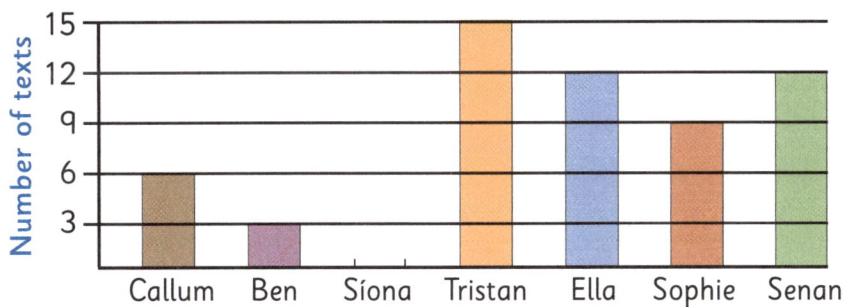

Number of texts: Callum, Ben, Síona, Tristan, Ella, Sophie, Senan

6. Study the multi-screen cinema timetable.

	Vacation in Venice	Dreadful Dan	Silly Summer
Start	14:10	14:30	15:04
Finish	15:32	16:03	16:48

(a) Calculate the length of each film in minutes.

(b) Calculate the average length of a film in minutes.

Challenge   If Sue fell asleep for $\frac{1}{8}$ of the film Silly Summer, for how many hours and minutes of the film was she awake?

Chapter 6: Multiplication 1 – Some new strategies

This **web** shows maths facts linked to the Maths Fact in the centre.

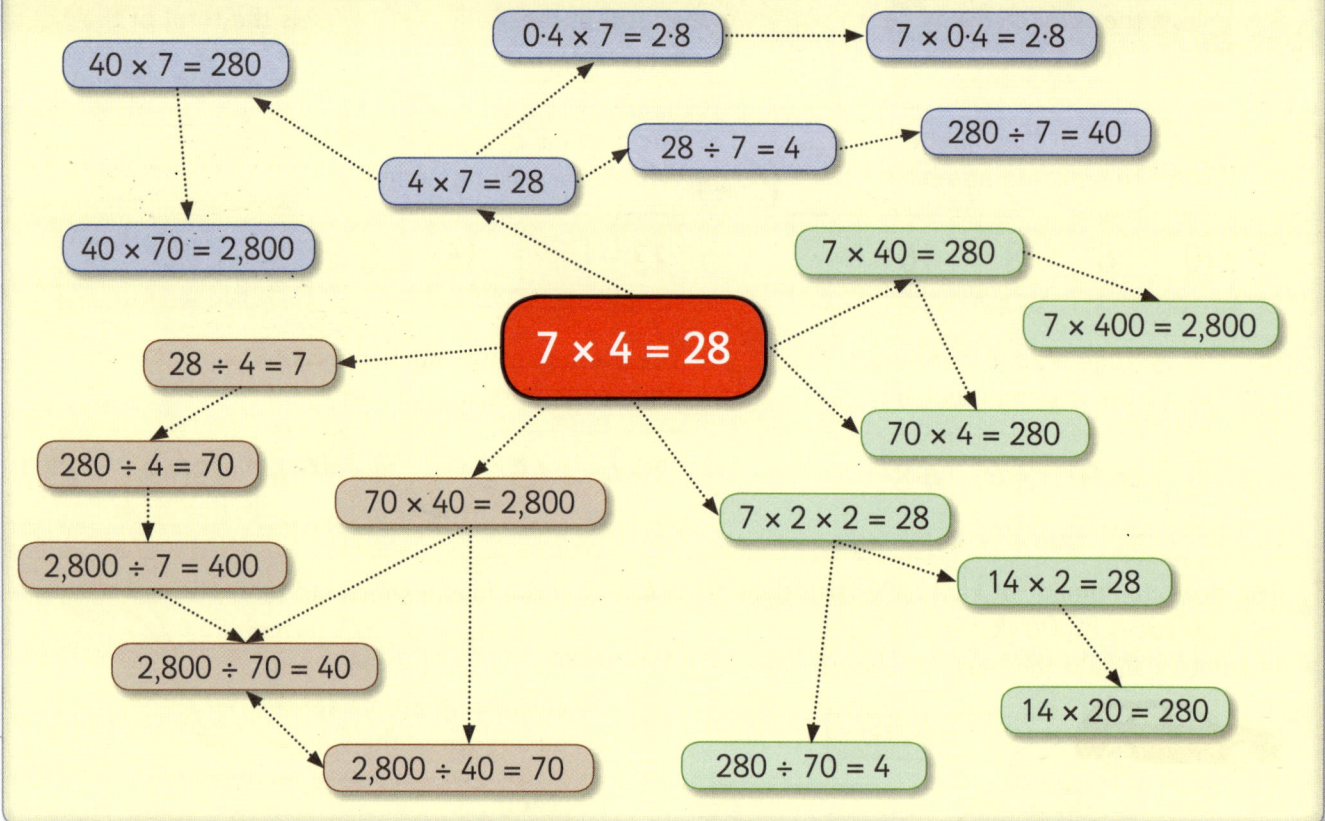

$40 \times 7 = 280$

$0{\cdot}4 \times 7 = 2{\cdot}8$

$7 \times 0{\cdot}4 = 2{\cdot}8$

$4 \times 7 = 28$

$28 \div 7 = 4$

$280 \div 7 = 40$

$40 \times 70 = 2{,}800$

$7 \times 40 = 280$

$7 \times 400 = 2{,}800$

$28 \div 4 = 7$

$7 \times 4 = 28$

$280 \div 4 = 70$

$70 \times 4 = 280$

$2{,}800 \div 7 = 400$

$70 \times 40 = 2{,}800$

$7 \times 2 \times 2 = 28$

$14 \times 2 = 28$

$2{,}800 \div 70 = 40$

$14 \times 20 = 280$

$2{,}800 \div 40 = 70$

$280 \div 70 = 4$

1. **Draw similar webs for these Maths Facts:**
   (a) $8 \times 6 = 48$ (b) $9 \times 5 = 45$ (c) $8 \times 9 = 72$ (d) $7 \times 6 = 42$

2. **Use the web strategy to help you do these:**
   (a) 5×60 _____   (b) 7×300 _____   (c) 80×3 _____   (d) 90×8 _____
   (e) $6 \times 3 \times 30$ _____   (f) 90×50 _____   (g) 8×90 _____   (h) 21×60 _____
   (i) 6×300 _____   (j) 900×5 _____   (k) 800×6 _____   (l) 50×90 _____

3. It took 7 men 4 days to lay 28km of cable. At this rate how much cable would be laid in (a) 40 days? and (b) 400 days?

4. It took 18 hours for 6 men to load 3 containers. How many hours would the same 6 men take to load 30 containers, if they continued to work at the same rate?

5. A bricklayer can lay 34 bricks in 1 hour. How many bricks should he lay in (a) 10 hours? and (b) 1,000 hours?

Maths Fact   3,300 metres above sea level is the upper limit of most mountain rainforests.

Challenge   Now complete this number sentence: $30 \times 10 \times$ ____ $= 3300$.

STRAND Number   **STRAND UNIT/ELEMENT** *Operations*
LANGUAGE *Multiplication strategies, the grid strategy, estimate, brackets, decimals*

Multiplication 1

Remember: When we **multiply a number by 10**, we move **all** digits **one place** to the **left**. ←

To multiply by **100**, move all the digits **2 places** to the left.

To multiply by **1,000**, move all the digits **3 places** to the left.

th	h	t	u	$\frac{1}{10}$	$\frac{1}{100}$	$\frac{1}{1000}$
			5 • 2	3	6	
		5	2 • 3	6		
	5	2	3 • 6			
5	2	3	6 •			

← (5·236 × 10)
← (5·236 × 100)
← (5·236 × 1,000)

Complete these.

1. 7·458   (a) × 10 = _____   (b) × 100 = _____   (c) × 1,000 = _____

2. 18·293   (a) × 10 = _____   (b) × 100 = _____   (c) × 1,000 = _____

3. 6·502   (a) × 10 = _____   (b) × 100 = _____   (c) × 1,000 = _____

4. 30·47   (a) × 10 = _____   (b) × 100 = _____   (c) × 1,000 = _____

Now, have a go at these.

5. (a) 6·832 × 1,000   (b) 9·176 × 1,000   (c) 2·877 × 1,000   (d) 5·378 × 1,000

6. (a) 14·52 × 1,000   (b) 73·36 × 1,000   (c) 80·45 × 1,000   (d) 91·06 × 1,000

7. (a) 316·9 × 1,000   (b) 550·8 × 1,000   (c) 40·40 × 1,000   (d) 0·274 × 1,000

8. Ivan earns €17·67 for every 10 windows he cleans in an office block. How much will he earn if he cleans:

   (a) 20 windows? _____   (b) 70 windows? _____   (c) 90 windows? _____

9. A metre of electrical cable costs €0·74. What is the cost of these lengths:

   (a) 1km? _____   (b) 6km? _____   (c) 9km? _____   (d) 12km? _____   (e) 18km? _____

10. A machine in a factory can produce 100 tins of dog food in an hour. How many tins are produced in:

    (a) 5·62 hours? _____   (b) 37·5 hrs? _____   (c) 640·8 hrs? _____

11. There are 52 oranges in each box. How many oranges are there in:

    (a) 3 boxes? _____   (b) 30 boxes? _____   (c) 300 boxes? _____

    (d) 600 boxes? _____   (e) 60 boxes? _____   (f) 6 boxes? _____

Maths Fact 52,000 square km of Amazon Rainforest is being destroyed, on average, each year.

Challenge How many square km of Amazon Rainforest are destroyed, on average, in periods of (a) 10 years? _____ (b) 100 years? _____

Multiplication 1 – The grid strategy

> There are 26 children in a class. How many are there in 37 such classes?

26 × 37 = ☆

- Break each number into tens and units.

  26 = 20 + 6 and 37 = 30 + 7

- Multiply each part of the first number 20 + 6
  by each part of the second number 30 + 7 .

- Add the products to get the answer: = 26 × 37 = 962

	20		6	
20 × 30	600	6 × 30	180	× 30
20 × 7	140	6 × 7	42	× 7

600 + 180 + 140 + 42 = 962

26 × 37 = 962

1. Now complete these grids. Make sure that you add the **four sections** in each case.

(a) 34 × 27 = ☆

30	4	
		× 20
		× 7

(b) 46 × 35 = ☆

40	6	
		× 30
		× 5

(c) 72 × 46 = ☆

70	2	
		× 40
		× 6

(d) 85 × 39 = ☆

80	5	
		× 30
		× 9

236 × 48 = ☆

We deal with 3-digit numbers in a similar way.

	200		30		6	
200 × 40	8,000	30 × 40	1,200	6 × 40	240	40
200 × 8	1,600	30 × 8	240	6 × 8	48	8

8,000 + 1,200 + 240 + 1,600 + 240 + 48 = 11,328

2. Complete these grids using the same strategy. Add the **six sections** in each case.

(a) 354 × 36 = ☆

300	50	4	
			× 30
			× 6

(b) 472 × 27 = ☆

			×
			×

(c) 326 × 75 = ☆

			×
			×

3. Use the grid method to solve:

276 crates are loaded onto each of 43 trucks. How many crates are loaded in total?

4. 29 postal workers each delivered 658 letters.

(a) How many letters were delivered in total?

(b) What would the total have been if there had been 2 less workers?

Maths Fact   500 pounds is the amount of money called a 'monkey' in English slang.

Challenge   How many pounds would you have if you had 67 'monkeys'? _____

Multiplication 1 – Let's look back

1. (a) 6·7 × 10 = _____   (b) 4·2 × 10 = _____   (c) 8·3 × 10 = _____   (d) 9·1 × 10 = _____

2. (a) 2·41 × 10 = _____   (b) 7·65 × 10 = _____   (c) 2·08 × 10 = _____   (d) 5·52 × 10 = _____

3. (a) 4·39 × 100 = _____   (b) 9·23 × 100 = _____   (c) 3·52 × 100 = _____   (d) 7·04 × 100 = _____

4. (a) 26·2 × 100 = _____   (b) 53·7 × 100 = _____   (c) 100 × 70·8 = _____   (d) 100 × 82·5 = _____

5. (a) 15·3 × 10 = _____   (b) 100 × 15·3 = _____   (c) 1·53 × 100 = _____   (d) 10 × 1·53 = _____

6. (a) 10 × 5·9 = _____   (b) 0·59 × 100 = _____   (c) 5·09 × 10 = _____   (d) 100 × 5·09 = _____

What is the total weight of 384 crates each weighing 42kg? Estimate first.

384 × 42 = ☆

Round 384 to 400
Round 42 to 40

Estimate: 400 × 40 = 16,000

Did you make a good estimate? Explain your reasoning.

Short way
```
    384
  ×  42
  -----
    768
  15360
  -----
 16,128
```

Complete these. Estimate first.

7. (a) 473 × 54 = _____   (b) 692 × 41 = _____   (c) 269 × 33 = _____   (d) 681 × 52 = _____

8. (a) 326 × 67 = _____   (b) 519 × 28 = _____   (c) 647 × 45 = _____   (d) 726 × 86 = _____

9. (a) 662 × 39 = _____   (b) 234 × 76 = _____   (c) 506 × 28 = _____   (d) 485 × 74 = _____

When multiplying decimals, round to the nearest whole number first to estimate, e.g. a stamp measures 3·2cm. Round 3·2cm to 3cm.

A What is the width of 5 such stamps?

3·2 × 5 = ☆

Estimate:
3 × 5
→ 15cm

Short way
```
  3·2cm
  ×  5
  ------
 16·0cm
```

B What is 79 times 86·85?

86·85 × 79 = ☆

Estimate:
87 × 80
→ 6,960

Short way
```
   86·85
  ×   79
  -------
   78165
  607950
  -------
 6,861·15
```

Complete these. Estimate first.

10. (a) 8·3 × 7 = _____   (b) 6·7 × 58 = _____   (c) 67·24 × 37 = _____

11. (a) 6·2 × 9 = _____   (b) 8·6 × 67 = _____   (c) 39·31 × 59 = _____

12. (a) 51·6 × 6 = _____   (b) 9·8 × 47 = _____   (c) 78·52 × 66 = _____

13. (a) 47·4 × 7 = _____   (b) 19·5 × 63 = _____   (c) 62·48 × 47 = _____

Maths Fact   The Gotthard Rail Tunnel is 800m below the Alps and is 57km long.

Challenge   What whole number must I multiply 57km by to get closest to 600km? _____

25

Multiplication 1

The record length of a python is 7·671 metres. What would be the total length of 26 such pythons?

7·671 × 26 = ☆

Estimate: 8 × 30 = 240

```
        7·6 7 1 m
    ×       2 6
    _____
    4 6 0 2 6      ← 7·671 × 6
+ 1 5·3 4 2 0      ← 7·671 × 20
    _____
1 9 9·4 4 6 m
```

Note: We must have the same number of decimal places in the answer as we have in the number we multiplied.

Now do these. Estimate first. You may use a calculator to check your answers.

1. (a) 6·842 × 73   (b) 8·753 × 64   (c) 5·968 × 58   (d) 9·254 × 47

2. (a) 2·917 × 39   (b) 4·257 × 87   (c) 3·577 × 67   (d) 7·818 × 62

3. (a) 8·084 × 76   (b) 5·706 × 28   (c) 83·72 × 49   (d) 17·27 × 94

4. (a) 34·49 × 64   (b) 274·6 × 37   (c) 638·2 × 81   (d) 760·8 × 47

5. (a) 5·619 × 23   (b) 42·88 × 58   (c) 726·3 × 71   (d) 6·029 × 93

6. What number is 47 times bigger than (a) 7·63? _____   (b) 35·28? _____

7. (a) Kevin's journey to work is 8·765km each day. How far does he travel to work during the month of May if he works 19 days during the month? _____ km

   (b) His return journey is 0·35km longer as he wants to avoid heavy traffic. What will be his total distance travelled to and from work during the 19 days he works in May? _____ km

8. A group of 63 scouts each paid €17·49 for a return ticket to their jamboree.

   (a) What was the total bill?

   (b) If 7 extra scouts had gone to the jamboree, what would the total bill have been then?

9. A coach travels 13·46km per litre of fuel. How far will the coach travel on 78 litres of fuel?

10. Gráinne is training for a triathlon. Each training day she runs 8·325km, swims 0·58km and cycles 27·065km. What distance does she travel for each event over a 17 day training period?

Maths Fact   Dick Fosbury won a gold medal at the 1968 Olympics for the high jump. This method of jumping became known as the 'Fosbury Flop'. He was the first to jump backwards over the bar. Fosbury cleared 2·24m.

Challenge   If Fosbury cleared 2·24 metres in each of 39 jumps, how many metres in total would he have cleared? _____

Multiplication 1

$(7{\cdot}635 + 14{\cdot}9 + 3{\cdot}287) \times 47 =$ ☆

Estimate: $26 \times 50 = 1{,}300$

Remember: When we use brackets ( ), we must complete the part inside the brackets first.

```
   7·635
  14·900
+  3·287
  25·822
```

```
     25·822
   ×     47
    180754
 + 1032880
  1,213·634
```

Now do these. Be careful with the signs! Estimate first.

1. $(5{\cdot}368 + 2{\cdot}758 + 8{\cdot}473) \times 53$

2. $(7{\cdot}249 + 6{\cdot}758 + 5{\cdot}215) \times 68$

3. $(8{\cdot}572 + 7{\cdot}636 - 4{\cdot}875) \times 74$

4. $(29{\cdot}76 + 68{\cdot}22 - 36{\cdot}49) \times 29$

5. $(319{\cdot}5 + 583{\cdot}8 - 482{\cdot}4) \times 38$

6. $(789{\cdot}1 + 345{\cdot}7 - 654{\cdot}3) \times 49$

7. $(27{\cdot}26 + 357{\cdot}6 - 295{\cdot}9) \times 57$

8. $(3{\cdot}79 + 467{\cdot}6 - 254{\cdot}8) \times 36$

9. $(725{\cdot}4 + 86{\cdot}7 - 334{\cdot}2) \times 100$

10. $(82{\cdot}6 + 77{\cdot}58 - 90{\cdot}3) \times 1{,}000$

11. In a distribution depot, boxes of meat weigh 37·58kg and 45·57kg. What is the total weight of meat packed onto delivery trucks with:

    (a) 57 of each box? _____   (b) 68 of each box? _____   (c) 100 of each box? _____

12. A school has a budget of €5,000 to buy new I.T. equipment. The principal buys a dozen tablets costing €345·78 each. How much money will there be left over? €_____

13. Paul and Anna are each paid €8·75 for each hour they work in part-time jobs. Paul works for 26 hours while Anna works 11 hours more than Paul. How much does each earn? €_____   €_____

14. A return flight to Madrid is on offer for €134·79. How much money is collected if:

    (a) 86 seats are sold?   (b) 93 seats are sold?   (c) 99 seats are sold?

15. Andrew earns €483·68 per week. He pays €127·77 in deductions each week. How much money will Andrew actually take home in wages over a 28-week period? €_____

16. Tim earns €47·28 per day. His mother earns five times this amount. How much does Tim's mother earn in a five day week? €_____

17. A ticket for a train journey from Cork to Dublin costs €34·96. How much would 56 tickets for the journey cost? €_____

Maths Fact   1·067m is the height of the hurdles in the men's 110 metre track race.

Challenge   In an athletics season during which an athlete cleared 87 of these hurdles, how many metres in total did he clear? _____ m

A quick look back 2

1. Write the value of the 4 in 134,765.

   _____

2. Write the value of the 9 in 937,582.

   _____

3. Add 60,000 to 437,156.

   _____

4. What is the total value of
   3 millions + 764 thousands + 195.

   _____

5. Write the missing amount to make up the jackpot total.

   €2,375,846

   €300,000   €70,000

   €5,000   €2,000,000

   €6   €40   _____

6. Write in our numerals the value of this Roman numeral amount: **MCMLXXVIII**.

   _____

7. Round 836,795 to the nearest thousand.

   _____

8. A helicopter costs €175,286. A better one costs €23,000 more. How much does the better helicopter cost?

   _____

9. What must be added to 499,992 to make 500,000?

   _____

10. A buyer needs another €9 to be able to buy the car. How much money has she?

    €60,000

    _____

11. What is the average of these four numbers:

    11 **19** **12** and **18** ?

    _____

12. The average height of the children is 130cm. If Kim is 138cm and Jim is 128cm, how tall is Tim?

    Tim   Kim   Jim

    _____ cm

13. The average of 6 numbers is 9. Five of the numbers are:

    8 **12** **9** **5** **7** **?**

    What is the sixth number?   _____

14. If 6 × 40 = 240, what is 6 × 400?

    _____

15. 6 × 2 × 30 = _____

16. What number is 100 times greater than 57?

    _____

17. €3·74 × 1,000 = € _____

18. 5 × 6 × 4 × 100 = _____

19. Elaine drove 965·84km in September. Evan drove one hundred times that distance last year. How far did Evan drive?

    _____ km

20. A lorry can carry 100 pallets, each holding 56 crates. How many crates altogether could two such lorries carry?

    _____

    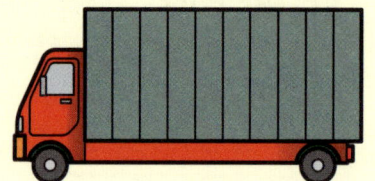

Chapter 7: Division 1 – Division strategies

Division is the **opposite** of multiplication.

1. Connect the facts on the left to the related facts on the right in each question.

A

3 × 12 = 36 •	• 8 × 4 = 32
55 ÷ 11 = 5 •	• 56 ÷ 7 = 8
7 × 8 = 56 •	• 36 ÷ 3 = 12
32 ÷ 4 = 8 •	• 11 × 5 = 55

B

42 ÷ 6 = 7 •	• 9 × 6 = 54
9 × 7 = 63 •	• 40 ÷ 5 = 8
5 × 8 = 40 •	• 63 ÷ 9 = 7
54 ÷ 9 = 6 •	• 6 × 7 = 42

We used a web for multiplication. Here is a web for division.

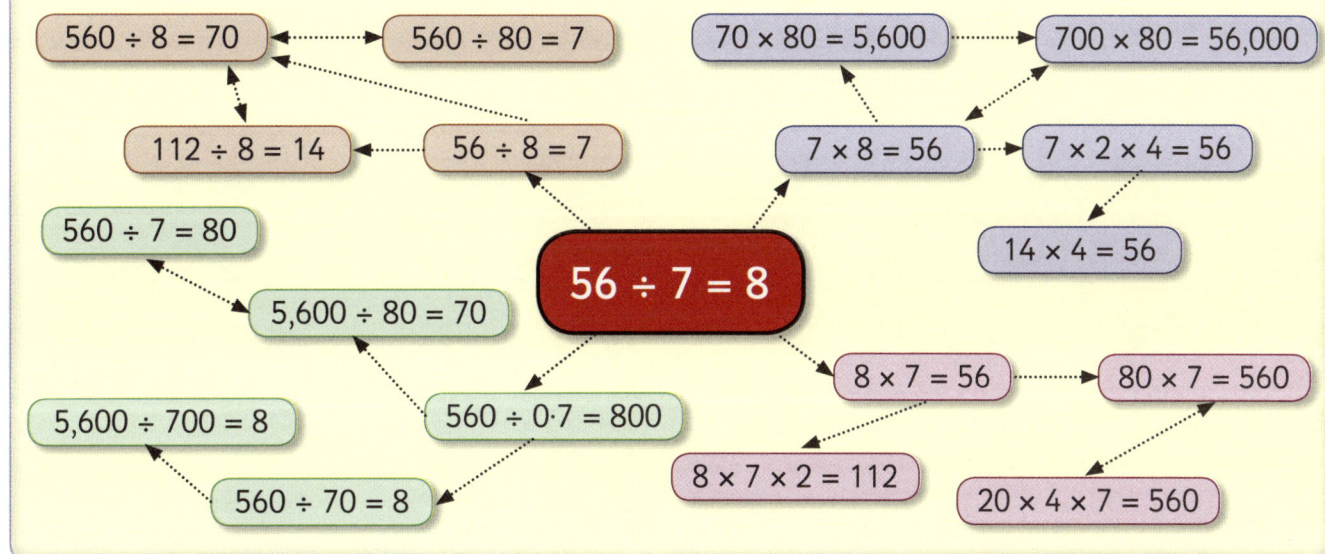

560 ÷ 8 = 70   560 ÷ 80 = 7   70 × 80 = 5,600   700 × 80 = 56,000

112 ÷ 8 = 14   56 ÷ 8 = 7   7 × 8 = 56   7 × 2 × 4 = 56

560 ÷ 7 = 80   14 × 4 = 56

5,600 ÷ 80 = 70   **56 ÷ 7 = 8**

5,600 ÷ 700 = 8   560 ÷ 0·7 = 800   8 × 7 = 56   80 × 7 = 560

560 ÷ 70 = 8   8 × 7 × 2 = 112   20 × 4 × 7 = 560

2. Draw your own web for (a) 36 ÷ 4 = 9   (b) 18 ÷ 3 = 6   (c) 48 ÷ 6 = 8

3. Use the web strategy to do these.

(a) 36 ÷ 9 = _____   (d) 18 ÷ 6 = _____   (g) 48 ÷ 8 = _____

(b) 360 ÷ 9 = _____   (e) 180 ÷ 6 = _____   (h) 480 ÷ 8 = _____

(c) 3,600 ÷ 90 = _____   (f) 1,800 ÷ 60 = _____   (i) 4,800 ÷ 80 = _____

4. Complete these number sentences.

(a) _____ ÷ 6 = 7   (b) _____ ÷ 4 = 12   (c) 35 ÷ _____ = 5

(d) 63 ÷ _____ = 9   (e) 36 ÷ _____ = 6   (f) 54 ÷ _____ = 9

(g) 48 ÷ _____ = 8   (h) 27 ÷ _____ = 9   (i) 81 ÷ _____ = 27

(j) 72 ÷ _____ = 9   (k) 72 ÷ _____ = 8   (l) _____ ÷ 9 = 11

Maths Fact   7·26kg is the weight of the heavy metal ball used by shot put athletes.

Challenge   What would be the weight of a shot put ball be if it was reduced in weight by one third? _____ kg

STRAND Number   **STRAND UNIT/ELEMENT** Operations
LANGUAGE Division strategies, the web strategy, divisor, factors, long division, estimate

29

Division 1

A To divide a number by 10, move all digits 1 place to the right.

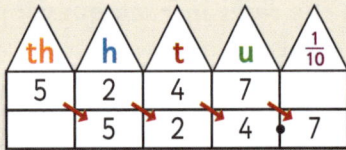

th	h	t	u	$\frac{1}{10}$
5	2	4	7	
	5	2	4 •	7

B To divide a number by 100, move all digits 2 places to the right.

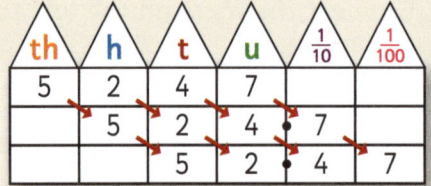

th	h	t	u	$\frac{1}{10}$	$\frac{1}{100}$
5	2	4	7		
	5	2	4 •	7	
		5	2 •	4	7

C To divide a number by 1,000, move all digits 3 places to the right.

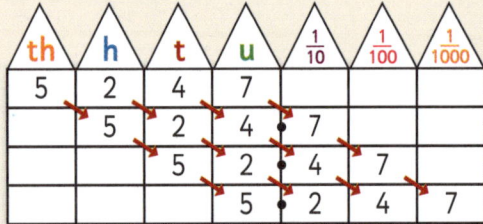

th	h	t	u	$\frac{1}{10}$	$\frac{1}{100}$	$\frac{1}{1000}$
5	2	4	7			
	5	2	4 •	7		
		5	2 •	4	7	
			5 •	2	4	7

> **Hot Tip!** The digits move right by the number of zeros in the divisor.

1. (a) 429 ÷ 10 (b) 643 ÷ 100 (c) 27·5 ÷ 10 (d) 27·5 ÷ 100

2. (a) 91·6 ÷ 100 (b) 15·2 ÷ 10 (c) 3,784 ÷ 1,000 (d) 6 ÷ 10

3. (a) 70 ÷ 100 (b) 3·7 ÷ 100 (c) 42·2 ÷ 1,000 (d) 621·3 ÷ 1,000

4. (a) 304 ÷ 1,000 (b) 0·8 ÷ 100 (c) 87 ÷ 100 (d) 0·54 ÷ 10

5. (a) 62m ÷ 100 (b) 52·7km ÷ 1,000 (c) 9kg ÷ 100 (d) 7·3l ÷ 10

6. A wine cellar in France holds 12,000 bottles of wine. There are 1,000 boxes of bottles. How many bottles are there in each box? _____

7. Over a period of 100 days, an electricity meter increased by 2,739 units. What was the average daily consumption of units of electricity? _____

8. The marathon distance is 42·2km. In a charity event, 10 runners shared the running distance equally.

   (a) How far in metres did each athlete run? _____ m

   (b) If 100 runners had shared the distance equally, how far in metres would each have run? _____ m

9. A builders' supplier sold 1,000 concrete blocks for €740.

   What was the cost: (a) per block? _____   (b) per 100 blocks? _____

   (c) per 10 blocks? _____   (d) per 700 blocks? _____   (e) per 60 blocks? _____

> **Maths Fact**   The longest man-made canal in the world (China's Grand Canal) is 1,800km.

> **Challenge**   Divide the length of China's Grand Canal into: (a) 10 equal lengths [____] ;
>
> (b) 100 equal lengths [____] ; (c) 1,000 equal lengths. [____]

Division 1 – Mental strategies (factors)

Another way of making division easier is to use the **factors** of the divisor. e.g. $540 \div 18 = \text{☆}$

Factors of 18 = (6 × 3) or (9 × 2)

A

$540 \div 18 = \text{☆}$

→ (540 ÷ 6) ÷ 3

→ 90 ÷ 3

= 30

B

$540 \div 18 = \text{☆}$

$6\overline{)540}$
$3\overline{)90}$
30

C

$540 \div 18 = \text{☆}$

→ (540 ÷ 9) ÷ 2

→ 60 ÷ 2

= 30

D

$540 \div 18 = \text{☆}$

$9\overline{)540}$
$2\overline{)60}$
30

Use a pair of factors of the divisor to do the following:

1. (a) 360 ÷ 18   (b) 720 ÷ 24   (c) 840 ÷ 35   (d) 848 ÷ 16

2. (a) 675 ÷ 15   (b) 693 ÷ 21   (c) 648 ÷ 36   (d) 476 ÷ 28

3. The Passage East car ferry carried a total of 450 cars in one day. If it took 15 cars on each trip, how many trips did the ferry make? _____

4. 432 golf balls were packaged into boxes containing 24 golf balls each. How many boxes were filled? _____

5. A mobile cinema can accommodate 384 customers. Each row has 24 seats. How many rows are there altogether? _____

6. 594 passengers are on a train to Sligo. There are 54 passengers in each carriage. How many carriages has the train altogether? _____

7. A wholesale fruit merchant has 945 bananas. The bananas are packed in boxes of 63. How many boxes are needed to pack all the bananas? _____

A number is divisible by **3** if the sum of its digits is a multiple of 3, e.g.

255·3 → (2 + 5 + 5 + 3 = 15)

A number is divisible by **6** if the sum of its digits is divisible by 3 and ends in an even digit, e.g.

5,814 → (5 + 8 + 1 + 4 = 18)

8. Divide each of the following numbers by 3. Some of the numbers can be divided evenly by 6. Divide those ones by 6 also.

(a) 483   (b) 19·32   (c) 8·25   (d) 75·3   (e) 52·62

(f) 195·3   (g) 827·4   (h) 63·54   (i) 30·93   (j) 72·42

Maths Fact   When hit by a top badminton player, a shuttlecock can reach a speed of 320km/h.

Challenge   Use factors to divide 320 by: (a) 40 and (b) 16.

Division 1 – Long division of 4 digits

The north stand of a stadium has 27 equal rows of seating. When full, the stand holds 9,342 fans. How many seats are there in each row?

Was 300 a good estimate? Explain.

Estimate:

9,342 ÷ 27

→ 9,000 ÷ 30

→ 900 ÷ 3

= 300

Answer = 346 seats

Long division

```
        346
27 ) 9342
   -  81↓
      124
    - 108↓
       162
     - 162
         0
```

Now do these. Estimate first. You may use a calculator to check your answers.

1. (a) 8,645 ÷ 35   (b) 7,344 ÷ 48   (c) 6,885 ÷ 27   (d) 8,284 ÷ 19

2. (a) 9,425 ÷ 25   (b) 7,130 ÷ 46   (c) 8,149 ÷ 29   (d) 9,386 ÷ 38

3. (a) 5,817 ÷ 21   (b) 6,768 ÷ 18   (c) 6,837 ÷ 43   (d) 9,588 ÷ 51

4. (a) 7,733 ÷ 19   (b) 6,846 ÷ 42   (c) 8,532 ÷ 36   (d) 6,992 ÷ 16

5. (a) 9,381 ÷ 53   (b) 7,232 ÷ 32   (c) 6,919 ÷ 37   (d) 7,938 ÷ 14

SUPERSTORE

6. An electrical store sold 37 fridges in a 'flash sale' and made €9,065. What was the sale price of each fridge? **sale**

7. The store took in €7,003 by selling 47 vacuum cleaners. What was the sale price of each? **sale**

8. 28 tablet computers were sold. They yielded €7,112 for the store. What was the sale price of each tablet? **sale**

9. A manager spent €43·68 posting cards to customers in Cork. If each card took a 78c stamp, how many cards were sent?

10. The same manager spent €87·75 posting cards to their 65 Swiss clients. What was the postage cost to Switzerland per card?

éire

11. The manager sent all of his 37 French clients calendars. Postage for this cost €99·16. What was the postage cost per calendar?

Maths Fact   650 people, on average, are mauled or killed by wild big cats each year.

Challenge   Based on the above figure, what is the average number of people killed or mauled by wild big cats each month? Round your answer to the nearest whole number. ☐

Division 1 – Long division

111·8 litres of water escaped from a leaking tap over a 13 day period. How many litres escaped daily?

111·8 ÷ 13 = ☆

Estimate: 110 ÷ 10 = 11

The tap leaked 8·6 litres per day.

Long division

```
        8·6
  13 ) 111·8
     −  104↓
          78
       −  78
           0
```

Hot Tip!
Always write the decimal points under or over each other when doing division.

Now do these using the **long division** method. Estimate first.

1. (a) 68·4 ÷ 36	(b) 89·1 ÷ 27	(c) 79·8 ÷ 19	(d) 82·8 ÷ 23
2. (a) 100·8 ÷ 28	(b) 64·6 ÷ 17	(c) 95·2 ÷ 56	(d) 62·9 ÷ 37
3. (a) 92·4 ÷ 28	(b) 101·5 ÷ 35	(c) 89·9 ÷ 29	(d) 89·9 ÷ 31
4. (a) 115·2 ÷ 18	(b) 215·8 ÷ 26	(c) 155·1 ÷ 47	(d) 190·4 ÷ 34
5. (a) 148·2 ÷ 39	(b) 197·1 ÷ 73	(c) 448·9 ÷ 67	(d) 244·4 ÷ 52

Sometimes we will get an answer that may be **less than one unit**.

8·74 ÷ 19 = ☆   Estimate: 10 ÷ 20 = 0·5

8·74m of material is used to make 19 flags. How many metres are used for each flag?

Long division

```
        0·46
  19 ) 8·74
     − 76↓
        114
     − 114
          0
```

Hot Tip!
Always write a **zero** in the units place before the decimal point.

Each flag requires 0·46m

Now complete these. Don't forget the zero before the decimal point.

6. (a) 9·46 ÷ 22	(b) 5·95 ÷ 35	(c) 7·56 ÷ 21	(d) 8·74 ÷ 38
7. (a) 9·66 ÷ 46	(b) 9·01 ÷ 53	(c) 9·62 ÷ 37	(d) 9·28 ÷ 29
8. (a) €9·99 ÷ 27	(b) €8·82 ÷ 14	(c) €6·76 ÷ 26	(d) €7·02 ÷ 18
9. (a) 5·55m ÷ 15	(b) 6·66m ÷ 37	(c) 9·89m ÷ 43	(d) 8·48m ÷ 16
10. (a) €9·36 ÷ 36	(b) €8·97 ÷ 13	(c) €6·67 ÷ 23	(d) €9·86 ÷ 34

Maths Fact   60,000 bees live in an average bee colony.

Challenge   How many bees would be in each colony, if we divided this number by 20?

Division 1 – Do I multiply or divide?

1. How many performances will there be in total? _____

2. What is the total seating capacity of the Olympia Theatre? _____

3. All the seats in the stalls and circle were sold for the 3 matinee performances. The upper circle was closed. How many seats in total were sold? _____

4. Only half of the circle seats were sold for Wednesday night. What was the value of the circle seats sold for that performance? € _____

5. Each show lasts 97 mins. At what time does each matinee end? [:]

6. For the opening night, circle tickets were reduced to €15 each. How many were sold at this price, if circle ticket sales yielded €5,640? _____

7. On the opening night, stalls ticket sales yielded receipts of €7,362. These tickets had been reduced by €4·50. How many tickets were sold? _____

8. Mr and Mrs Casey brought their triplets to the Friday night show. They bought stalls tickets and got the children's tickets at half price. What was the total cost for the Casey family? € _____

9. €292·50 was taken in on Friday by sales of "Magical Calculators" in the Olympia shop. If 78 calculators were sold, what did each cost? € _____

10. What amount would have been received in ticket sales, if all tickets for the Monday show had been sold at full price? € _____

11. €9,826 was taken in on Tuesday 12th. $\frac{3}{10}$ of this was donated to charity. How much was donated to charity? € _____

12. How many shows would be performed over a period of 1,118 minutes if each performance lasted only 86 minutes? _____

13. On Thursday night, $\frac{1}{4}$ of the stall seats, $\frac{1}{8}$ of the circle seats and $\frac{1}{2}$ of the upper circle seats were sold. How many seats were empty? _____

The Olympia Theatre presents

Tom and the Magical Calculator

by The Maths Theatrical Society

Mon 11th March – Mon 18th March
[No show Sun 17th March]

Show each evening @ 8pm

Matinees:
Thurs, Fri, Sat, @ 2.30pm

Ticket Prices:
Stalls: €22·50   Circle: €17·50   Upper Circle: €12·50

Olympia Theatre, Dublin: Opened 1879

Seating Capacity:
Stalls: 516   Circle: 408   Upper Circle: 316

Maths Fact

London's famous Royal Albert Hall opened in 1871 and has a capacity of 5,272 seats.

Challenge

(a) If one-quarter of the seats in the Royal Albert Hall were not sold for an event, what was the attendance? _____

(b) How much more than a full Olympia theatre is this? _____

Chapter 8: Lines and angles

1. What type of angle is made in each picture? Choose from the list.

acute	right	obtuse	straight	reflex

(a)   (b)   (c)   (d)   (e)

_____   _____   _____   _____   _____

2.
Outside scale   **Inside scale**

140°

(i) Read the measure of each angle and write it in degrees.
(ii) Say whether the **inside scale** or **outside scale** is used.

(a)   (b)

(c)   (d)   (e)

3. Use your protractor to measure the following angles.   *Use either scale!*

(a) _____   (b) _____   (c) _____   (d) _____

Draw a 50° angle.

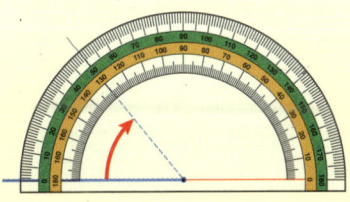

1. Draw a line. Mark one end of the line.
2. Place the centre point of the protractor on this mark.
3. Count from 0° to 50°. Make a new mark at 50°.
4. Join your two marks with a straight line to form your angle.

4. Use your protractor and pencil to draw the following angles.

(a) 30°	(b) 60°	(c) 45°	(d) 75°	(e) 95°	(f) 15°	(g) 135°	(h) 175°
(i) 28°	(j) 144°	(k) 63°	(l) 99°	(m) 104°	(n) 132°	(o) 78°	(p) 8°

STRAND Shape and space   **STRAND UNIT/ELEMENT** Lines and angles
LANGUAGE Angle, acute, right, straight, obtuse, reflex, rotation, protractor, inside scale, outside scale, measure, estimate, triangle, side, trapezium, quadrilateral, clockwise, anti-clockwise.

Lines and angles

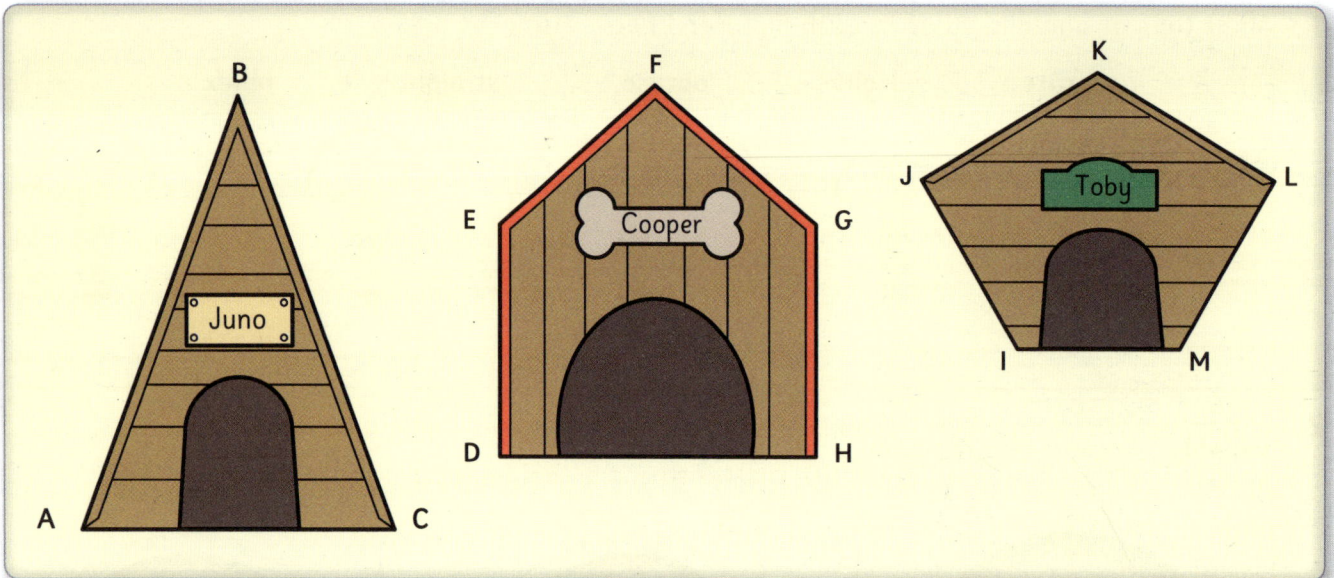

1. Measure the angles in each kennel. Complete the tables below.

Juno's Kennel			
Angle	Estimate	Measure	Type of angle
A			
B			
C			

Estimate first. Then use your protractor to measure.

Cooper's Kennel			
Angle	Estimate	Measure	Type of angle
D			
E			
F			
G			
H			

Toby's Kennel			
Angle	Estimate	Measure	Type of angle
I			
J			
K			
L			
M			

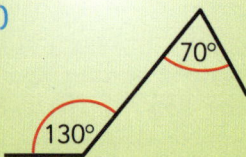 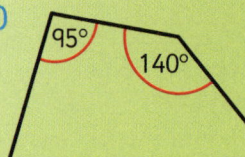 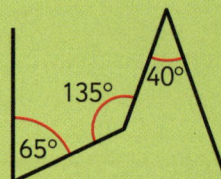

2. Draw kennels where the point of the roof has an angle of:

   (a) 90°   (b) 130°   (c) 65°   (d) 145°   (e) 80°

Challenge

Draw the following angle pictures in your copy. Use your protractor and ruler.

(a) 70° 130°

(b) 95° 140°

(c) 135° 65° 40°

The lines can be any length!

Lines and angles

Draw the following triangle: One side measures **5cm**. Another side measures **3cm**. The angle between them measures **100°**. Complete the triangle.

Step 1

5cm

Draw your first line – **5cm**.

Step 2

5cm

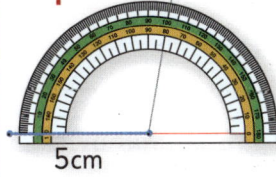

From one end of the line, measure a **100° angle**.

Step 3

100°   3cm

5cm

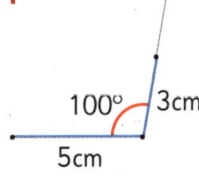

Make the 100° angle. The new line must measure **3cm**.

Step 4

3cm

5cm

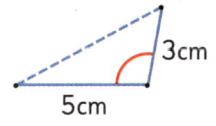

Join the two lines to complete the triangle.

1. Draw the following triangles in your copy.

	Line	Line	Angle between them
(a)	4cm	5cm	120°
(b)	6cm	8cm	85°
(c)	9cm	4cm	40°

	Line	Line	Angle between them
(d)	5·5cm	5cm	70°
(e)	7·3cm	5·4cm	110°
(f)	4·8cm	3.5cm	65°

Draw the following triangle: One side measures **5cm**. The angle at one end of this line measures **70°**. The angle at the other end measures **50°**.

Step 1

5cm

Draw your first line – **5cm**.

Step 2

5cm

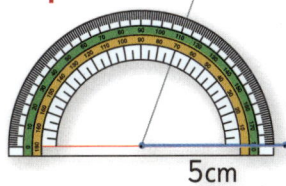

Draw a **70°** angle from the left side of the line (inside scale).

Step 3

70°

50°

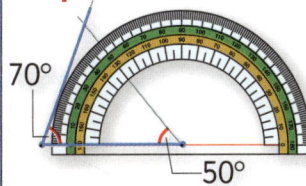

Draw a **50°** angle from the right side of the line (outside scale).

Step 4

70°   50°

5cm

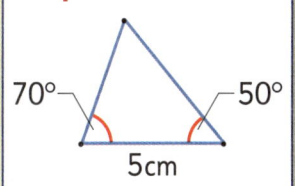

Extend both new lines until they meet.

2. Draw the following triangles in your copy.

	Line	Angle	Angle
(a)	6cm	40°	80°
(b)	7cm	65°	65°
(c)	8cm	75°	25°

	Line	Angle	Angle
(d)	5·6cm	55°	90°
(e)	6·2cm	100°	46°
(f)	7·7cm	73°	68°

Challenge

Draw this quadrilateral, accurately, in your copy. Use real size measurements.

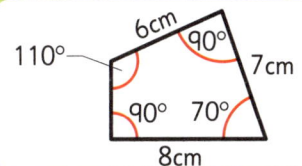

110°   6cm   90°   7cm
90°   70°
8cm

Lines and angles

1. What is the measure of each angle in an equilateral triangle?

   _____ degrees

2. Without using a protractor, (i) calculate the size of the **unknown** angles and, (ii) say whether the angles are **acute**, **right-angled** or **obtuse**.

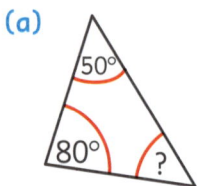

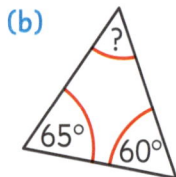

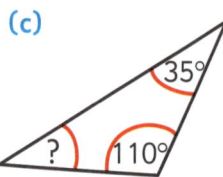

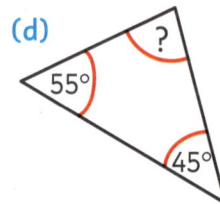

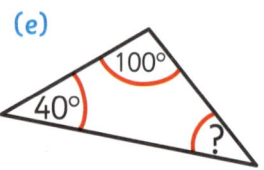

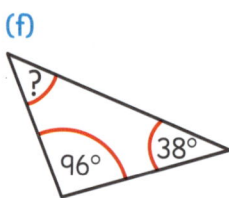

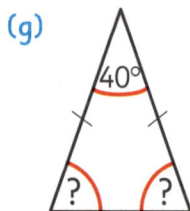

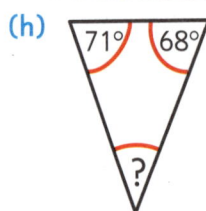

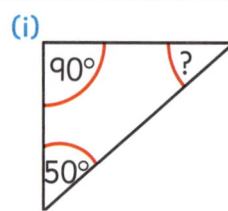

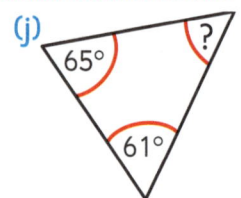

   (a) 50° 80° ?

   (b) ? 65° 60°

   (c) 35° ? 110°

   (d) 55° ? 45°

   (e) 100° 40° ?

   (f) ? 96° 38°

   (g) 40° ? ?

   (h) 71° 68° ?

   (i) 90° ? 50°

   (j) ? 65° 61°

3.

   (a) Name the: (i) blue 2-D shape (ii) the yellow 2-D shape.

   (b) When combined, the two shapes form a _____.

   (c) How many degrees are in the blue shape? _____.

   (d) How many degrees are in the yellow shape? _____.

   (e) How many degrees altogether are in the rectangle? _____.

   All quadrilaterals can be divided into two triangles, so the angles of all quadrilaterals have 360°.

4. Without using a protractor, (i) calculate the measure of each **unknown** angle, and (ii) say whether the angle is **acute**, **right** or **obtuse**.

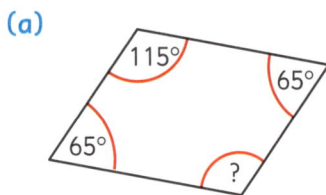

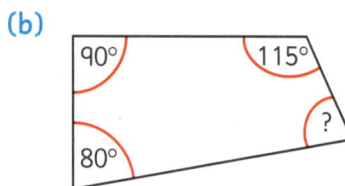

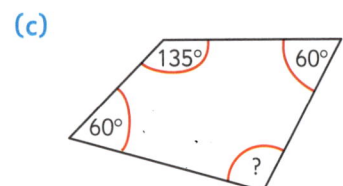

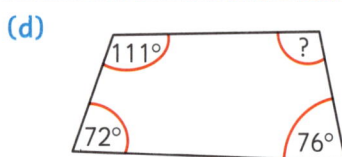

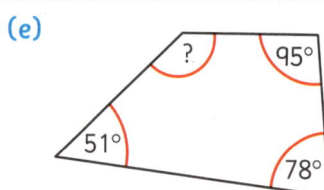

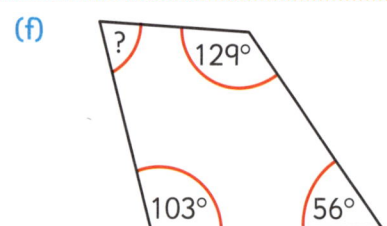

   (a) 115° 65° 65° ?

   (b) 90° 115° 80° ?

   (c) 135° 60° 60° ?

   (d) 111° ? 72° 76°

   (e) ? 95° 51° 78°

   (f) ? 129° 103° 56°

Lines and angles

Remember, a protractor is a semi-circle. A semi-circle has 180°, so a circle has 360°.

1. How many degrees has the ice-skater (rotated) in each picture.

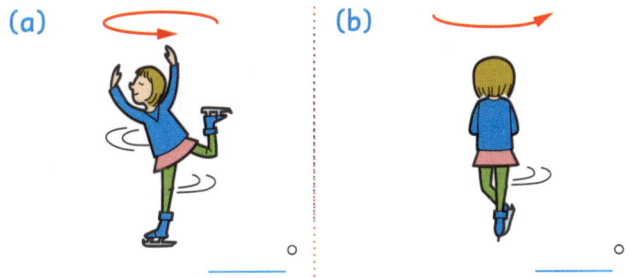

    (a) _____ °   (b) _____ °

    (c) _____ °   (d) _____ °   (e) _____ °   (f) _____ °

    Key
    → = $\frac{1}{4}$ turn
    → = $\frac{1}{2}$ turn
    → = $\frac{3}{4}$ turn
    → = full turn

2. (a) Through how many degrees does the minute hand of a clock turn in:
    (i) 1 hour?   (ii) $\frac{1}{4}$ hour?   (iii) $\frac{3}{4}$ hour?   (iv) $\frac{1}{2}$ hour?   (v) $1\frac{1}{12}$ hour?
    (vi) 1 minute?   (vii) 5 minutes?   (viii) 20 minutes.

    (b) Through how many degrees does the minute hand turn from:
    (i)   12:00 → 12:25   (ii)   06:25 → 06:40   (iii) 11:20 → 11:30
    (iv) 21:15 → 21:50   (v)   12:55 → 13:40   (vi) 04:50 → 05:19
    (vii) 19:20 → 19:55   (viii) 17:45 → 18:35   (ix) 22:40 → 23:50

3. (a) Is the wheel rotating in a clockwise or anti-clockwise direction?

    (b) Which colour carriage will the white carriage replace after a:
    (ii) $\frac{1}{2}$ turn?   (ii) $\frac{3}{4}$ turn?   (iii) $\frac{1}{8}$ turn?
    (iv) $\frac{5}{8}$ turn?   (v) $\frac{1}{4}$ turn?   (vi) $\frac{3}{8}$ turn?
    (vii) $1\frac{1}{4}$ turns?   (viii) $1\frac{4}{8}$ turns?   (ix) $2\frac{5}{8}$ turns?
    (x) $2\frac{1}{2}$ turns?   (xi) $2\frac{3}{4}$ turns?   (xii) $3\frac{7}{8}$ turns?

    (c) Through how many degrees must the wheel spin for the:
    (i)   red carriage to reach the top?   (ii) green carriage to reach the bottom?
    (iii) pink carriage to reach the bottom?   (iv) orange and purple carriages to swap places?

    (d) Which colour carriage will the orange carriage replace after the wheel has rotated:
    (i)   90°   (ii) 45°   (iii) 270°   (iv) 315°   (v) 180°

    (vi) 225°   (vii) 135°   (viii) 360°   (ix) 540°   (x) 405°

Lines and angles

1. Calculate the number of degrees in the **unknown** angles, without using a protractor.

(a)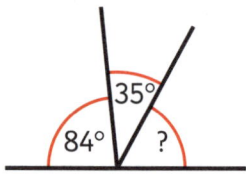

(b)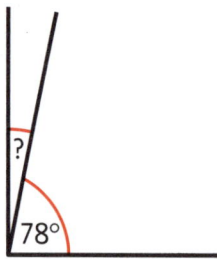

(c)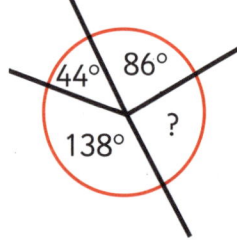

(d)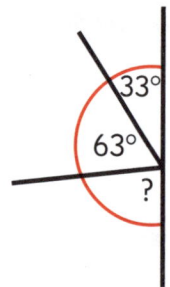

(e)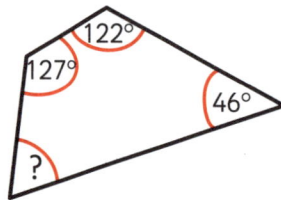

(f)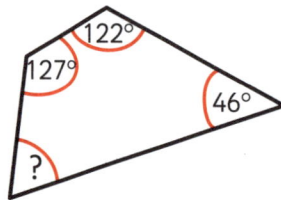

(g)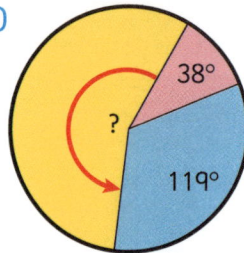

(h)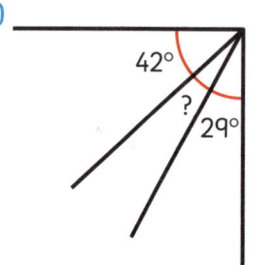

(i)

(j)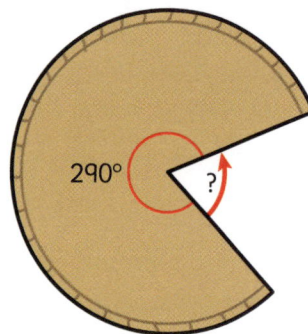

(k)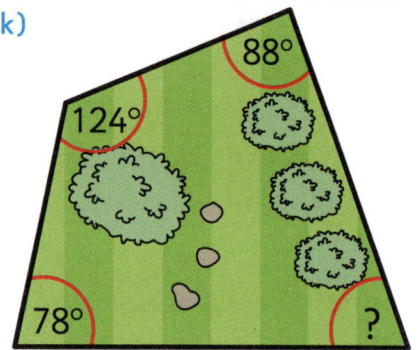

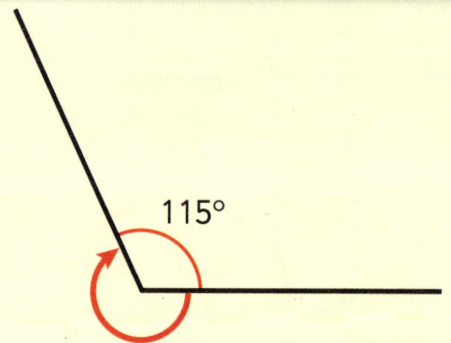

Drawing a reflex angle of 245°.

1. Subtract your angle from 360°.

   $360° - 245° = 115°$

2. Use your protractor to measure and draw a 115° angle.

3. Mark in your 245° reflex angle.

115°

2. Use your protractor to draw the following **reflex** angles:

(a) 260°	(b) 300°	(c) 190°	(d) 275°	(e) 340°
(f) 316°	(g) 199°	(h) 324°	(i) 293°	(j) 352°

3. Using your protractor, measure the following **reflex** angles.

(a) _____   (b) _____   (c) _____   (d) _____

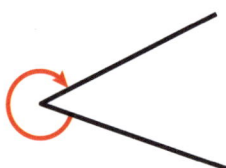

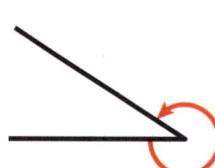
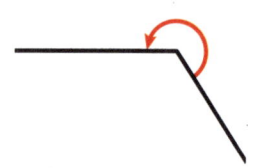

Chapter 9: Fractions 1

Quick quiz – Finding fractions!

(a) $\frac{5}{9}$ of 18 = _____

(b) If $\frac{5}{7}$ = 10, then $\frac{7}{7}$ = _____

(c) Find $\frac{1}{12}$ of 36. _____

(d) If $\frac{2}{3}$ = 8, $\frac{3}{4}$ = _____

(e) If 15 = $\frac{3}{5}$, 10 = _____

(f) $\frac{5}{9}$ of _____ = 45

---

1. **Improper fractions** and **mixed numbers**.

Sort these into their correct category below:

$\frac{3}{4}$,　$1\frac{1}{2}$,　5,　$\frac{6}{5}$,　$2\frac{7}{9}$,　$\frac{5}{3}$,　$\frac{15}{23}$,　$\frac{18}{7}$,　13,　$\frac{13}{5}$,　$\frac{5}{53}$,　$1\frac{3}{10}$,　$\frac{45}{1000}$.

(a) Whole numbers	(b) Fractions	(c) Mixed numbers	(d) Improper fractions

---

2. **Mixed numbers.** Tick ☑ if true, ☒ if false.

(a) $3\frac{1}{4} = \frac{12}{4}$ ☐

(b) $\frac{13}{5} = 2\frac{3}{5}$ ☐

(c) $\frac{27}{9} = 3$ ☐

(d) $\frac{45}{11} = 4\frac{5}{11}$ ☐

(e) $2\frac{1}{10} = \frac{21}{10}$ ☐

(f) $10\frac{1}{2} = \frac{12}{10}$ ☐

(g) $\frac{15}{3} = 6$ ☐

(h) $7\frac{1}{2} = \frac{15}{7}$ ☐

---

3. **Equivalent fractions.**

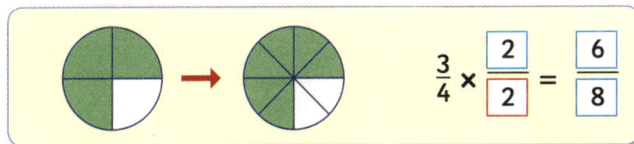

$\frac{3}{4} \times \frac{\boxed{2}}{\boxed{2}} = \frac{\boxed{6}}{\boxed{8}}$

> I concentrate on the denominator.
> $4 \times \boxed{2} = 8$
> I must now multiply the numerator by 2 also.

(a) $\frac{2}{3} \times \frac{\boxed{}}{\boxed{}} = \frac{\boxed{}}{6}$

(b) $\frac{4}{5} \times \frac{\boxed{}}{\boxed{}} = \frac{\boxed{}}{20}$

(c) $\frac{1}{4} \times \frac{\boxed{}}{\boxed{}} = \frac{\boxed{}}{16}$

(d) $\frac{4}{7} \times \frac{\boxed{}}{\boxed{}} = \frac{\boxed{}}{21}$

(e) $\frac{3}{5} \times \frac{\boxed{}}{\boxed{}} = \frac{\boxed{}}{25}$

(f) $\frac{5}{8} \times \frac{\boxed{}}{\boxed{}} = \frac{\boxed{}}{24}$

---

4. Use your head! Work out these to make **equivalent fractions**!

(a) $\frac{1}{2} = \frac{\boxed{}}{14}$

(b) $\frac{2}{3} = \frac{\boxed{}}{9}$

(c) $\frac{7}{8} = \frac{\boxed{}}{16}$

(d) $\frac{4}{5} = \frac{\boxed{}}{15}$

(e) $\frac{1}{3} = \frac{\boxed{}}{12}$

(f) $\frac{3}{4} = \frac{\boxed{}}{20}$

(g) $\frac{1}{6} = \frac{\boxed{}}{24}$

(h) $\frac{2}{5} = \frac{\boxed{}}{25}$

(i) $\frac{5}{7} = \frac{\boxed{}}{21}$

(j) $\frac{5}{8} = \frac{\boxed{}}{40}$

(k) $\frac{7}{8} = \frac{\boxed{}}{24}$

(l) $\frac{5}{9} = \frac{\boxed{}}{45}$

(m) $\frac{2}{3} = \frac{\boxed{}}{15}$

(n) $\frac{4}{5} = \frac{\boxed{}}{40}$

(o) $\frac{5}{12} = \frac{\boxed{}}{36}$

---

5. Find the pairs of cards that match! Colour each pair the same colour:

$\frac{1}{2}$　$\frac{3}{5}$　$\frac{3}{7}$　$\frac{1}{5}$　$\frac{6}{10}$　$\frac{8}{12}$　$\frac{4}{20}$　$\frac{9}{30}$　$\frac{5}{50}$　$\frac{7}{14}$　$\frac{9}{21}$　$\frac{1}{10}$　$\frac{6}{18}$　$\frac{2}{3}$　$\frac{1}{3}$　$\frac{3}{10}$

STRAND **Number**   STRAND UNIT/ELEMENT *Fractions*
LANGUAGE *Fractions, mixed numbers, equivalent/equivalence, compare, numerator, denominator, number line, common denominators, addition, subtraction, multiplication of segments*

Equivalent fractions

A: Using equivalent fractions – which is bigger?

How do we compare (a) $\frac{2}{3}$ and (b) $\frac{3}{4}$?

Remember: $\frac{3}{7}$ ➞ numerator / denominator

We list the **multiples** of each **denominator** until we find a **common** one.

(a) $\frac{2}{3} = \frac{4}{6} = \frac{6}{9} = \boxed{\frac{8}{12}}$

(b) $\frac{3}{4} = \frac{6}{8} = \boxed{\frac{9}{12}}$

12 is the **first common multiple**. It is called a **common denominator**.

$\frac{2}{3} = \frac{8}{12}$ $\frac{3}{4} = \frac{9}{12}$ so $\frac{3}{4} > \frac{2}{3}$

We can also see this from the following diagrams:

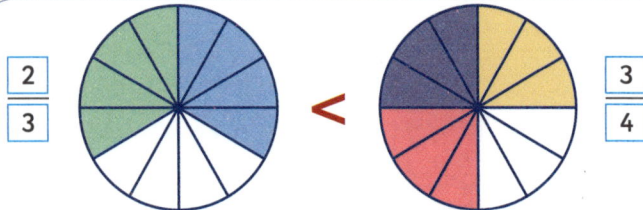

$\frac{2}{3}$ < $\frac{3}{4}$

Always use the smallest or **lowest common denominator**.

B: Which is bigger: $\frac{2}{5}$ or $\frac{1}{4}$? Find a **common denominator** first.

(a) $\frac{2}{5} = \frac{4}{10} \quad \frac{6}{15} \quad \boxed{\frac{8}{20}}$

(b) $\frac{1}{4} = \frac{2}{8} = \frac{3}{12} = \frac{4}{16} = \boxed{\frac{5}{20}}$

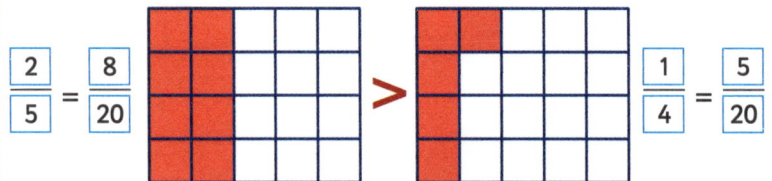

$\frac{2}{5} = \frac{8}{20}$ > $\frac{1}{4} = \frac{5}{20}$

---

1. Which would you prefer? Use a **common denominator** to help you find out.

   (a) $\frac{1}{4}$ or $\frac{2}{6}$ of [€10] $\boxed{\frac{}{}}$

   (b) $\frac{1}{6}$ or $\frac{2}{9}$ of [€20] $\boxed{\frac{}{}}$

   (c) $\frac{2}{3}$ or $\frac{3}{5}$ off the price of a jumper. $\boxed{\frac{}{}}$

   (d) To score $\frac{3}{4}$ or $\frac{4}{5}$ of your shots. $\boxed{\frac{}{}}$

   (e) $\frac{5}{6}$ or $\frac{7}{9}$ of a prize fund. $\boxed{\frac{}{}}$

   (f) $\frac{3}{5}$ or $\frac{5}{8}$ off your homework. $\boxed{\frac{}{}}$

2. Equivalent fractions on the number line:

   (a) Write these fractions on the number line. $\frac{3}{4}$ $\frac{1}{2}$ $\frac{5}{6}$ $\frac{2}{3}$ $\frac{1}{4}$ $\frac{1}{6}$ $\frac{1}{3}$

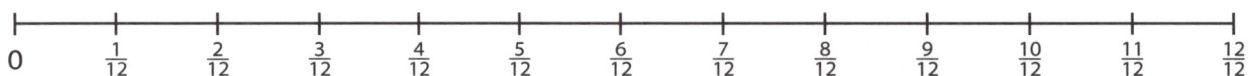

   0   $\frac{1}{12}$ $\frac{2}{12}$ $\frac{3}{12}$ $\frac{4}{12}$ $\frac{5}{12}$ $\frac{6}{12}$ $\frac{7}{12}$ $\frac{8}{12}$ $\frac{9}{12}$ $\frac{10}{12}$ $\frac{11}{12}$ $\frac{12}{12}$

   (b) Write these fractions on the number line. $\frac{1}{4}$ $\frac{1}{2}$ $\frac{7}{20}$ $\frac{2}{5}$ $\frac{1}{20}$ $\frac{3}{10}$ $\frac{3}{4}$ $\frac{7}{10}$ $\frac{4}{5}$ $\frac{9}{10}$

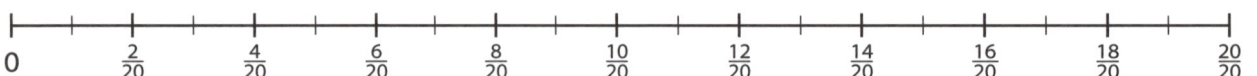

   0   $\frac{2}{20}$ $\frac{4}{20}$ $\frac{6}{20}$ $\frac{8}{20}$ $\frac{10}{20}$ $\frac{12}{20}$ $\frac{14}{20}$ $\frac{16}{20}$ $\frac{18}{20}$ $\frac{20}{20}$

Fractions 1 – Addition and subtraction

Using equivalent fractions – addition.

Step 1: Find the common denominator.

$2\frac{5}{6}$
$+5\frac{7}{9}$

$\frac{5}{6} = \frac{10}{12} = \frac{15}{18}$ $\frac{7}{9} = \frac{14}{18}$

The common denominator is **18**.

Step 2:

$2\frac{5}{6} \rightarrow 2\frac{15}{18}$
$5\frac{7}{9} \rightarrow +5\frac{14}{18}$
$\phantom{5\frac{7}{9} \rightarrow} 7\frac{29}{18} \rightarrow 8\frac{11}{18}$

---

1. Now do these. First find a common denominator.

(a) $3\frac{2}{3}$
$+2\frac{3}{4}$

(b) $6\frac{4}{5}$
$+1\frac{1}{2}$

(c) $1\frac{1}{4}$
$+3\frac{3}{5}$

(d) $2\frac{6}{7}$
$+3\frac{2}{3}$

(e) $2\frac{1}{3}$
$+4\frac{8}{9}$

(f) $3\frac{3}{4}$
$+4\frac{5}{7}$

(g) $2\frac{1}{4}$
$+4\frac{7}{9}$

(h) $3\frac{5}{6}$
$+4\frac{2}{5}$

(i) $4\frac{7}{10}$
$+2\frac{3}{4}$

(j) $2\frac{5}{8}$
$+1\frac{3}{5}$

(k) $1\frac{3}{8}$
$+2\frac{11}{12}$

(l) $3\frac{1}{8}$
$+4\frac{4}{7}$

2. What is the total weight in kg and fractions of a kg of the two boxes of apples? _____

$2\frac{3}{4}$ kg $1\frac{7}{12}$ kg

3. What is the total length in metres and fractions of a metre of these two planks of wood combined? _____

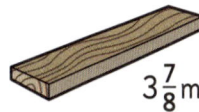

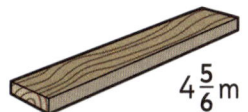

$3\frac{7}{8}$ m $4\frac{5}{6}$ m

Using equivalent fractions – subtraction.

Step 1: Find the common denominator.

$3\frac{1}{6}$
$-\frac{3}{4}$

$\frac{1}{6} = \frac{2}{12}$ $\frac{3}{4} = \frac{6}{8} = \frac{9}{12}$

The common denominator is **12**.

Step 2:

$3\frac{1}{6} \rightarrow 3\frac{2}{12} \rightarrow {}^{2}\cancel{3}\frac{14}{12}$
$-\frac{3}{4} \rightarrow -\frac{9}{12} \rightarrow -\frac{9}{12}$
$\phantom{-\frac{3}{4} \rightarrow -\frac{9}{12} \rightarrow} 2\frac{5}{12}$

---

4. (a) $4\frac{1}{4}$
$-\frac{2}{3}$

(b) $7\frac{3}{4}$
$-\frac{5}{6}$

(c) $5\frac{3}{8}$
$-\frac{11}{16}$

(d) $4\frac{1}{2}$
$-2\frac{2}{3}$

(e) $3\frac{5}{6}$
$-1\frac{8}{9}$

(f) $3\frac{1}{4}$
$-1\frac{3}{5}$

(g) $5\frac{7}{8}$
$-3\frac{5}{6}$

(h) $5\frac{1}{2}$
$-2\frac{7}{11}$

(i) $9\frac{3}{4}$
$-3\frac{9}{10}$

(j) $6\frac{3}{7}$
$-1\frac{3}{4}$

(k) $8\frac{1}{5}$
$-3\frac{5}{8}$

(l) $1\frac{1}{4}$
$-\frac{2}{5}$

Problem-solving and simplifying fractions

Use equivalent fractions to add or subtract.

1. Jemma is $\frac{1}{2}$ way up the mountain. Aoife has climbed $\frac{4}{5}$ of the way. How much higher up is Aoife than Jemma? ☐

2. Jack has $\frac{2}{3}$ of his homework finished. Tina has completed $\frac{3}{4}$ of hers. Who has (i) more completed?, and (ii) how much more?
   (i) _____ (ii) ☐

3. Clare has $\frac{5}{9}$ of the race completed. Maria has completed $\frac{1}{6}$ more of the race than Clare. What fraction of the race has Maria still to complete? ☐

4. A zookeeper fed $14\frac{1}{2}$ fish to the sealions. He gave $3\frac{2}{5}$ fish to the penguins. How many fish had the zookeeper at first? _____

5. A shopkeeper sold $5\frac{7}{8}$ pizzas in the morning and $9\frac{3}{5}$ pizzas in the afternoon. How many more pizzas did she sell in the afternoon? _____

6. Paul ate $3\frac{7}{9}$ pancakes. Priscilla ate $4\frac{1}{4}$ pancakes. How many pancakes did they eat between them? _____

Simplifying fractions

We **simplify** fractions to make them easier to understand and to use: $\frac{12}{20} = \frac{?}{5}$

$$\frac{12}{20} \div \frac{4}{4} = \frac{3}{5}$$

When we divide a fraction by 1 unit, we make no change to its value.

7. Now simplify these fractions.

   (a) $\frac{5}{10}$ = _____
   (b) $\frac{6}{18}$ = _____
   (c) $\frac{15}{20}$ = _____
   (d) $\frac{60}{70}$ = _____
   (e) $\frac{14}{21}$ = _____
   (f) $\frac{25}{40}$ = _____

8. Simplify the **fraction part** of these **mixed numbers**. Write the simplified answers.

   (a) $3\frac{10}{15}$ = _____
   (b) $4\frac{12}{16}$ = _____
   (c) $2\frac{12}{20}$ = _____
   (d) $9\frac{15}{60}$ = _____

   (e) $5\frac{9}{24}$ = _____
   (f) $7\frac{21}{28}$ = _____
   (g) $6\frac{35}{42}$ = _____
   (h) $8\frac{49}{63}$ = _____

   (i) $1\frac{36}{48}$ = _____
   (j) $5\frac{28}{63}$ = _____
   (k) $3\frac{35}{50}$ = _____
   (l) $8\frac{32}{48}$ = _____

   (m) $13\frac{8}{36}$ = _____
   (n) $17\frac{35}{42}$ = _____
   (o) $14\frac{45}{60}$ = _____
   (p) $15\frac{20}{45}$ = _____

9. Find the matching pairs. Colour each pair the same colour.

   $5\frac{3}{9}$ $5\frac{25}{40}$ $5\frac{3}{4}$ $5\frac{2}{7}$ $5\frac{1}{3}$ $5\frac{9}{21}$ $5\frac{5}{8}$ $5\frac{3}{7}$ $5\frac{9}{12}$ $5\frac{12}{42}$

Multiplying a fraction by a whole number

Simplify fractions ending in one or more zeros.

(a) $\dfrac{70}{100} \div \dfrac{10}{10} = \dfrac{7}{10}$ (b) $\dfrac{90}{200} \div \dfrac{10}{10} = \dfrac{9}{20}$ (c) $\dfrac{300}{1000} \div \dfrac{100}{100} = \dfrac{3}{10}$

The quick way is to cross off the zeros: $\dfrac{3\cancel{0}}{10\cancel{0}} = \dfrac{3}{10}$; $\dfrac{7\cancel{00}}{10\cancel{00}} = \dfrac{7}{10}$

1. What fraction of each picture is coloured? Simplify.

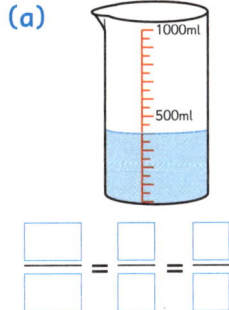

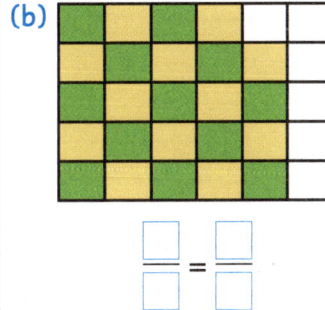

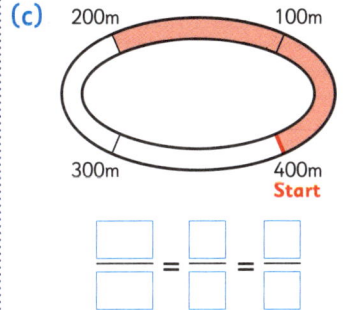

$\dfrac{20}{60} = \dfrac{2}{6} = \dfrac{1}{3}$

(a) $\dfrac{\square}{\square} = \dfrac{\square}{\square} = \dfrac{\square}{\square}$

(b) $\dfrac{\square}{\square} = \dfrac{\square}{\square}$

(c) $\dfrac{\square}{\square} = \dfrac{\square}{\square} = \dfrac{\square}{\square}$

2. Now try these.

(a) $\dfrac{10}{100} = \dfrac{\square}{\square}$ (b) $\dfrac{100}{1000} = \dfrac{\square}{\square}$ (c) $\dfrac{90}{1000} = \dfrac{\square}{\square}$ (d) $\dfrac{240}{1000} = \dfrac{\square}{\square}$

(e) $\dfrac{70}{200} = \dfrac{\square}{\square}$ (f) $\dfrac{500}{800} = \dfrac{\square}{\square}$ (g) $\dfrac{190}{1000} = \dfrac{\square}{\square}$ (h) $\dfrac{800}{1000} = \dfrac{\square}{\square}$

3. Add or subtract. Then simplify your answer, where possible.

$8\dfrac{1}{2} \rightarrow \overset{7}{\cancel{8}}\dfrac{\overset{1}{\ }5}{10}$

$-1\dfrac{7}{10} \rightarrow -1\dfrac{7}{10}$

$\overset{\star}{\underline{\qquad}}$ $6\dfrac{8}{10} = 6\dfrac{4}{5}$

(a) $4\dfrac{2}{3}$
$+ 2\dfrac{1}{12}$

(b) $3\dfrac{2}{5}$
$+ 1\dfrac{4}{10}$

(c) $3\dfrac{3}{4}$
$- 1\dfrac{5}{20}$

(d) $5\dfrac{7}{12}$
$+ 2\dfrac{5}{6}$

Multiplying fractions by whole numbers. Example: $\dfrac{1}{2} \times 5 = \star$

$\bigcirc \times 5 \rightarrow \bigcirc \bigcirc \bigcirc$ $\dfrac{1}{2} \times 5 \rightarrow \dfrac{1}{2} \times \dfrac{5}{1} \rightarrow \dfrac{5}{2} = 2\dfrac{1}{2}$

$\bigoplus \times 3 \rightarrow \bigoplus \bigoplus \bigoplus = 2\dfrac{1}{4}$ $\dfrac{3}{4}$ of $3 \rightarrow \dfrac{3}{4} \times \dfrac{3}{1} \rightarrow \dfrac{9}{4} = 2\dfrac{1}{4}$

4. (a) $\dfrac{3}{5} \times 3 = \underline{\quad} = \underline{\quad}$ (b) $\dfrac{3}{4} \times 5 = \underline{\quad} = \underline{\quad}$ (c) $\dfrac{2}{3}$ of $10 = \underline{\quad} = \underline{\quad}$

(d) $\dfrac{4}{5} \times 6 = \underline{\quad} = \underline{\quad}$ (e) $\dfrac{3}{7}$ of $21 = \underline{\quad} = \underline{\quad}$ (f) $\dfrac{2}{9} \times 20 = \underline{\quad} = \underline{\quad}$

5. (a) $\dfrac{2}{3}$ of $12 = \underline{\quad} = \underline{\quad}$ (b) $\dfrac{7}{8} \times 6 = \underline{\quad} = \underline{\quad}$ (c) $\dfrac{5}{9}$ of $8 = \underline{\quad} = \underline{\quad}$

(d) $\dfrac{11}{12} \times 7 = \underline{\quad} = \underline{\quad}$ (e) $\dfrac{8}{9}$ of $12 = \underline{\quad} = \underline{\quad}$ (f) $\dfrac{6}{7} \times 9 = \underline{\quad} = \underline{\quad}$

(g) $9 \times \dfrac{3}{5} = \underline{\quad} = \underline{\quad}$ (h) $\dfrac{11}{12}$ of $5 = \underline{\quad} = \underline{\quad}$ (i) $7 \times \dfrac{8}{11} = \underline{\quad} = \underline{\quad}$

Fractions 1 – Multiplying fractions by fractions

Aaron had an orange with eight segments. He broke off $\frac{1}{2}$ of it and ate $\frac{3}{4}$ of that. How much of the orange did he eat?

$$\times \quad \frac{3}{4} \quad = $$

$$\frac{1}{2} \quad \times \quad \frac{3}{4} \quad = \quad \frac{3}{8}$$

Here's how we multiply a fraction by a fraction.

numerator × numerator
denominator × denominator

1. Now try these.

(a) $\times \frac{1}{3} = $

$\frac{2}{5} \times \frac{1}{3} = \frac{\square}{\square}$

(b) $\times \frac{3}{4} = $

$\frac{5}{6} \times \frac{3}{4} = \frac{\square}{\square}$

(c) $\frac{2}{3} \times \frac{1}{2} = \frac{\square}{\square}$ (d) $\frac{1}{5} \times \frac{2}{3} = \frac{\square}{\square}$ (e) $\frac{1}{2}$ of $\frac{1}{4} = \frac{\square}{\square}$ (f) $\frac{2}{3}$ of $\frac{5}{8} = \frac{\square}{\square}$ (g) $\frac{3}{5}$ of $\frac{3}{4} = \frac{\square}{\square}$

I find it easier to simplify by **cancelling** before multiplying.

(a) $\frac{6}{7} \times \frac{7}{1} = \frac{42}{7} = 6$

or $\frac{6}{\cancel{7}_1} \times \frac{\cancel{7}^1}{1} = \frac{6}{1} = 6$

(b) $\frac{8}{9} \times \frac{3}{4} = \frac{24}{36} = \frac{2}{3}$

or $\frac{^2\cancel{8}}{_3\cancel{9}} \times \frac{^1\cancel{3}}{_1\cancel{4}} = \frac{2}{3}$

2. Simplify these first to find the answer more easily and faster!

(a) $\frac{2}{5} \times \frac{10}{1}$ (b) $\frac{1}{2} \times \frac{4}{5}$ (c) $\frac{5}{6}$ of 18   (d) $\frac{4}{5} \times \frac{5}{8} = $ (e) $\frac{3}{7} \times \frac{7}{9}$

(f) $\frac{9}{12} \times \frac{2}{3}$ (g) $11 \times \frac{7}{11}$ (h) $\frac{5}{8}$ of 12   (i) $\frac{5}{9}$ of $\frac{12}{15}$ (j) $\frac{8}{15} \times \frac{9}{20}$

3. Find the answers and write them on the number line below.

(a) $\frac{2}{6} \times \frac{3}{8}$ (b) $\frac{3}{8} + \frac{6}{12}$ (c) $2\frac{2}{8} - 1\frac{7}{8}$ (d) $\frac{8}{8} \times \frac{24}{32}$ (e) $\frac{6}{8} \times \frac{4}{12}$

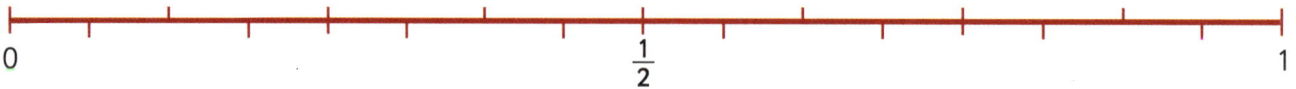

0 ——————————— $\frac{1}{2}$ ——————————— 1

4. Joe took $\frac{3}{7}$ of an hour to climb a hill. It took him $\frac{7}{15}$ of that time to go back down. How long did it take Joe to go back down? _____

5. Jim had 25 bales of hay. His cows ate $\frac{3}{4}$ of them. He gave $\frac{4}{5}$ of what was left to Sam. How many bales did Sam get? _____

6. Match the pairs of cards that have equal value. Colour the matching pairs the same colour.

| $\frac{3}{5} \times \frac{2}{3}$ | $\frac{5}{16}$ | $\frac{4}{9} \times \frac{7}{8}$ | $\frac{1}{2}$ | $\frac{3}{8} \times \frac{5}{6}$ | $\frac{2}{5}$ | $\frac{6}{15} \times \frac{5}{4}$ | $\frac{7}{18}$ |

Challenge Abbie was sick. She spent $\frac{5}{8}$ of a full day (24 hours) in bed. She spent $\frac{6}{15}$ of her time in bed reading. How long did Abbie spend reading? [____]

A quick look back 3

1. Divide 54,670 by 10.

   _____

2. Share €26,475 equally among 100 winners of a jackpot. Each gets

   € _____ .

3. How many times can I take 15 oranges from 300 oranges?

   _____

4. $375 \div 15 =$ ☆

   → $(375 \div 5) \div 3 =$ _____

5. The first three multiples of 9 are 9 18 27. The first three multiples of 4 are 4 8 12. What is the lowest common multiple of 4 and 9? _____

6. If I share 75 apples equally among 4 children, how many will each get and how many apples are left?

   _____ R _____

7. A water butt holds 800l. How many times can I draw 25 litres from it?

   _____

8. A return bus ticket costs €37·50. How many such tickets can I buy with €375?

   _____

9. How many right angles are there in this shape?

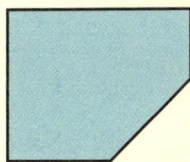

   _____

10. Put the correct sign (< or >) in the ◯.

    An acute angle is ◯ a right angle.

11. What name do we call this angle?

    _____

12. How many right angles can you see **inside** this shape?

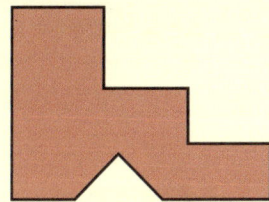

    _____

13. Calculate the size of the unknown angle.

    55° 70° ?

    _____

14. How many degrees in the unknown angle?

    ? 65° 59°

    _____

15. Through how many degrees does a ballerina turn if she makes $\frac{3}{4}$ of a full turn?

    _____

16. What is the total number of degrees in all of the angles of a quadrilateral?

    _____

17. Calculate the number of degrees in the unknown angle?

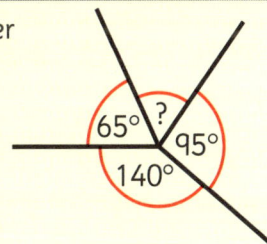

    65° ? 95° 140°

    _____

18. Which is bigger and by how much $\frac{3}{4}$ or $\frac{2}{3}$?

    _____ by _____

19. Simplify this fraction: $\frac{35}{40}$ $\frac{\square}{\square}$

20. Complete and write as a mixed number.

    $\frac{3}{4} \times 7 = \frac{\square}{\square} = $ _____ $\frac{\square}{\square}$

Chapter 10: 2-D shapes – Polygons

A polygon is a shape with 3 or more straight sides.

Many polygons get their name from Latin or Greek.

3 = tri (Latin)	4 = quad (Latin)	5 = penta (Greek)	6 = hex (Greek)
7 = hept (Greek)	8 = oct (Latin)	9 = nona (Latin)	10 = dec (Latin)

1. Using the above information, name each of the following polygons:

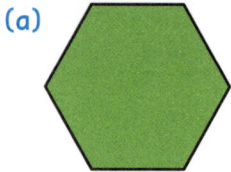

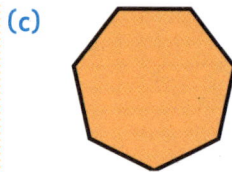

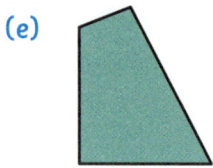

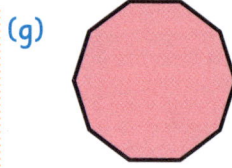

(a)   (b)   (c)   (d)

triangle
quadrilateral
pentagon
hexagon
heptagon
octagon
nonagon
decagon

(e)   (f)   (g)   (h)

Some quadrilaterals have special names.

square   rectangle   rhombus

parallelogram   trapezium   kite

If it doesn't have a special name, it is simply a quadrilateral.

This is a kite.

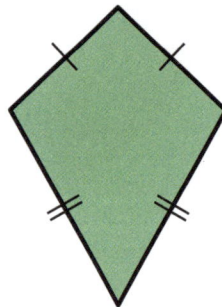

Discuss how you would recognise a kite shape.

2. Name the following quadrilaterals.

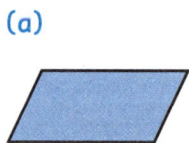

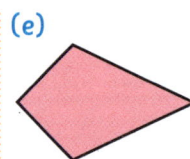

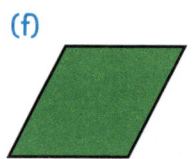

(a)   (b)   (c)   (d)   (e)   (f)

3. Label each triangle.   isosceles   scalene   equilateral   right-angled

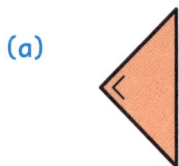

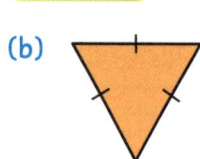

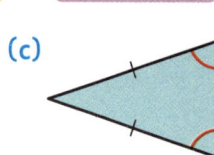

(a)   (b)   (c)   (d)

STRAND Shape and space   **STRAND UNIT/ELEMENT** 2-D shapes

LANGUAGE Polygon, straight sides, quadrilateral, square, rectangle, rhombus, parallelogram, trapezium, kite, pentagon, hexagon, heptagon, octagon, nonagon, decagon, tangram, irregular, angles, acute, right, obtuse, tessellate, rotational, reflected, intersect, hexomino, pentomino, symmetrical

2-D shapes – Polygons

Regular polygons...
- have equal, straight sides.
- have equal angles.
- are always symmetrical.

Irregular polygons...
- have straight sides.
- sides are not all equal.
- are not always symmetrical.

1. Copy and complete this grid.

	Shape	Name	Angles	Regular or irregular	Is it symmetrical?
(b)					
(c)					no
(d)		isosceles triangle			
(e)			2 acute 2 obtuse		
(f)					
(g)		heptagon		irregular	
(h)					

2. List all the 2-D shapes you can find on these flags.

(a) Philippines   (b) Congo   (c) Seychelles   (d) Kuwait   (e) Guyana

Challenge 1

(i) Use your protractor to measure one angle of this regular pentagon.

(ii) How many degrees in total are in a pentagon? _____

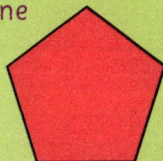

Challenge 2

Without using a protractor, calculate the unknown angle.

_____

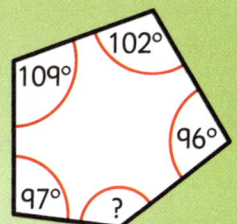

2-D shapes – Symmetry

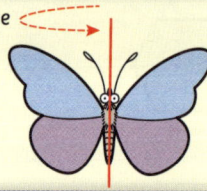

Symmetrical shapes can be folded so that each half fits exactly on the other.

fold line

The fold line is called the line of symmetry.

1. Identify the symmetrical picture in each question.

(a) (i)   (ii)

(b) (i)   (ii)   (iii)

(c) (i)   (ii)

(d) (i)   (ii)   (iii)

  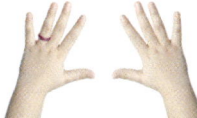  

2. Complete the symmetrical shapes. The red lines are the lines of symmetry.

(a)   (b)   (c)

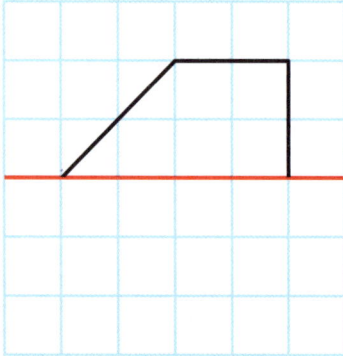 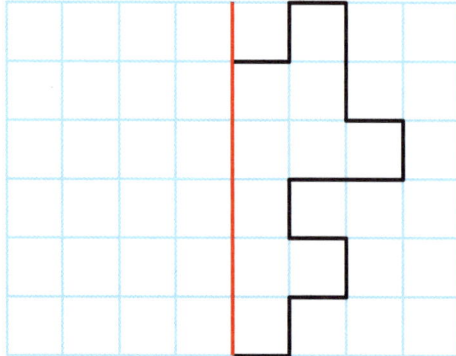 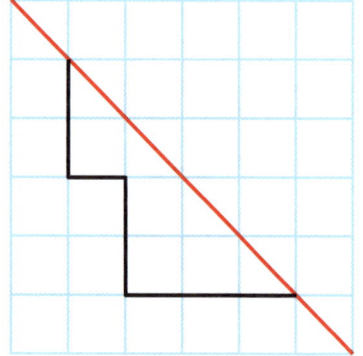

3. Complete these symmetrical patterns. Colour the squares the correct colour.

(a)   (b)   (c)

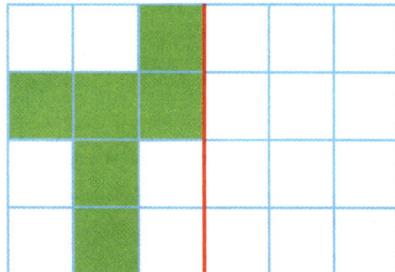 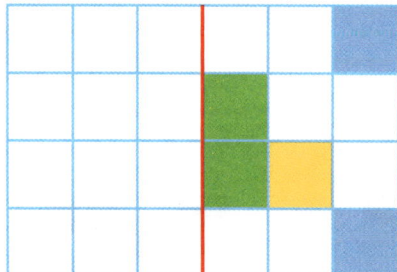 

(d)   (e)   (f)

Take care when there are two lines of symmetry.

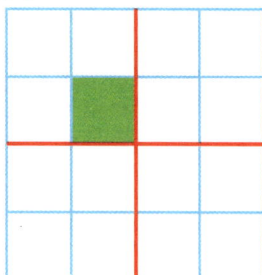  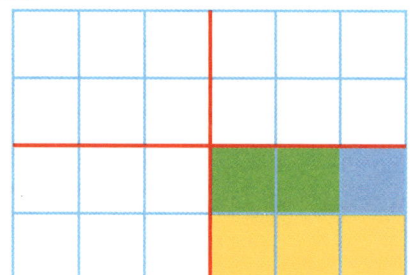

2-D shapes – Tessellations

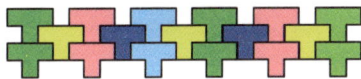

Tessellating shapes fit together perfectly, without leaving any gaps.

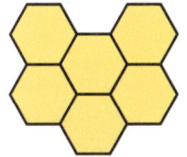

1. List or draw examples of tessellating shapes in the environment.
Look around your home or school for examples.

2. Some shapes tessellate when **combined** with others. List all the different **2-D shapes** you see in the following tessellating patterns.

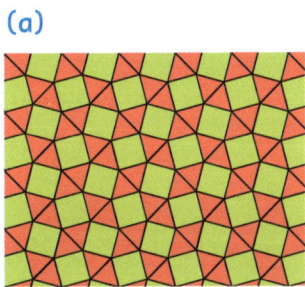

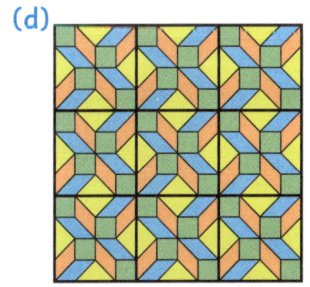

(a)

(b)

(c)

(d)

Simple tessellation	Rotational tessellation	Reflected tessellation
A shape is simply slid across a level surface.	The shape is turned or rotated to fit.	The shape is flipped over to face in the opposite direction or as seen in a mirror.

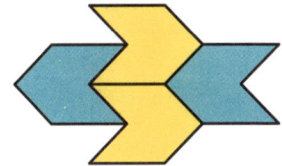

3. What type(s) of tessellation is used in the following patterns?

   simple   rotational   reflected

Some patterns here have more than one type of tessellation!

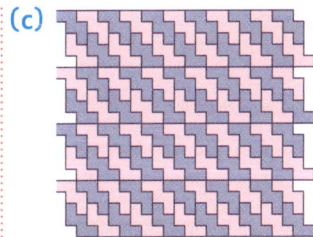

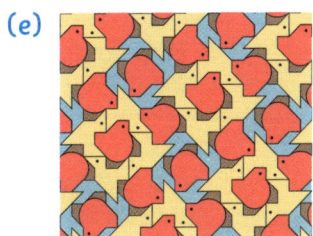

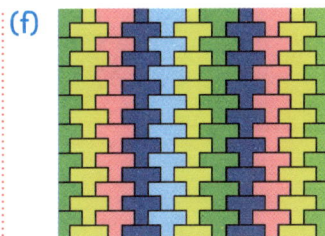

(a)

(b)

(c)

(d)

(e)

(f)

4. Copy and continue these tessellating patterns on squared paper.

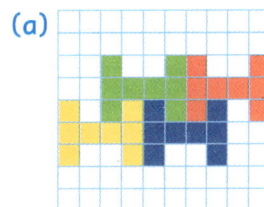

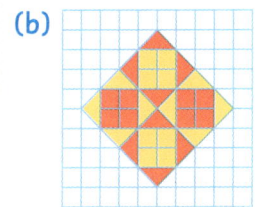

(a)

(b)

2-D shapes – Puzzles

Hexominoes are shapes made by joining 6 squares together. There are 35 different hexomino shapes.

We looked at pentominoes in 5th class. They are made up of 5 squares.

1. (i) Using squared paper, draw the following hexominoes in your copy.

   (ii) Draw in the line(s) of symmetry.

   (a)   (b)   (c)

   (d)   (e)   (f)   (g)

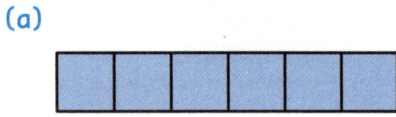

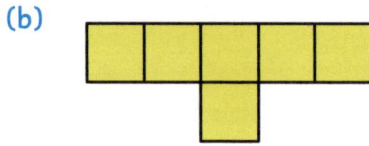

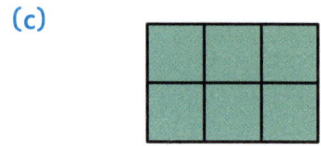

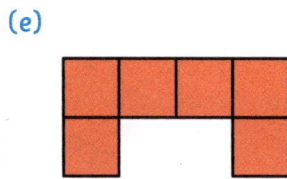

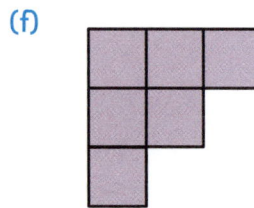

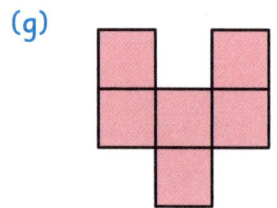

2. Copy and continue these tessellating hexomino patterns. Use squared paper.

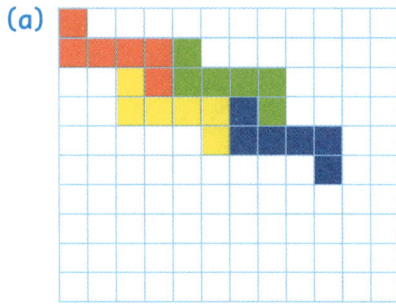

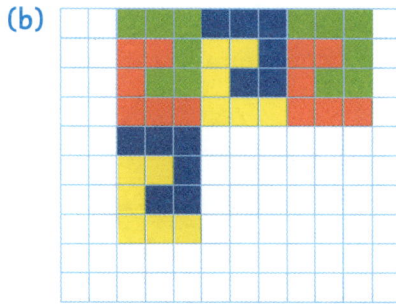

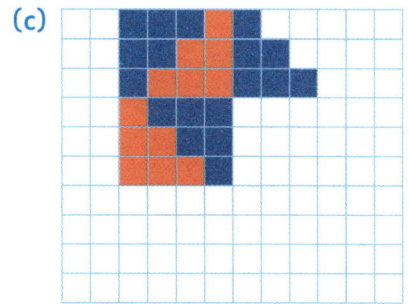

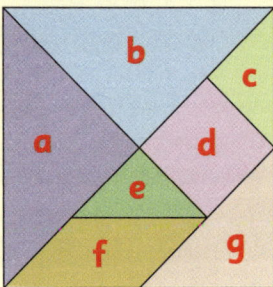

   (a)   (b)   (c)

The tangram is an ancient Chinese puzzle made up of seven 2-D shapes called tans.

3. What 2-D shape has each tan?

   a = right-angled triangle

   b = _____

   c = _____

   d = _____

   e = _____

   f = _____

   g = _____

4. Use your own tangram pieces to make each of the following shapes.
   The first tan has been placed for you! You must use all seven tans each time.

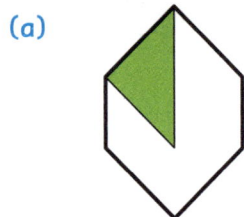

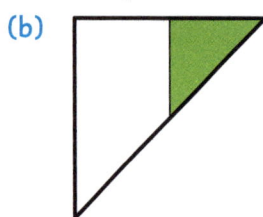

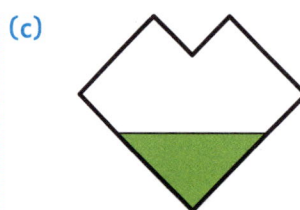

   (a)   (b)   (c)

   What 2-D outline has each shape?

Challenge   There are 35 hexominoes in total. 9 of them are shown in questions 1 and 2. Draw at least nine more hexominoes using squared paper.

52

2-D shapes – Co-ordinates

Co-ordinates are used in mapping. They are pairs of numbers.
These numbers tell us the exact location of an object.

Remember these steps.

What object is found at (2, 3)?

Step 1: The first co-ordinate moves across the grid.
Count 2 squares across.

Step 2: The second co-ordinate moves up the grid.
Count 3 squares up.

(2, 3) = strawberry

1. **Name the objects located at the following co-ordinates:**
   (a) (4, 2)   (b) (2, 1)   (c) (5, 3)   (d) (2, 4)   (e) (4, 4)
   (f) (2, 5)   (g) (3, 4)   (h) (4, 3)   (i) (1, 1)   (j) (3, 5)

2. **Give co-ordinates for the following objects.**
   (a) mobile phone   (b) ladybird   (c) knife   (d) duck
   (e) fish   (f) hand   (g) chair   (h) flower   (i) watch
   (j) tree   (k) spoon   (l) ring   (m) leaf   (n) pot

In most grids, the co-ordinates are **on** the lines rather than in the spaces as in the grids above.
The co-ordinates are where two lines intersect (meet).

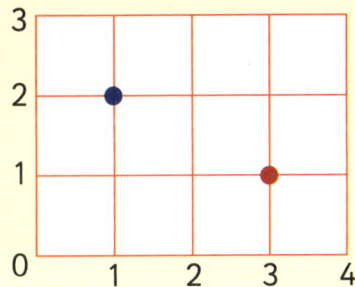

Co-ordinates will pinpoint the exact location of the dots.

The blue dot is at (1, 2).

The red dot is at (3, 1).

3. Write the co-ordinates for each of the four corners of the parallelogram.

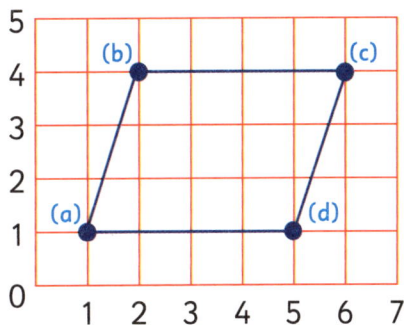

4. Write the co-ordinates for each dot.

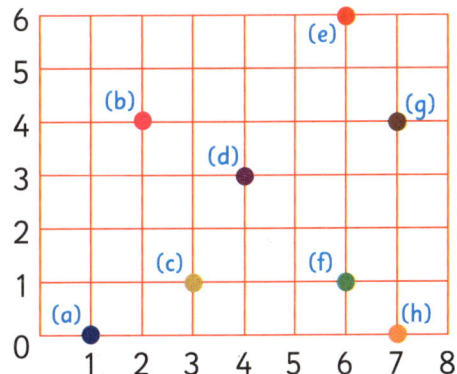

2-D shapes – Co-ordinates

Here is a 5 × 5 square grid. The following co-ordinates were plotted (marked):

(1, 1) → (4, 4) → (4, 1) → (1, 1)

The co-ordinates were joined in order by straight lines.

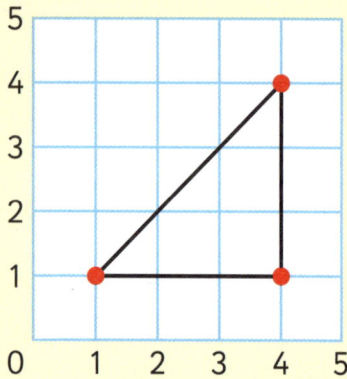

right-angled triangle

1. Draw a 5 × 5 square to plot (mark) each of the following shapes.

   (i) Join the co-ordinates to draw each 2-D shape.

   (ii) Colour and name each shape. Use squared paper to help you plot the shapes.

   (a) (1, 1) → (1, 4) → (4, 4) → (4, 1) → (1, 1)

   (b) (1, 1) → (2, 4) → (5, 1) → (1, 1)

   (c) (1, 1) → (2, 3) → (4, 3) → (5, 1) → (1, 1)

   (d) (0, 4) → (5, 5) → (4, 2) → (1, 1) → (0, 4)

   (e) (1, 0) → (0, 2) → (1, 4) → (3, 4) → (4, 2) → (3, 0) → (1, 0)

   Don't forget to join the dots in the correct order.

2. Name the object or creature located at each of the following co-ordinates.

   (a) (2, 4)   (b) (4, 3)
   (c) (7, 7)   (d) (5, 8)
   (e) (4, 6)   (f) (9, 8)

3. Give the co-ordinates for the following objects or creatures.

   (a) lighthouse   (b) bench
   (c) lifeguard hut   (d) whale
   (e) tent   (f) rock pool

4. Create your own grid and draw items that you like on it. Ask a friend to give the co-ordinates for the items.

5. (i) Copy and complete these shapes using the green lines as lines of symmetry.

   (ii) List all the co-ordinates of each completed shape.

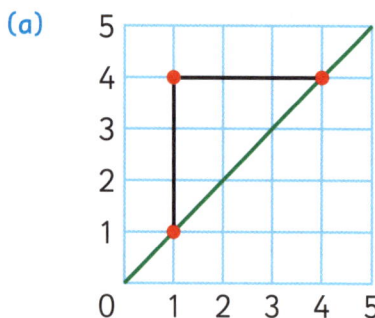

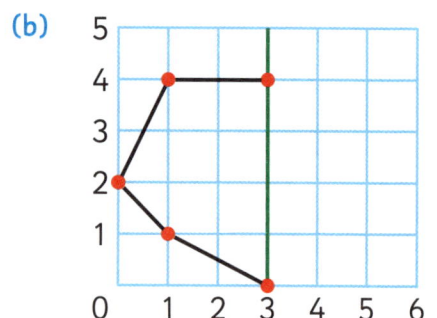

   (a)

   (b)

54

Chapter 11: Fractions 2

Dividing Fractions

A How many halves are there in 3? $3 \div \frac{1}{2} = \boxed{\star}$ (Divide 3 into halves)

$3 \div \frac{1}{2} = 6$ (There are 6 halves in 3).

B How many quarters are there in 4? $4 \div \frac{1}{4} = \boxed{\star}$ (Divide 4 into quarters)

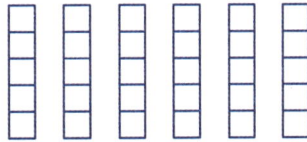

$4 \div \frac{1}{4} = 16$ quarters (There are 16 quarters in 4).

1. Now try these. Colour the corrrect amount in each case.

   (a) $2 \div \frac{1}{4} = $ _____

   (b) $6 \div \frac{1}{5} = $ _____

   (c) $3 \div \frac{1}{8} = $ _____

2. Draw your own shapes to help you do these. Colour the correct amount.

   (a) $2 \div \frac{1}{3}$
   (b) $1 \div \frac{1}{10}$
   (c) $3 \div \frac{1}{5}$
   (d) $3 \div \frac{1}{4}$

   (e) $5 \div \frac{1}{2}$
   (f) $2 \div \frac{1}{6}$
   (g) $3 \div \frac{1}{3}$
   (h) $4 \div \frac{1}{8}$

   Did you notice any pattern? Explain.

Dividing fractions using reciprocals.

What is a reciprocal? A reciprocal is the number we multiply a fraction by to get 1.

Examples: (a) $\frac{1}{5} \times \frac{5}{1} = 1$ (b) $\frac{2}{3} \times \frac{3}{2} \rightarrow \frac{6}{6} = 1$ (c) $\frac{7}{12} \times \frac{12}{7} \rightarrow \frac{84}{84} = 1$

How many quarters are there in 5? $\frac{5}{1} \div \frac{1}{4} = \boxed{\star}$

We can write it like this:
$$\frac{\frac{5}{1}}{\frac{1}{4}}$$

$\rightarrow$ Now we use a reciprocal
$$\frac{\frac{5}{1} \times \frac{4}{1}}{\frac{1}{4} \times \frac{4}{1}} \rightarrow \frac{\frac{5}{1} \times \frac{4}{1}}{1}$$

$\rightarrow$ We finish by multiplying:
$$\frac{5}{1} \times \frac{4}{1} \rightarrow \frac{20}{1} = 20$$

3. Use the reciprocal method when doing these.

   (a) $1 \div \frac{1}{7} = $ _____
   (b) $2 \div \frac{1}{2} = $ _____
   (c) $3 \div \frac{1}{6} = $ _____
   (d) $2 \div \frac{1}{10} = $ _____

   (e) $4 \div \frac{1}{5} = $ _____
   (f) $5 \div \frac{1}{9} = $ _____
   (g) $10 \div \frac{1}{8} = $ _____
   (h) $20 \div \frac{1}{6} = $ _____

4. When doing these, be sure to simplify your answers.

   (a) $4 \div \frac{2}{3} = $ _____
   (b) $2 \div \frac{2}{5} = $ _____
   (c) $8 \div \frac{2}{3} = $ _____
   (d) $8 \div \frac{4}{5} = $ _____

   (e) $10 \div \frac{2}{5} = $ _____
   (f) $12 \div \frac{3}{4} = $ _____
   (g) $20 \div \frac{5}{6} = $ _____
   (h) $25 \div \frac{5}{8} = $ _____

STRAND **Number**   STRAND UNIT/ELEMENT *Fractions*
LANGUAGE *Division, dividing, sharing, pattern, reciprocal, compare, ratios, unitary method, simplify*

Fractions 2 – Ratio

Fractions – solve the problems!

1. (a) If a coffee shop uses $\frac{1}{30}$ of a litre of milk in each cup they sell, how many cups of coffee can they make from a 2-litre carton of milk? _____

   (b) Jill swam $\frac{1}{5}$ km each week for a year. How far did she swim altogether? _____

   (c) An oak sapling is 3 metres tall. How long will it take to double in size if it grows $\frac{1}{4}$ of a metre each year? _____

   (d) Katie jogs $\frac{1}{2}$ km each day. How far should she jog in 35 days? _____

Ratio is a way of comparing different quantities.

We can see that $\frac{3}{5}$ are girls and $\frac{2}{5}$ are boys.
We say that the ratio of girls to boys is **3 : 2**

$\frac{4}{5}$ of the children have black hair and $\frac{1}{5}$ have red hair.
The **ratio** of children with black to red hair is **4 : 1**

2. Work out the ratio shown in each of these pictures starting with the **smaller** amounts!

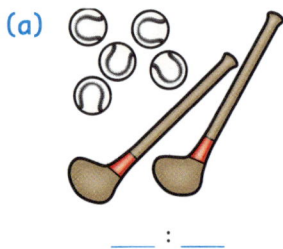

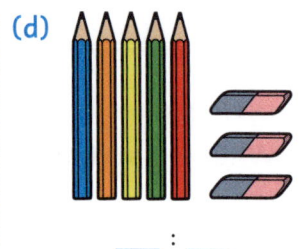

   (a) ___ : ___

   (b) ___ : ___

   (c) ___ : ___

   (d) ___ : ___

3. A farmer has 63 cows and 81 sheep. Write the ratio of cows to sheep in its lowest terms. ___ : ___

4. A gardener has 84 cabbages and 60 carrots. Write the ratio of carrots to cabbages in its lowest terms. ___ : ___

5. There are 18 cats and 27 rabbits in a pet shop. Write the ratio of cats to rabbits in its lowest terms. ___ : ___

6. There were 72 red marbles and 96 blue marbles in a box. Write the ratio of red marbles to blue marbles in its lowest terms. ___ : ___

7. There are 144 boys and 132 girls in a school. Write the ratio of boys to girls in its lowest terms. ___ : ___

Challenge Sofia won €585 and Simona won €975 in a raffle. Write the ratio of Sofia's prize to Simona's prize in its lowest terms. ☐ : ☐

Fractions 2 – More ratios

Ratios in your classroom

1. **Work these out and simplify where possible.**

   (a) Children with fair hair to children with black hair. ___ : ___

   (b) Right-handed children to left-handed children. ___ : ___

   (c) Eleven-year-olds to twelve-year-olds. ___ : ___

   (d) Children with brown eyes to children with blue eyes. ___ : ___

   (e) Children who support Manchester Utd to children who support Chelsea. ___ : ___

   (f) Children who walk to school to children who come to school by car. ___ : ___

Using ratios

Ann shared a bag of dog food between her labrador and her poodle in the ratio **3:1**.
If she had a 1kg bag, how much did each dog get?

The ratio is **3:1**. The labrador got 3 of every 4 parts, while the poodle got 1 of every 4 parts.
Another way of saying this is that the labrador got $\frac{3}{4}$ and the poodle got $\frac{1}{4}$.
Out of a 1kg bag, the labrador got $\frac{3}{4}$ (750g) and the poodle got $\frac{1}{4}$ (250g).

---

2. The ratio of walking to driving on a doctor's journey to work is 1:9.
   If the journey is 20km long, how far does she drive? _____ .

3. A farmer has a ratio of 5:2 for sheep to cows on his farm.
   If there are 35 animals altogether, how many sheep are there? _____

4. The ratio of boys to girls in a class is 6:5.
   If there are 18 boys in the class, how many girls are there? _____

5. Ali spends and saves her money in the ratio 5:2. If she spends €15 buying a ball, how much does she save? €_____

6. There are 15 doctors and 60 nurses in a hospital.
   Write this as a ratio and simplify it. _____

7. First prize in an art competition was €85, second prize was €50 and third prize was €15.
   Write the ratio of the third prize to the first prize in its lowest terms. ___ : ___

8. The ratio of Joe's money to Jane's is 4:5. If Jane has €180, how much money has Joe? €_____

9. The distance from Fred's house to the school is 4cm on a map drawn to the scale 10cm:1km.
   How many metres is Fred's house from the school? _____

Challenge The ratio of males to females in a factory is 7:5. If there are 98 males, how many people work in the factory altogether? [_____] .

Fractions 2 – Unitary method

$\frac{37}{100}$ of the children in a school picked art as their favourite subject. If 111 children picked art, how many children altogether are in the school?

$\frac{37}{100}$ = 111 children

$\frac{1}{100}$ = 3   (111 ÷ 37 = 3)

$\frac{100}{100}$ = 300 children in the school

1. Use the **unitary method** to find the whole amount if:

   (a) $\frac{2}{5}$ = 8   (b) $\frac{3}{7}$ = 12   (c) $\frac{4}{5}$ = 20   (d) $\frac{7}{12}$ = 49   (e) $\frac{8}{9}$ = 72

   (f) $\frac{13}{20}$ = 39   (g) $\frac{11}{50}$ = 77   (h) $\frac{6}{25}$ = 24   (i) $\frac{9}{11}$ = 99   (j) $\frac{5}{8}$ = 45

2. (a) If Tony spent $\frac{2}{5}$ of his pocket money buying football cards and still had €6 left, how much money had he before he went shopping? €_____

   (b)  A carton of orange juice that has 200ml left in it is $\frac{4}{7}$ full. How much does a full carton hold? _____ml

---

Express one number as a fraction of another.

Sarah has saved €10 to buy Christmas presents and Sam has saved €15. Express Sarah's savings as a fraction of Sam's.

$\frac{10}{15}$ ÷ $\frac{5}{5}$ = $\frac{2}{3}$ Sarah's savings are $\frac{2}{3}$ of Sam's.

3. Express these as **fractions** of each other and simplify, using the **smaller** number as the **numerator**.

   (a)    (b)

   (c)    (d)

Challenge Cathy spent €35 in one shop and €49 in another. Dan spent a total of €56. Express the amount Dan spent as a fraction of the amount Cathy spent.

Simplify your answer. □/□

Fractions 2

Monster Quiz

1. What is the ratio of monsters with legs to monsters without legs? _____

2. What fraction of the monsters have more than two eyes? _____

3. Of the monsters with two eyes, what is the ratio of those with arms to those without arms? _____

4. If the purple monster lived $2\frac{2}{5}$ light years from Earth and the orange monster lived $3\frac{5}{6}$ light years from Earth, how many light years in total did they travel to get here? _____

5. The green monster weighs $10\frac{1}{6}$ kg and the red monster weighs $7\frac{3}{4}$ kg. How much lighter is the red monster? _____ kg

6. If you brought the monsters to an Italian restaurant and bought them $\frac{5}{13}$ of a pizza for each eye they had, how many pizzas would you have to buy altogether? _____

7. If you wanted to leave a tip of $\frac{2}{15}$ of the bill and the food cost €105, how much would you pay in total? €_____

8. Which monster has $\frac{15}{20}$ of the number of eyes that the red monster has? _____

9. Write the total number of eyes that the brown and red monsters have as a fraction of the total number of eyes of the blue and green monsters in its lowest terms. _____

10. The red monster weighs $7\frac{3}{4}$ kg. The yellow monster weighs $5\frac{11}{12}$ kg. How many kg lighter is the yellow monster? Write the answer in its lowest terms. _____ kg

Fractions 2

The Garden Sale

1. If Mam is selling the television for $\frac{2}{5}$ of its original price and put a tag of €44 on it, how much did she buy it for originally? €_____

2. If Jerry uses $\frac{3}{4}$ of a lemon in each drink and sells 20 drinks, how many lemons does he use? _____

   Lemonade

3. The twenty books at the sale are split between thrillers and comedy in the ratio of 2:3. How many of each are there? _____ _____

4. If the medium weight weighs $\frac{8}{9}$ kg and the small weight weighs $\frac{3}{4}$ of that, how heavy is the small weight? _____kg

5. Dad has $11\frac{5}{6}$ m of rope. He needs another $1\frac{4}{9}$ m of rope to tie it around the trees. How much rope will he need altogether? _____

6. What is the ratio of dresses with spots to other dresses hanging on the rope? _____

7. If $\frac{2}{5}$ of the dresses were sold before the official start of the sale, how many dresses were there to begin with? _____

8. The tricycle is on sale for $\frac{5}{6}$ of its original price and the skateboard is on sale for $\frac{9}{10}$ of the tricycle's sale price. If the skateboard is on sale for €24, how much did the tricycle cost when new? €_____

9. One lady bought $\frac{2}{5}$ of the dresses before the sale officially began. Express the number of dresses she bought as a ratio of the number that are hanging on the line. _____ : _____

Challenge A bottle of lemonade cost €1·20 and was sold in plastic containers for 40c each. Each bottle contained $4\frac{1}{4}$ containers. What profit was made if 12 bottles worth of lemonade was sold in containers? €_____

Chapter 12: Learning through the calculator

Keyboard Pattern!

1. Digits are arranged on a calculator keyboard as shown.

(a)

3-digit fun!

Follow these steps!

Make 3-digit numbers by using the digits (from top down) in any column. Example: 963.

Subtract the number in the column beside it: Example: 963 – 852 = _____.

Repeat for the other column.

Now do the same but read the numbers from the bottom up.

What do you notice about the answer in each case?

(b)

2-digit fun!

Follow these steps!

Choose any digit on the keyboard. Use the number directly above or below it to form a 2-digit number. Example: 41.

Reverse the digits: 14.

Subtract the numbers.

Now do the same with other examples.

What do you notice about the answer in each case?

Exploring Number Pattern

Explore these patterns on the calculator. Predict the answers for **2 (h)** and **3 (h)**.

2.

(a) $1 \times 8 + 1 = 9$

(b) $12 \times 8 + 2 = 98$

(c) $123 \times 8 + 3 =$

(d) $1234 \times 8 + 4 =$

(e) $12345 \times 8 + 5 =$

(f) $123456 \times 8 + 6 =$

(g) $1234567 \times 8 + 7 =$

(h) $12345678 \times 8 + 8 =$

3.

(a) $9 \times 9 = 81$

(b) $98 \times 9 = 882$

(c) $987 \times 9 =$

(d) $9876 \times 9 =$

(e) $98765 \times 9 =$

(f) $987654 \times 9 =$

(g) $9876543 \times 9 =$

(h) $98765432 \times 9 =$

4. Explore these patterns related to 9 times tables. Predict the answers. Then check using the calculator.

$9 \times 1 = 9$	$99 \times 1 = 99$	$999 \times 1 = 999$
$9 \times 2 = 18$	$99 \times 2 = 198$	$999 \times 2 = 1998$
$9 \times 3 = 27$	$99 \times 3 = 297$	$999 \times 3 = 2997$
$9 \times 4 =$	$99 \times 4 =$	$999 \times 4 =$
$9 \times 5 =$	$99 \times 5 =$	$999 \times 5 =$
$9 \times 6 =$	$99 \times 6 =$	$999 \times 6 =$
$9 \times 7 =$	$99 \times 7 =$	$999 \times 7 =$
$9 \times 8 =$	$99 \times 8 =$	$999 \times 8 =$
$9 \times 9 =$	$99 \times 9 =$	$999 \times 9 =$

Calculator problem-solving

The Broken Key

The 3 key on David's calculator is broken.
However, he can still work out the answer to 38 + 13 by:

(a) Key in 4 0 $-$ 2 $+$ 1 0 $+$ 2 $+$ 1 $=$ 51, **or**

(b) Key in 2 0 $+$ 1 8 $+$ 1 5 $-$ 2 $=$ 51

Can you find the correct answers in another way?

1. Help David calculate the answers to these on his broken calculator.

(a) 93 + 103
(b) 303 + 333
(c) 83 – 31
(d) 308 – 131

(e) 3 × 19
(f) 30 × 26
(g) 51 ÷ 3
(h) 105 ÷ 3

Missing Operations

Write the correct operation sign (+, –, × or ÷) to make these number sentences true.

$$(72 \bigcirc 8) \bigcirc 9 = 81 \rightarrow (72 ÷ 8) × 9 = 81$$

2. (a) $(16 \bigcirc 24) \bigcirc 4 = 380$

(b) $(66 \bigcirc 11) \bigcirc 345 = 381$

(c) $3{,}875 \bigcirc 3{,}487 \bigcirc 2 = 776$

(d) $(235 \bigcirc 5) \bigcirc 5 = 1{,}170$

(e) $(2{,}498 \bigcirc 6) \bigcirc 2{,}361 = 12{,}627$

(f) $7{,}429 \bigcirc 5{,}431 \bigcirc 4{,}123 = 16{,}983$

Missing Digits

3. Write the missing digits.

(a)
```
   3 2 □
 +   2 □ 8
 ─────────
   6 2 3
```

(b)
```
       4 , 6 7 2
 +  □ □ , □ □ □
 ───────────────
   1 7 , 5 4 8
```

(c)
```
   5 , □ □ □
 - 3 , 7 9 8
 ───────────
   1 , 2 0 2
```

(d)
```
   6 3 , 8 7 1
 - 4 □ , 6 □ 9
 ─────────────
   2 0 , 1 8 2
```

Calculate percentages on the calculator.

Sporty's Superstore is having an end of season sale. Use your calculator to work out a 15% reduction on the football boots. Round the reduction to two decimal places. €79.99

Steps	Example	Answer	Round to 2 decimal places
Step 1: Enter the price into the calculator. →	€79.99		
Step 2: Press × (multiply sign). →	×		
Step 3: Press the percentage required. →	15		
Step 4: Press the percentage key. →	%	€11·9985	€12·00

4. Now find the reductions on the following items in the shop. Round to 2 decimal places.

Take 20% off the marked price	Take 33% off the marked price	Take 70% off the marked price
Tracksuit €45·49	Treadmill €1,500	Rugby ball €28·99
Runners €75·99	Weights bench €300	Squash racket €110
Football jersey €60·99	Bicycle €350	Football €49·99

Calculator problem-solving

Change the underlined digit to zero in one step. $384{,}759 - 80{,}000 =$ ☆

Press ③ ⑧ ④ ⑦ ⑤ ⑨ ⊖ ⑧ ⓪ ⓪ ⓪ ⓪ ⊜

③ ⓪ ④ ⑦ ⑤ ⑨ will appear on the screen.

---

1. Change the underlined digits to zero.

(a) 3,48<u>7</u>	(b) 2,8<u>3</u>9	(c) 5,<u>5</u>96	(d) <u>2</u>,948
(e) 2<u>8</u>,374	(f) 84,37<u>4</u>	(g) 9<u>8</u>,457	(h) 27,9<u>5</u>2
(i) 506,9<u>3</u>8	(j) <u>3</u>84,959	(k) 283,<u>7</u>50	(l) 498,3<u>7</u>2

---

2. Write down the keys you press to reach the **target number**. You may press the keys in any order and as often as you wish.

	Keys	Target number	Fewest goes possible
(a)	3, 4, ×, ÷, =	16	③ ⓧ ④ ⓧ ④ ÷ ③ ⊜
(b)	9, 7, +, −, =	20	
(c)	4, 7, +, −, =	14	
(d)	6, 8, −, ×, ÷, =	5	
(e)	3, 9, ×, ÷, +, =	13	
(f)	6, 12, +, −, ×, =	426	
(g)	8, 20, −, ×, =	96	
(h)	6, 15, +, ×, ÷, =	16	

> You may have to make large numbers before getting the correct small number.

---

3. Consecutive numbers are numbers that come directly after one another.

Step 1: Add 5 consecutive numbers: 10, 11, 12, 13, 14 → 10 + 11 + 12 + 13 + 14 = 60.

Step 2: Find the average number: 60 ÷ 5 = 12 (the middle number).

> **Note:** The average of any odd number of consecutive numbers will always be the middle number.

Now try this with other amounts of consecutive odd numbers and check if the average is the middle number. Does it work for consecutive even numbers?

---

4. Add as many **consecutive numbers** as you wish **starting with 1**:

1 + 2 + 3 + 4 + 5 + 6 + 7 + 8 + 9 + 10 = 55

Now try adding numbers 1 + 2 + 3 + 4 +..........+ 25 on the calculator.

Check if the quick way gives the same answer. 0·5 × 25 × 26 = 325

> When we are adding 10 consecutive numbers, the quick way of working it out is to multiply
>
> 0·5 × 10 × 11 = 55 .

Which Consecutive Numbers?

5. What three consecutive numbers add up to:

(a) 75? (b) 291? (c) 1071? (d) 1470? (e) 4638?

Challenge A pile of 40 sheets of paper measures 50mm in thickness. How many sheets would be needed to make a pile:

(a) 2·5cm high? _____ (b) 100cm high? _____ (c) 5m high? _____

Chapter 13: Decimals

A full block represents one unit.

1. Write the (i) **fraction** and (ii) **decimal fraction** for each of the coloured amounts.
   Note: this cube represents one unit.

   (i) fraction: $\frac{1}{1}$

   (ii) decimal: 1·0

   (a)
   (i) _____
   (ii) _____

   (b)
   (i) _____
   (ii) _____

   (c)
   (i) _____
   (ii) _____

2. Make the following using uniblocks (or draw them on a page).

   (a) $\frac{7}{10}$ (b) 0·09 (c) $\frac{23}{100}$ (d) 1·2 (e) $2\frac{6}{1000}$ (f) $1\frac{37}{1000}$

   (g) 2·45 (h) 1·304 (i) $1\frac{43}{100}$ (j) 0·315 (k) $2\frac{403}{1000}$ (l) 1·23

Changing fractions to decimals:

$1\frac{3}{10}$ → (one decimal place) →

$6\frac{47}{100}$ → (two decimal places) →

$2\frac{75}{1000}$ → (three decimal places) →

u		$\frac{1}{10}$	$\frac{1}{100}$	$\frac{1}{1000}$
1	·	3		
6	·	4	7	
2	·	0	7	5

→ 1·3
→ 6·47
→ 2·075

---

3. Now write these in **decimal** form:

   (a) $\frac{45}{100}$ (b) $2\frac{3}{10}$ (c) $1\frac{375}{1000}$ (d) $4\frac{3}{100}$

   (e) $7\frac{45}{100}$ (f) $6\frac{23}{1000}$ (g) $\frac{4}{10}$ (h) $\frac{6}{1000}$

   (i) $9\frac{99}{100}$ (j) $\frac{7}{100}$ (k) $3\frac{3}{1000}$ (l) $4\frac{44}{1000}$

Changing decimals to fractions:

0·7 → (one decimal place) → $\frac{?}{10}$ → 0·7 = $\frac{7}{10}$

2·05 → (two decimal places) → $2\frac{?}{100}$ → 2·05 → $2\frac{05}{100} = 2\frac{5}{100}$

1·059 → (three decimal places) → $1\frac{?}{1000}$ → 1·059 → $1\frac{059}{1000} = 1\frac{59}{1000}$

---

4. Now change these **decimal numbers** to **fractions**:

   (a) 0·9 (b) 0·07 (c) 2·19 (d) 0·002 (e) 3·1 (f) 4·029
   (g) 5·051 (h) 2·001 (i) 4·44 (j) 5·207 (k) 0·006 (l) 1·111

Simplifying fractions:

(a) $\frac{700}{1000} = \frac{7}{10} = 0·7$

(b) $1\frac{60}{100} = 1\frac{6}{10} = 1·6$

(c) $4\frac{750}{1000} = 4\frac{75}{100} = 4·75$

---

5. Now write these as **fractions** or **mixed numbers** in their lowest terms.

   (a) $\frac{90}{100}$ (b) 0·40 (c) $2\frac{500}{1000}$ (d) 3·540 (e) $1\frac{600}{1000}$ (f) $3\frac{800}{1000}$

   (g) 2·080 (h) 5·250 (i) $1\frac{990}{1000}$ (j) 0·020 (k) 4·80 (l) 8·090

STRAND Number **STRAND UNIT/ELEMENT** Decimals

LANGUAGE Decimal number/fraction/form, uniblocks, simplify, simplifying, ordering, sequences, calculator, rounding, adding, addition, subtracting, subtraction, problem-solving, bar-line graph

Decimals – Changing more fractions to decimals

Changing fractions to decimals:

(a) $\dfrac{6}{25} \times \dfrac{4}{4} \longrightarrow \dfrac{24}{100} = 0 \cdot 24$ (b) $\dfrac{3}{4} \times \dfrac{25}{25} \longrightarrow \dfrac{75}{100} = 0 \cdot 75$ (c) $\dfrac{13}{20} \times \dfrac{5}{5} \longrightarrow \dfrac{65}{100} = 0 \cdot 65$

1. Change these fractions to decimals.

   (a) $\dfrac{4}{5}$ _____   (b) $\dfrac{1}{4}$ _____   (c) $\dfrac{11}{20}$ _____   (d) $\dfrac{21}{25}$ _____   (e) $\dfrac{2}{5}$ _____   (f) $\dfrac{31}{50}$ _____   (g) $\dfrac{19}{20}$ _____

2. Find the mistakes.

   There are 6 mistakes. Can you find them? Then write out all eight answers correctly.

   (a) $0 \cdot 77 = \dfrac{77}{1000}$ (b) $3\dfrac{30}{100} < 3 \cdot 33$ (c) $4\dfrac{4}{100} > 4 \cdot 040$ (d) $\dfrac{10}{100} < \dfrac{11}{1000}$

   (e) $6\dfrac{660}{1000} = 6 \cdot 066$ (f) $2 \cdot 20 < 2\dfrac{20}{100}$ (g) $\dfrac{70}{100} = \dfrac{700}{1000}$ (h) $0 \cdot 099 > \dfrac{900}{100}$

Changing any fraction to a decimal:

We can use division to change any fraction to a decimal:

(a) $\dfrac{7}{1000} \longrightarrow 1000 \overline{)7 \cdot 000}\;^{0 \cdot 007} = 0 \cdot 007$ (b) $\dfrac{3}{8} \longrightarrow 8\overline{)3 \cdot 000}\;^{0 \cdot 375} = 0 \cdot 375$

> Keep adding zeros until you get a final answer!

3. Use division to change these fractions to decimals.

   (a) $\dfrac{1}{2}$ (b) $\dfrac{3}{5}$ (c) $\dfrac{3}{4}$ (d) $\dfrac{1}{20}$ (e) $\dfrac{8}{50}$ (f) $\dfrac{7}{8}$ (g) $\dfrac{11}{25}$ (h) $\dfrac{5}{8}$

Sometimes the fraction won't divide evenly:

(a) $\dfrac{1}{3} = 3\overline{)1 \cdot 000000}\;^{0 \cdot 333333}$ (b) $\dfrac{5}{12} = 12\overline{)5 \cdot 00000}\;^{0 \cdot 41666}$

> These numbers will keep on going, so we can stop after 2 or 3 decimal places.

4. Use the division method to solve these problems (stop after 3 decimal places).

   (a) If you needed $\dfrac{5}{6}$ kg of flour to make some scones, how many grammes would you put on the scales? _____

   (b) The 100 metre record was recently $9\dfrac{7}{12}$ seconds. Write this time in decimal form. _____

   (c) The Jack Lynch Tunnel in Cork is about $\dfrac{7}{11}$ km long. How many metres is that? _____

   (d) How many millilitres are there in a drink of $\dfrac{2}{3}$ l? _____

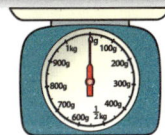

---

5. Show these **fractions** as **decimals** on the number line: $\dfrac{1}{2}, \dfrac{1}{3}, \dfrac{1}{4}, \dfrac{1}{5}, \dfrac{1}{6}, \dfrac{1}{7}, \dfrac{1}{8}, \dfrac{1}{9}, \dfrac{1}{10}, \dfrac{1}{12}.$

0·0   0·25   0·5

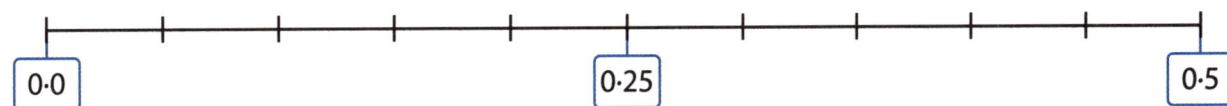

6. Draw a number line and show the following fractions on it in decimal form:

   $\dfrac{1}{8}, \dfrac{2}{8}, \dfrac{3}{8}, \dfrac{4}{8}, \dfrac{5}{8}, \dfrac{6}{8}, \dfrac{7}{8}, \dfrac{8}{8}.$

Decimals – Ordering decimals

1. Put these groups of numbers in order of size, starting with the **smallest** each time.

   (a) 0·11, 0·1, 0·101, 0·111

   (b) 7·0, 7·077, 7·77, 7·707

   (c) 0·34, 0·43, 0·104, 0·133

   (d) 1·506, 1·06, 1·501, 1·605

2. Write the next **three terms** in each of these decimal number sequences.

   (a) 4·175, 4·185, 4·195, _____, _____, _____.

   (b) 0·706, 0·807, 0·908, _____, _____, _____.

   (c) 0·040, 0·080, 0·160, _____, _____, _____.

   (d) 1·035, 1·025, 1·015, _____, _____, _____.

   (e) 0·678, 1·789, 2·900, _____, _____, _____.

   (f) 5·801, 5·856, 5·911, _____, _____, _____.

Calculator challenge!

Use your calculator to find 5 **fractions** with a value between

0·4 and 0·5 (example $\frac{5}{11}$ = 0·4545).

(a) ☐/☐ (b) ☐/☐ (c) ☐/☐ (d) ☐/☐ (e) ☐/☐

Rounding decimals.

When rounding a decimal number, always look to the **next digit** to see if we round **up** or **down**:

5 or higher rounds up. 4 or lower rounds down. That's the rule!!!

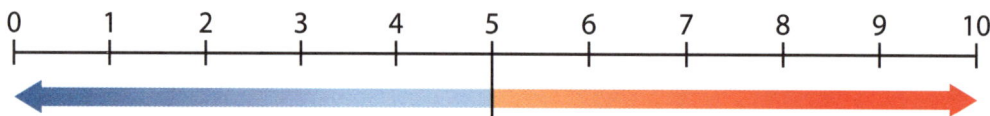

0 1 2 3 4 5 6 7 8 9 10

   (a) Round 2·4915 to the nearest **whole number**: 2·4915 → 4 rounds down so, answer = 2·0.

   (b) Round 2·4915 to **one decimal place**: 2·4915 → 9 rounds up so, answer = 2·5.

   (c) Round 2·4915 to **two decimal places**: 2·4915 → 1 rounds down so, answer = 2·49.

   (d) Round 2·4915 to **three decimal places**: 2·4915 → 5 rounds up so, answer = 2·492.

3. Have a go at rounding these numbers to:

   (i)   A whole number: (a) 8·48 (b) 0·51 (c) 40·73 (d) 3·495 (e) 1·49 (f) 7·045

   (ii) One decimal place: (a) 5·85 (b) 9·95 (c) 6·071 (d) 2·248 (e) 9·046 (f) 7·797

   (iii) Two decimal places: (a) 9·003 (b) 3·715 (c) 15·505 (d) 0·009 (e) 8·888 (f) 7·797

   (iv) Three decimal places: (a) 4·3526 (b) 4·2805 (c) 10·2009 (d) 8·0999 (e) 30·0373

4. Now try these:

   (a) Round 5·471 to one decimal place.

   (b) Round 4·499 to the nearest whole number.

   (c) Round 0·8895 to three decimal places.

   (d) Round 10·506 to two decimal places.

   (e) Round 6·096 to two decimal places.

   (f) Round 5·5555 to three decimal places.

Challenge   Find the sum of 3·765, 4·624 and 1·897 by first rounding each number to two decimal places. ☐

Decimals – Adding and subtracting decimals

Adding and subtracting decimals.

$9.3 + 4.85 - 5.971 =$ ☆

Estimate: $9 + 5 - 6 = 8$

```
   9·30
 + 4·85
 ──────
  14·150
 − 5·971
 ──────
   8·179
```

Add in **zeros** to make it easier to add and subtract.

1. Now do these. (Estimate first.)

   (a) $7 + 3.529 + 4.08$

   (b) $9.09 - 4.321$

   (c) $10 + 3.045 + 1.49$

   (d) $23 - 0.09 - 14.807$

   (e) $0.09 + 10 + 2.975$

   (f) $50 + 0.95 - 4.956$

Decimal problems – add or subtract.

2. Emma is packing 5·07kg of clothes, 2·901kg of books and a $2\frac{9}{1000}$kg laptop for her holiday. Calculate how much under or over the 10kg limit she is.

3. Rose ran $\frac{7}{10}$ km on Friday, 1·03km on Saturday and 2·415km on Sunday. What was the average distance she ran per day? (Round to 3 decimal places).

4. Elsie put $\frac{3}{50}$kg of raisins, $\frac{25}{100}$kg of nuts, 0·079kg of butter and some flour into a bowl to make scones. If the total mixture weighed 1kg, how much flour was in the bowl?

5. Find the total weight in kilogrammes of three bags of carrots weighing 4·75kg, 3·87kg and $\frac{38}{100}$kg respectively.

6. By how much is the sum of $1\frac{7}{100}$ and $4\frac{9}{10}$ greater than $3\frac{78}{1000}$?

7. Scott drank 4·35 litres of water and $5\frac{28}{100}$ litres of juice over three days. How many more millilitres must he drink to achieve a total of 12 litres?

8. By how much is the sum of 5·07 and $8\frac{19}{1000}$ greater than the sum of $2\frac{7}{10}$ and 9·004?

9. Rowan carried two shopping bags each weighing $4\frac{39}{1000}$kg. Amelia's two bags weighed 3·09kg and $4\frac{7}{100}$kg. Who carried more weight and how much more?

10. Ava put 1·003l of orange juice and 79ml of lemon juice into a jug. If she drank 489ml of it, how much was left?

Challenge John poured 2·56l of water into an empty bucket. Sarah poured in 1·67l. Sofia poured in $3\frac{3}{4}$l. Jane also poured some water into the bucket. If there are $12\frac{1}{2}$l in the bucket now, how much water did Jane pour into it? _____ l

Decimals – Check what you have learned

The following are the results for 6 children in a high jump competition.

1. Jack $1\frac{2}{9}$m; Abbie $1\frac{17}{20}$ m; Conor $\frac{15}{20}$ m; Brian $1\frac{500}{1000}$m; Aoife $1\frac{1}{8}$m; Katie $1\frac{10}{25}$m.

   (a) Convert each jump to decimals (up to two decimal places).

   (b) Draw each of their results on the bar-line graph as accurately as you can.

   (c) Work out the difference between the best and worst jumps.

   (d) Round each jump to one decimal place.

   (e) How much less than 2 metres was the best jump?

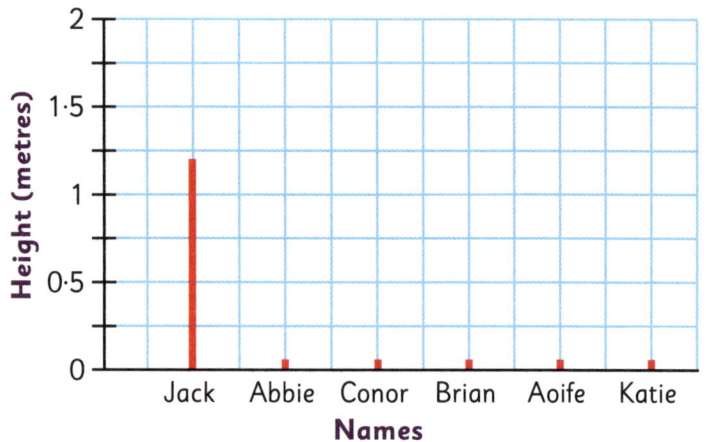

2. **What gets wetter as it dries?**

   To solve this riddle, find the decimal form of each of these questions and arrange the answers in ascending order. This will spell out the answer.

   $L = \frac{80}{1000} + \frac{6}{10} + \frac{6}{1000}$ $A = \frac{1}{11}$ $W = \frac{31}{50} - 0\cdot303$

   $O = 2\cdot1 - 1\cdot801$ $T = \frac{250}{1000}$ $E = 0\cdot7 + 0\cdot093 - 0\cdot199$

   Answer: ☐ ☐ ☐ ☐ ☐ ☐

3. (a) Each number in the **blue** box has been rounded to the nearest hundredth in the **orange** box. Match them.

Blue	Orange
0·527	0·46
0·459	0·50
0·454	0·53
0·500	0·51
0·506	0·45

   (b) Each number in the **yellow** box has been rounded to the nearest thousandth in the **green** box. Match them.

Yellow	Green
0·7465	0·477
0·4774	0·475
0·7029	0·751
0·4747	0·747
0·7506	0·703

4. $\frac{2}{5}$ of the population of a town were children and there were equal numbers of men and women. If there were 564 children in the town, what was its population? (Use the decimal method.)

5. Cathy got €178·50 more than Conor when a prize was shared between them in the ratio of $0\cdot45 : \frac{55}{100}$. What was the value of the prize?

> **Challenge** A prize of €980 was shared among Pat, Niall and Brian in the ratio $0\cdot45 : 0\cdot35 : 0\cdot2$. If Brian got €196, how much did Pat and Niall get?
>
> (Note: Pat got the largest share.) € _____   € _____

A quick look back 4

1. How much is $\frac{7}{9}$ of 18? _____

2. If $\frac{5}{8}$ of a number is 40, what is the number? _____

3. $\frac{6}{7} = \frac{\square}{21}$

4. Use the lowest common denominator to add $\frac{1}{6}$ and $\frac{4}{9}$. → $\frac{\square}{\square} + \frac{\square}{\square} = \frac{\square}{\square}$

5. Use equivalent fractions to subtract $\frac{4}{5}$ from $\frac{7}{8}$. → $\frac{\square}{\square} - \frac{\square}{\square} = \frac{\square}{\square}$

6. $\frac{25}{40}$ of the oranges in a box were good. Write the fraction that was good in its lowest terms (Simplify). $\frac{\square}{\square} = \frac{\square}{\square}$

7. Write $\frac{3}{4} \times 18$ as a mixed number in its lowest terms. _____

8. Paul spent $\frac{3}{4}$ of his money and Pamela spent $\frac{8}{9}$ of hers. Multiply the fraction that Paul spent by the fraction that Pamela spent. Simplify the answer. $\frac{\square}{\square} = \frac{\square}{\square}$

9. A triangle that has no equal sides is called a _____ triangle.

10. This 2D-shape is called a _____ .

11. Which shape is best for tessellating: (a), (b) or (c)? _____

   (a) ⬤   (b) ⬤   (c) ▮

12. Write the reciprocal of $\frac{4}{7}$. _____

13. There were 16 men and 24 women in a choir. What was the ratio of men to women? (Answer in lowest terms.) ____ : ____

14. The ratio of cows to sheep on a farm is 3:5. If the farmer has 64 animals altogether, how many sheep has she? _____

15. Express 16 as a fraction of 36 in simplified form. $\frac{\square}{\square} = \frac{\square}{\square}$

16. Write 1·8 as a mixed number (fractions) in its lowest terms. _____

17. Write 17·682 to the nearest tenth by rounding. _____

18. 19·37 + 4·5 = _____

19. Olivia ran $4\frac{3}{5}$ km on Monday and 3,295m on Tuesday. How many km did she run altogether? (Answer in decimal form.) _____ km

20. Joe's suitcase weighed $\frac{1}{10}$ more than the amount allowed by the airline. If it weighed 33kg, what is the allowed weight? _____ kg

Chapter 14: Number theory – Factors (divisors)

Factors are whole numbers that are multiplied to get a **product**.
Factors are also called **divisors**.

$$3 \times 4 = 12$$
$$\text{factor} \times \text{factor} = \text{product}$$

The area of a rectangular pool is 12m². List all possible whole number dimensions of the pool.

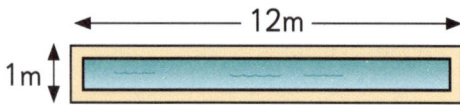

1m × 12m = 12m²
1 and 12 are **factors** of 12.
(1, 12) is a **related pair of factors** of 12.

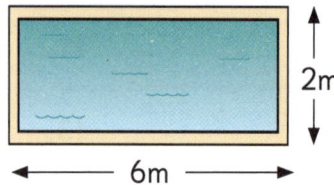

2m × 6m = 12m²
2 and 6 are **factors** of 12.
(2, 6) is a **related pair of factors** of 12.

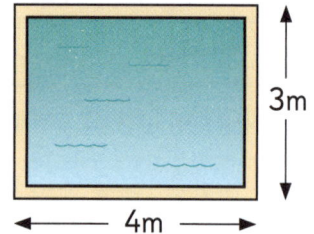

3m × 4m = 12m²
3 and 4 are **factors** of 12.
(3, 4) is a **related pair of factors** of 12.

List the **related pair of factors** of 12.

Factors of all numbers include the number itself and 1.

1   2   3   4   6   12

Related pairs of factors of 12 ➔ (1, 12), (2, 6), (3, 4)

Factors of 12 are 1, 2, 3, 4, 6, 12.

Tip: When finding the factors of a number, for example 24, you can stop searching when you reach half of the number. Half of 24 is 12. The only factor left is 24 itself.

1. (i) Write the related pairs of **factors** of these numbers and
   (ii) list the factors of each number in ascending order.

	Number	(i) related pairs of factors	(ii) factors in ascending order
(a)	6	(1, 6) (2, 3)	1, 2, 3, 6
(b)	8		
(c)	11		
(d)	16		
(e)	20		
(f)	24		
(g)	26		
(h)	29		
(i)	36		

STRAND **Number**   STRAND UNIT/ELEMENT *Number theory*
LANGUAGE *Factors, divisors, common factors, multiples, highest common factor (HCF), lowest common multiple (LCM), prime numbers, composite numbers, exponents, square number, square root*

Common factors and multiples

List (i) the related pairs of factors and (ii) all the factors of 18 and 24.

Related pairs of factors of 18: (1, 18) (2, 9) and (3, 6).
Related pairs of factors of 24: (1, 24) (2, 12) (3, 8) and (4, 6).

Factors of 18 = 1, 2, 3, 6, 9, 18.
Factors of 24 = 1, 2, 3, 4, 6, 8, 12, 24.

The common factors of 18 and 24 are 1, 2, 3, 6.

The highest common factor of 18 and 24 is 6.

1. (i) List the factors of each of the following groups of numbers in ascending order.
   (ii) Ring the common factors for each group. (iii) Write the highest common factor (HCF).

   (a) 6 and 24 | (b) 8 and 30 | (c) 18 and 45 | (d) 10 and 40 | (e) 40 and 50

   (f) 45 and 60 | (g) 24 and 36 | (h) 20 and 28 | (i) 18 and 27 | (j) 16 and 24

   (k) 6, 9 and 15 | (l) 11, 22 and 33 | (m) 8, 12 and 32 | (n) 14, 35 and 42 | (o) 36, 44 and 56

2. Multiples. Complete the table.

Number of cars	1	2	3	4	5	6	7	8	9	10	11	12
Number of wheels	4	8										

Multiples of 4 = (4, 8, 12, 16, 20, 24, ...)

To find the multiples of a 4 on a 🖩 press ④ ＋ ＋ ＝ ＝ ＝ ...

3. Write out the first 10 multiples of each of the following numbers. Use the 🖩 to check.
   (a) 6 | (b) 7 | (c) 8 | (d) 10 | (e) 13 | (f) 20 | (g) 100

4. Write the 1st, 3rd, 6th, 8th and 10th multiple of each of the following. Use the 🖩 to check.

	Number	1st multiple	3rd multiple	6th multiple	8th multiple	10th multiple
(a)	2					
(b)	3					
(c)	5					
(d)	9					
(e)	11					
(f)	12					
(g)	15					

Challenge   There are 7 days in a week. Which of the following numbers of days make up an exact number of weeks. Ring the correct numbers.

7,   11,   14,   19,   22,   28,   34,   35,   39,   40,   49,   51,   53,   63,   67

Lowest common multiple (LCM)

1	2	3	X	5	6	7	X	9	10
11	12	13	14	15	16	17	18	19	20
21	22	23	24	25	26	27	28	29	30
31	32	33	34	35	36	37	38	39	40
41	42	43	44	45	46	47	48	49	50
51	52	53	54	55	56	57	58	59	60
61	62	63	64	65	66	67	68	69	70
71	72	73	74	75	76	77	78	79	80
81	82	83	84	85	86	87	88	89	90
91	92	93	94	95	96	97	98	99	100

The multiples of 4 are marked with an X and the multiples of 6 are marked with a ◯.

1. (a) What is the first number that has both an X and a ◯ on it?

_____.

(b) List all the numbers on the hundred square that have both an X and a ◯ on them.

_____

These numbers are called the **common multiples** of 4 and 6.

12 is the first common multiple of 4 and 6. We call this the **lowest common multiple** (LCM) of 4 and 6.

(i) Write out the first 10 multiples of 3 and 5. (ii) Circle the **common multiples** of 3 and 5.

Multiples of 3 = 3, 6, 9, 12, 15, 18, 21, 24, 27, 30.
Multiples of 5 = 5, 10, 15, 20, 25, 30, 35, 40, 45, 50.

15 and 30 are **common multiples** of 3 and 5, but 15 is the **lowest common multiple**.

2. (i) List the first 10 multiples of each of these pairs of numbers.
(ii) Circle the **common multiples**. (iii) Find the **lowest common multiple** (LCM).

(a) 2 and 5 (b) 3 and 8 (c) 5 and 6 (d) 7 and 8 (e) 6 and 9 (f) 4 and 5 (g) 6 and 7

3. Paul cycles every 12 days and Tina cycles every 9 days. If they both cycle today, how many days will it be until they both cycle again on the same day? _____

4. Eggs come in boxes of 12 and bread rolls come in packs of 10. What is the least number of boxes of eggs and packs of bread rolls that can be bought to make egg rolls with no eggs or bread rolls left over (1 egg is used in each bread roll)? _____ _____

5. Imogen paints every 4th room in a hotel and Patrick paints every 7th room. Which room will be the first that they both paint together? _____

6. Elsa has football training every 5th day and Rose has it every 7th day. What is the first day on which they will both have training? _____

7. For the school concert, Hugo has to play the triangle on every 6th beat and Dara has to play the bodhrán on every 9th beat. On which beat do they both play together? _____

Challenge Una is organising a barbecue. Burgers come in packs of 10 and burger buns come in packs of 6. (a) What is the least number of packs of each she could buy to have the same number of each? ___ ___ (b) There are 55 people invited to the barbecue. How many packs of each must she buy to have a bun burger for each person? ___ ___

Prime and composite numbers

If a number has only itself and 1 as factors, it is a **prime number**.
The factors of 7 are 7 and 1.
7 is a **prime** number.

If a number has more than 2 factors, it is a **composite number**. The factors of 6 are 6 and 1 as well as 2 and 3.
6 is a **composite** number.

Helpful tests to determine if numbers are prime or composite.
These tests will help you to find out if a number is **composite**.

	Divisible	The Test	Example
(a)	by 2?	If the last digit is even.	528 ✓ 8 is even
(b)	by 4?	If the last two digits are ÷ 4.	536 ✓ 36 ÷ 4 = 9
(c)	by 8?	If the last three digits are ÷ 8.	3,576 ✓ 576 ÷ 8 = 72
(d)	by 5?	If the last digit is 0 or 5.	685 ✓ Last digit is 5

	Divisible	The Test	Example
(e)	by 3?	If the sum of the digits ÷ 3.	372 ✓ 3 + 7 + 2 = 12 and 12 ÷ 3 = 4
(f)	by 6?	If it's an even number and the sum of its digits is ÷ 3.	792 ✓ 792 is even 7 + 9 + 2 = 18 and 18 ÷ 3 = 6
(g)	by 9?	If the sum of the digits is ÷ 9.	6,894 ✓ 6 + 8 + 9 + 4 = 27 and 27 ÷ 9 = 3
(h)	by 10?	If the last digit is 0.	5790 ✓ Last digit is 0

1. Circle the divisors of each number. Use the divisibility tests to help you!

	Number	Divisible by
(a)	48	①②③④ 5 ⑥⑧ 9 10
(b)	426	1 2 3 4 5 6 8 9 10
(c)	1,738	1 2 3 4 5 6 8 9 10

	Number	Divisible by
(d)	1,812	1 2 3 4 5 6 8 9 10
(e)	5,816	1 2 3 4 5 6 8 9 10
(f)	3,556	1 2 3 4 5 6 8 9 10

2. Now work out whether the following numbers are **prime** or **composite**. Tick the correct box.

	Number	Prime	Composite
(a)	7		
(b)	18		
(c)	45		
(d)	67		

	Number	Prime	Composite
(e)	131		
(f)	156		
(g)	419		
(h)	578		

	Number	Prime	Composite
(i)	1,741		
(j)	1,332		
(k)	5,000		
(l)	4,032		

Challenge Liam cooks the dinner on prime number days in November, starting on November 2nd. Bernie cooks the dinner on composite number days.

(a) On which dates will Liam cook during this month?

(b) On which dates will Bernie cook?

(c) Is this schedule fair? Explain.

Remember: the digit 1 is neither prime nor composite!

Mon	Tue	Wed	Thu	Fri	Sat	Sun
		1	2	3	4	5
6	7	8	9	10	11	12
13	14	15	16	17	18	19
20	21	22	23	24	25	26
27	28	29	30			

Exponents

Using **exponents** is a quick way to multiply a digit by itself a number of times. Exponents are also called **indices** or **powers**.

$2^5 = $ ☆

exponent/index/power

$2^5 = 2 \times 2 \times 2 \times 2 \times 2 = 32$

base number

We say that 2^5 is 'two to the power of five'.

Two to the power of five means 2 multiplied by itself 5 times.

---

1. Complete the table. What number pattern can you see?

		Exponent	Value
(a)	2×2	2^2	4
(b)	$2 \times 2 \times 2$	2^3	8
(c)	$2 \times 2 \times 2 \times 2$		
(d)	$2 \times 2 \times 2 \times 2 \times 2$		
(e)	$2 \times 2 \times 2 \times 2 \times 2 \times 2$		
(f)	$2 \times 2 \times 2 \times 2 \times 2 \times 2 \times 2$		
(g)	$2 \times 2 \times 2 \times 2 \times 2 \times 2 \times 2 \times 2$		
(h)	$2 \times 2 \times 2 \times 2 \times 2 \times 2 \times 2 \times 2 \times 2$		

2. Complete the table. Use your 🖩 to help you.

		Exponent	Value
(a)	$3 \times 3 \times 3$	3^3	27
(b)	$4 \times 4 \times 4 \times 4 \times 4$	4^5	
(c)	$5 \times 5 \times 5 \times 5 \times 5 \times 5 \times 5$		
(d)	$7 \times 7 \times 7 \times 7 \times 7 \times 7$		
(e)	$9 \times 9 \times 9 \times 9 \times 9 \times 9$		
(f)	$10 \times 10 \times 10 \times 10 \times 10$		
(g)	$15 \times 15 \times 15$		

3. Find the value of the following. Use your 🖩 to help you.

(a) 3^5 (b) 7^4 (c) 8^3 (d) 6^6 (e) 2^9 (f) 4^7 (g) 1^8

4. Now do these. Use your 🖩 to help you.

(a) $2^8 + 2^2$ (b) $3^7 + 2^9$ (c) $4^4 + 5^2$ (d) $5^4 + 3^6$ (e) $6^2 + 9^2$ (f) $3^4 + 2^6$

Challenge   Jake works in a cinema. He has to clean 8 rows of seats. Each row has 8 seats.

(a) How many seats has he to clean? _____

Now write the answer as a power using (i) base 2 _____ and (ii) base 8 _____ .

(b) Jake will spend 2 minutes cleaning each seat. (i) How long will it take him to clean all the seats if he takes no breaks? _____ (ii) Write this as a power using base 2. _____

Special exponents

When a number has an exponent of 2, we call it a **square number**.
When a number is multiplied by itself, the product is a square number.

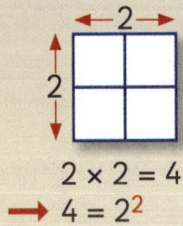

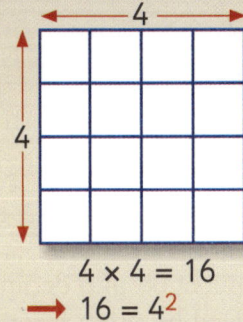

$2 \times 2 = 4$
$\rightarrow 4 = 2^2$

$3 \times 3 = 9$
$\rightarrow 9 = 3^2$

$4 \times 4 = 16$
$\rightarrow 16 = 4^2$

1. Complete the table.

	Number	Multiplied by itself	Symbol	Square number
(a)	1	1 × 1	1^2	1
(b)	2	2 × 2	2^2	
(c)	3			
(d)	4			
(e)	5			
(f)	6			
(g)	7			

	Number	Multiplied by itself	Symbol	Square number
(h)	8			
(i)	9			
(j)	10			
(k)	11			
(l)	12			
(m)	13			
(n)	14			

2. Colour all the square numbers on a hundred square. Use squared paper.

3. Work out the following. Use a calculator to check your answers.
   (a) 18^2 (b) 23^2 (c) 38^2 (d) 44^2 (e) 51^2 (f) 58^2 (g) 64^2 (h) 79^2 (i) 83^2 (j) 96^2 (k) 100^2

4. Now do these.
   (a) $3^2 + 5^2$ (b) $4^2 + 6^2$ (c) $7^2 + 2^2$ (d) $6^2 + 8^2$ (e) $9^2 + 10^2$

Square roots

$3^2 = 9$ or 3 squared equals 9.
The square root (base) of 9 is 3.
We write this as: $\sqrt{9} = 3$

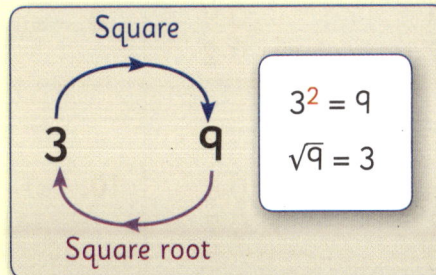

Square

$3^2 = 9$
$\sqrt{9} = 3$

$12^2 = 144$
$\sqrt{144} = 12$

5. Now find the square roots of the following.
   (a) $\sqrt{4}$ (b) $\sqrt{16}$ (c) $\sqrt{100}$ (d) $\sqrt{49}$ (e) $\sqrt{81}$ (f) $\sqrt{64}$ (g) $\sqrt{9}$ (h) $\sqrt{121}$ (i) $\sqrt{25}$ (j) $\sqrt{1}$

6. The calculator has a $\sqrt{}$ key that helps you calculate the square root of any number. Key in the following numbers followed by the $\sqrt{}$ key to find the square root of each.
   (a) $\sqrt{256}$ (b) $\sqrt{225}$ (c) $\sqrt{400}$ (d) $\sqrt{529}$ (e) $\sqrt{625}$ (f) $\sqrt{900}$ (g) $\sqrt{1600}$

Chapter 15: Multiplication 2 – Decimal × decimal

Brain awakener! Do the following. Estimate first.

1. (a) 54·37 × 100 = | (b) 6·158 × 1,000 = | (c) 39·245 × 100 = | (d) 0·51 × 1,000 =

2. (a) 147 × 38 = | (b) 5·72 × 63 = | (c) 5,326 × 44 = | (d) 6,392 × 36 =

3. (a) 4·18 × 56 = | (b) 7·63 × 34 = | (c) 2·57 × 75 = | (d) 8·39 × 87 =

4. (a) 26·57 × 28 = | (b) 47·38 × 65 = | (c) 73·46 × 84 = | (d) 78·06 × 94 =

A Multiplication of a decimal by decimal may be solved by using **fractions**.

$$0·2 × 0·8 \rightarrow \frac{2}{10} × \frac{8}{10} \rightarrow \frac{16}{100} = 0·16$$

B The **vertical method** is done like this.

```
    0·2
×   0·8
———————
   0·16
```

5. **Complete these. Change to fractions first.**

(a) $0·5 × 0·3 \rightarrow \dfrac{\square}{10} × \dfrac{\square}{10} \rightarrow \dfrac{\square}{100} = \underline{\hspace{1cm}}$

(b) $0·4 × 0·9 \rightarrow \dfrac{\square}{10} × \dfrac{\square}{\square} \rightarrow \dfrac{\square}{\square} = \underline{\hspace{1cm}}$

(c) $0·7 × 0·6 \rightarrow \dfrac{\square}{\square} × \dfrac{\square}{\square} \rightarrow \dfrac{\square}{\square} = \underline{\hspace{1cm}}$

(d) $0·5 × 0·5 \rightarrow \dfrac{\square}{\square} × \dfrac{\square}{\square} \rightarrow \dfrac{\square}{\square} = \underline{\hspace{1cm}}$

(e) $0·3 × 0·4 \rightarrow \dfrac{\square}{\square} × \dfrac{\square}{\square} \rightarrow \dfrac{\square}{\square} = \underline{\hspace{1cm}}$

(f) $0·8 × 0·6 \rightarrow \dfrac{\square}{\square} × \dfrac{\square}{\square} \rightarrow \dfrac{\square}{\square} = \underline{\hspace{1cm}}$

6. (a) 0·6 | (b) 0·3 | (c) 0·1
   × 0·8 | × 0·9 | × 0·5

   (d) 0·7 | (e) 0·4 | (f) 0·6
   × 0·7 | × 0·8 | × 0·7

Remember: factor × factor = product

```
    7          0·7          0·7
×   4      ×     4      ×   0·4
————       ———————      ———————
   28          2·8         0·28
```

Did you notice that we have the same number of digits after the decimal point in the **product** as we have in the **two factors combined?**

Complete these.

7. (a)   9 | (b) 0·9 | (c) 0·9
     × 2 | × 2 | × 0·2

8. (a)   3 | (b) 0·3 | (c) 0·3
     × 6 | × 6 | × 0·6

9. (a)   8 | (b) 0·8 | (c) 0·8
     × 7 | × 7 | × 0·7

10. (a)   4 | (b) 0·4 | (c) 0·4
      × 9 | × 9 | × 0·9

Maths Fact The smallest known bee species is the 0·2cm (2mm) Trigona Duckei bee.

Challenge A typical bee colony has 60,000 bees in it. What would be the total length in metres of a colony of Trigona Duckei bees standing in a line? _____ m

STRAND **Number**   STRAND UNIT/ELEMENT *Multiplication*
LANGUAGE *Decimal, multiply, decimal places, factor, product, vertical method*

Multiplication 2 – Decimal × decimal

When we multiply a decimal number by a decimal number, how do we know where to put the decimal point in the answer? Study the following examples to find out.

A

(a)
$$\begin{array}{r} 57 \\ \times\ 6 \\ \hline 342 \end{array}$$

(b)
$$\begin{array}{r} 5 \cdot 7 \\ \times\ 6 \\ \hline 34 \cdot 2 \end{array}$$

(c)
$$\begin{array}{r} 5 \cdot 7 \\ \times\ 0 \cdot 6 \\ \hline 3 \cdot 42 \end{array}$$

B

(a)
$$\begin{array}{r} 26 \\ \times\ 13 \\ \hline 78 \\ 260 \\ \hline 338 \end{array}$$

(b)
$$\begin{array}{r} 2 \cdot 6 \\ \times\ 13 \\ \hline 78 \\ 260 \\ \hline 33 \cdot 8 \end{array}$$

(c)
$$\begin{array}{r} 2 \cdot 6 \\ \times\ 1 \cdot 3 \\ \hline 78 \\ 260 \\ \hline 3 \cdot 38 \end{array}$$

Now do these. You may use a calculator to check your answers.

1. (a)
$$\begin{array}{r} 3 \cdot 8 \\ \times\ 7 \\ \hline \end{array}$$
  (b)
$$\begin{array}{r} 3 \cdot 8 \\ \times\ 0 \cdot 7 \\ \hline \end{array}$$

2. (a)
$$\begin{array}{r} 4 \cdot 9 \\ \times\ 23 \\ \hline \end{array}$$
  (b)
$$\begin{array}{r} 4 \cdot 9 \\ \times\ 2 \cdot 3 \\ \hline \end{array}$$

3. (a)
$$\begin{array}{r} 5 \cdot 6 \\ \times\ 37 \\ \hline \end{array}$$
  (b)
$$\begin{array}{r} 5 \cdot 6 \\ \times\ 3 \cdot 7 \\ \hline \end{array}$$

Now do these. You may use a calculator to check your answers.

4. (a) 2·6 × 0·3 (b) 3·5 × 0·7 (c) 1·8 × 0·6 (d) 3·3 × 0·5

5. (a) 4·2 × 0·4 (b) 3·7 × 0·2 (c) 5·7 × 0·3 (d) 8·2 × 0·6

6. (a) 5·7 × 0·6 (b) 8·5 × 0·5 (c) 2·7 × 1·3 (d) 3·6 × 1·4

7. (a) 2·2 × 3·6 (b) 4·8 × 2·3 (c) 5·5 × 2·3 (d) 7·4 × 1·7

8. (a) 3·9 × 4·6 (b) 5·7 × 3·7 (c) 8·5 × 6·3 (d) 9·4 × 7·2

9. Elizabeth jumped a distance of 3·7m in the long jump.
   Niall jumped 1·2 times that distance. How far did Niall jump? _____ m

10. Sarah had €4·70. Her mother gave her €1·40. She wants to go on a
    school tour. The tour costs 3·7 times the amount of money that she now has.
    How much will the school tour cost her? €_____

11. Anita can throw a shot put a distance of 4·9 metres. Terry can throw it 1·5 times that distance.
    How much less than 12m is Terry's throw? _____ m

12. Brian aims to beat his pole vault personal best of 5·3m by vaulting 1·3 times that
    height next season. What height is he targeting? _____ m

Maths Fact   A monster truck drove up a ramp and went 61·57 metres into the air to clear a Boeing 727 jet.

Challenge   How many metres would the monster truck have cleared if it completed
7 such jumps. _____ m

Multiplication 2 – Bigger numbers

It is **really important** to have the correct number of decimal places in the answer.

A   6·7 × 2·3 = ☆

Estimate: 7 × 2 = 14

$$\begin{array}{r} 6·\mathbf{7} \\ \times\ 2·\mathbf{3} \\ \hline 201 \\ 134\mathbf{0} \\ \hline 15·41 \end{array}$$

B   27·5 × 9·4 = ☆

Estimate: 30 × 9 = 270

$$\begin{array}{r} 27·\mathbf{5} \\ \times\ 9·\mathbf{4} \\ \hline 1100 \\ 2475\mathbf{0} \\ \hline 258·50 \end{array}$$

C   58·4 × 7·3 = ☆

Estimate: 60 × 7 = 420

$$\begin{array}{r} 58·\mathbf{4} \\ \times\ 7·\mathbf{3} \\ \hline 1752 \\ 4088\mathbf{0} \\ \hline 426·32 \end{array}$$

Now do these. Estimate first. You may use a calculator to check your answers.

1. (a) 7·4 × 3·6   (b) 5·8 × 2·7   (c) 6·9 × 4·5   (d) 8·3 × 6·9

2. (a) 8·5 × 4·6   (b) 3·6 × 7·5   (c) 22·6 × 3·7   (d) 40·7 × 4·8

3. (a) 14·8 × 6·5   (b) 36·7 × 5·6   (c) 72·3 × 6·2   (d) 78·4 × 7·4

4. (a) 55·6 × 7·5   (b) 85·7 × 8·2   (c) 96·5 × 4·9   (d) 139·6 × 3·8

5. (a) 283·7 × 6·7   (b) 563·5 × 8·7   (c) 267·8 × 9·5   (d) 708·4 × 7·8

Now try these. Always estimate first.

6. Joan would win a prize if she got a number that is 7·8 times greater than 6·9. What number must she get in order to win the prize? _____

7. Jamie can lift 37·6kg. Paulie can lift 2·9 times that weight.

   (a) What weight can Paulie lift? _____kg

   (b) What is the difference between the two lifts? _____kg

8. | meter |
   | 2 | 8 | 9 | 5 | 3 | 4 |

   The school's Green Committee reads the electricity meter every day. The school used 76·4 units each day. How many units did it use in $4\frac{1}{2}$ days? _____

9. Calculate the difference between 276·1 and 613·4 and then multiply the result by 8·9. _____ Now work out the difference between your estimate and the actual answer. _____

10. John was asked to multiply 364·2 by 5·7. He got an answer of 2234·04. His answer was incorrect. Find (a) the correct answer _____ and (b) by how much his answer was too big? _____

Maths Fact   High heels are not new. In 16th century, Venice high platform shoes of up to 0·76m were fashionable. They were called Chopines.

Challenge   What would be the total height of 23 of these high platform shoes? _____ m

Multiplication 2 – Decimal × decimal

Multiplying numbers with a different amount of decimal places can cause confusion!

3·67 × 4·8 = ☆   Estimate: 4 × 5 = 20

Hot Tip! Multiply as normal ignoring the decimal points. When you come to the answer, count the number of digits after the decimal points in the **two factors**. You must have the same number of digits after the decimal point in the **product**.

```
    3·67
 ×   4·8
   2936
 14680
 17·616
```

Remember: factor × factor = product.

Do these. Always estimate first. You may use a calculator to check your answers.

1. (a) 5·63 × 4·2   (b) 7·24 × 5·8   (c) 8·71 × 6·3   (d) 6·65 × 7·4

2. (a) 4·72 × 5·7   (b) 6·83 × 3·9   (c) 9·27 × 8·4   (d) 7·08 × 8·6

3. (a) 17·39 × 2·6   (b) 35·64 × 7·5   (c) 62·58 × 4·9   (d) 81·78 × 6·3

4. (a) 263·4 × 3·7   (b) 448·6 × 6·7   (c) 562·7 × 9·5   (d) 925·7 × 4·8

5. (a) 65·8 × 0·46   (b) 87·3 × 0·58   (c) 342·8 × 0·73   (d) 569·8 × 0·29

6. Ciarán and Darragh were asked to multiply 67·4 × 8·9. Darragh misheard and multiplied by 9·8 instead. What was the difference between their answers? _____

7. Charles de Gaulle airport in Paris has a runway of 4·2km in length. If this runway was 2·87 times longer, how long would it be then? _____ km

8. Maria weighs 63·52kg. Marcus is 1·4 times heavier. What is their combined weight? _____ kg

9. Add 37·4 and 6·8 and multiply the answer by 1·9. _____

10. Tom got a score of 19·68 for his dive during a competition. This was multiplied by 3·7 for degree of difficulty. What was his total score for that dive? _____

11. Shauna put 9·3 litres of diesel fuel into her car. How much did it cost Shauna if diesel was on sale at €1·36 per litre? €_____

12. What is the difference between 57·6 × 0·67 and 65·7 × 0·76? _____

13. A shopkeeper bought 36 football jerseys costing €8·95 each. She had €276·52 left. How much money had she before she bought the football jerseys? €_____

Maths Fact The Mamenchisaurus dinosaur had the longest neck of all the dinosaurs. It measured 9·8 metres.

Challenge Calculate the length of a garden that is 3·47 times the length of the neck of the Mamenchisaurus. _____ m

Chapter 16: Division 2

Dividing **decimal numbers** is almost identical to dividing numbers without a decimal point. We just remember to include the decimal point. Look at these examples. The only difference will be the inclusion of the decimal point.

```
A        147
     63)9261
       - 63
          296
        - 252
           441
         - 441
             0
```

```
B        1·47
     63)92·61
       - 63
          296
        - 252
           441
         - 441
             0
```

```
C        0·147
     63)9·261
       - 63
          296
        - 252
           441
         - 441
             0
```

Try these. Always estimate first. Use your calculator to check the answers.

1. (a) 6·403 ÷ 19 (b) 88·20 ÷ 36 (c) 72·36 ÷ 27 (d) 6·222 ÷ 17

2. (a) 422·4 ÷ 16 (b) 8·064 ÷ 48 (c) 6·358 ÷ 17 (d) 74·88 ÷ 26

3. (a) 8·346 ÷ 78 (b) 710·1 ÷ 27 (c) 886·6 ÷ 22 (d) 85·76 ÷ 67

4. (a) 7·384 ÷ 26 (b) 887·3 ÷ 19 (c) 82·68 ÷ 52 (d) 805·8 ÷ 34

5. (a) 9·360 ÷ 52 (b) 69·56 ÷ 47 (c) 8·103 ÷ 37 (d) 82·25 ÷ 35

Now solve these problems. Be careful where you place the decimal point!

6. The weighbridge showed a weight of 3720kg for the bales of hay. If each bale weighs 15kg, how many bales were weighed? _____

7. A music superstore paid €372·60 for a stock of 81 new tin whistles. What did each tin whistle cost them? €_____

8. A consignment of 45 cement bags had a total weight of 837·9kg. What was the weight of each cement bag? _____kg

9. Paul has to share a prize of €132·80 equally among 16 winners. How much will each get? €_____

10. Divide 842·7 by the sum of 25 + 28. _____

11. Divide 6·762 by the difference between (12 × 12) and (19 × 5). _____

12. Simona scored a total of 840·6 after playing 18 games of **Pinball Wizard** on her games console. What was her average score per game? _____

13. Griff divided 22·62 by 58. What answer should he get? _____

Maths Fact   It takes 29·50 years for the planet Saturn to complete an orbit of the sun.

Challenge   Check which of these numbers divides into the Maths Fact number of 29·50 without going beyond 2 places of decimals? (a) 15   (b) 18   (c) 25

STRAND Number   **STRAND UNIT/ELEMENT** Division
LANGUAGE Division, 4-digit decimal numbers, decimal places, decimal point, divisor, whole number

Division 2 – Dividing a decimal by a decimal

$4·2 ÷ 0·7 =$ ☆

A $\dfrac{4·2}{0·7} × \dfrac{10}{10} \longrightarrow \dfrac{42}{7} = 6$

B $4·2 ÷ 0·7$
× 10   × 10
$42 ÷ 7 = 6$

When dividing by a decimal number, make the divisor into a whole number first!

Now do these.

1. (a) $3·5 ÷ 0·5$ (b) $2·1 ÷ 0·7$ (c) $4·8 ÷ 0·6$ (d) $5·6 ÷ 0·8$ (e) $6·3 ÷ 0·9$

$1·48 ÷ 3·7 =$ ☆

C $\dfrac{1·48}{3·7} × \dfrac{10}{10} \longrightarrow \dfrac{14·8}{37} = 0·4$

D $1·48 ÷ 3·7$
× 10   × 10
$14·8 ÷ 37 = 0·4$

$$\begin{array}{r} 0·4 \\ 37\overline{)14·8} \\ 148 \\ \hline 0 \end{array}$$

2. **Now do these.**

(a) $1·56 ÷ 2·6 =$ _____
(b) $1·65 ÷ 3·3 =$ _____
(c) $1·88 ÷ 4·7 =$ _____
(d) $4·96 ÷ 6·2 =$ _____
(e) $6·08 ÷ 7·6 =$ _____

Try these mentally.

3. (a) $3·2 ÷ 0·8$ (b) $2·8 ÷ 0·7$ (c) $4·8 ÷ 0·8$ (d) $5·6 ÷ 0·7$ (e) $6·3 ÷ 0·9$

4. (a) $6·5 ÷ 0·5$ (b) $3·6 ÷ 0·4$ (c) $2·7 ÷ 0·3$ (d) $4·5 ÷ 0·9$ (e) $7·2 ÷ 0·8$

E $41·6 ÷ 2·6 =$ ☆

$2·6\overline{)41·6}$ → $26\overline{)416}$ →

$$\begin{array}{r} 16 \\ 26\overline{)416} \\ 26 \\ \hline 156 \\ 156 \\ \hline 0 \end{array}$$

F $6·66 ÷ 3·7 =$ ☆

$3·7\overline{)6·66}$ → $37\overline{)66·6}$ →

$$\begin{array}{r} 1·8 \\ 37\overline{)66·6} \\ 37 \\ \hline 296 \\ 296 \\ \hline 0 \end{array}$$

Now do these.

5. (a) $1·36 ÷ 1·7$ (b) $3·45 ÷ 2·3$ (c) $1·44 ÷ 0·8$ (d) $60·8 ÷ 3·8$ (e) $37·8 ÷ 4·2$

6. (a) $59·2 ÷ 1·6$ (b) $6·21 ÷ 2·3$ (c) $9·52 ÷ 2·8$ (d) $8·74 ÷ 1·9$ (e) $8·97 ÷ 2·3$

7. (a) $1·836 ÷ 5·1$ (b) $12·54 ÷ 3·3$ (c) $1·628 ÷ 4·4$ (d) $1·625 ÷ 2·5$ (e) $36·66 ÷ 4·7$

8. (a) $220·4 ÷ 3·8$ (b) $13·34 ÷ 4·6$ (c) $1·105 ÷ 1·7$ (d) $19·78 ÷ 2·3$ (e) $2·184 ÷ 5·6$

9. (a) $126·9 ÷ 2·7$ (b) $15·66 ÷ 2·9$ (c) $3·055 ÷ 4·7$ (d) $1·914 ÷ 5·8$ (e) $15·87 ÷ 2·3$

Maths Fact   5·6 metres is the record length of a venomous snake, called a King Cobra.

Challenge   How many sections of 0·7m could be cut from a piece of ribbon that is the same length as the King Cobra mentioned above? _____

Division 2 – Dividing a decimal by a decimal

$84.48 \div 2.4 = \boxed{\star}$

A

$\dfrac{84.48}{2.4} \times \dfrac{10}{10} \longrightarrow \dfrac{844.8}{24} = \boxed{\star}$

$84.48 \div 2.4 = 35.2$

B

$84.48 \div 2.4$

$\downarrow \times 10 \quad \downarrow \times 10$

$844.8 \div 24 = \boxed{\star}$

```
        35.2
   24)844.8
       72
      ----
       124
       120
      ----
        48
        48
      ----
        00
```

Now do these.

1. (a) $43.69 \div 1.7$ (b) $89.24 \div 2.3$ (c) $74.52 \div 2.7$ (d) $65.55 \div 1.9$ (e) $96.22 \div 3.4$

$9.045 \div 0.27 = \boxed{\star}$

C

$\dfrac{9.045}{0.27} \times \dfrac{100}{100} \longrightarrow \dfrac{904.5}{27} = \boxed{\star}$

$9.045 \div 0.27 = 33.5$

D

$9.045 \div 0.27$

$\downarrow \times 100 \quad \downarrow \times 100$

$904.5 \div 27 = \boxed{\star}$

```
        33.5
   27)904.5
       81
      ----
        94
        81
      ----
       135
       135
      ----
       000
```

Now do these. Don't forget to make the divisor into a whole number first.

2. (a) $9.731 \div 0.37$ (b) $7.252 \div 0.28$ (c) $7.137 \div 0.39$ (d) $9.761 \div 0.43$ (e) $8.142 \div 0.23$

3. (a) $2.856 \div 0.17$ (b) $3.984 \div 0.16$ (c) $7.656 \div 0.24$ (d) $7.196 \div 2.8$ (e) $8.208 \div 2.7$

4. (a) $9.614 \div 0.22$ (b) $9.682 \div 0.47$ (c) $9.462 \div 0.38$ (d) $618.8 \div 2.6$ (e) $85.14 \div 3.3$

5. (a) $6.615 \div 0.45$ (b) $5.82 \div 0.24$ (c) $1.258 \div 0.37$ (d) $9.152 \div 0.16$ (e) $7.506 \div 2.7$

6. (a) $0.7682 \div 0.23$ (b) $9.381 \div 0.53$ (c) $9.828 \div 2.7$ (d) $0.7936 \div 0.32$ (e) $7.644 \div 4.9$

7. How many times is 0.87 contained in 8.004?   8. How many times can I take 4.5 from 117?

9. Sophie spent €12.90 downloading tunes costing 86c each. How many tunes did she download? _____

10. During a charity swim, a total distance of 2.800km was covered equally by 35 swimmers. What decimal fraction of a km did each swimmer cover? _____

11. A chemist used 9.246 litres of a chemical to fill 69 test tubes equally with the liquid. What decimal fraction of a litre was used for each tube? _____

Challenge   269.1m was the length of the Titanic. That is about the length of 2.5 football pitches placed end to end. Using these figures, find the approximate length of a football pitch. _____ m

Division 2 – Money, money, money!

1. (a) €52·20 ÷ 0·36 (b) €64·26 ÷ 0·27 (c) €15·12 ÷ 0·42

 (d) €14·11 ÷ 0·17 (e) €21·84 ÷ 0·24 (f) €17·48 ÷ 0·38

2. (a) €23·56 ÷ 0·62 (b) €13·20 ÷ 0·55 (c) €12·74 ÷ 0·26

 (d) €15·75 ÷ 0·35 (e) €11·68 ÷ 0·16 (f) €11·88 ÷ 0·27

3. (a) €16·94 ÷ 0·22 (b) €30·74 ÷ 0·58 (c) €27·72 ÷ 0·63

 (d) €40·64 ÷ 0·16 (e) €22·95 ÷ 0·27 (f) €24·57 ÷ 0·63

Usually, the 3rd decimal place in an answer is so small that mostly we can ignore it. This one thousandth part may be rounded to leave us with an answer rounded to two decimal places.

| 26·735 → 26·74 | 48·947 → 48·95 | 68·642 → 68·64 | 73·808 → 73·81 |

Now do the following. Round the answers to two places of decimals.

4. (a) 63·24 ÷ 5·8 (b) 85·21 ÷ 2·6 (c) 3·952 ÷ 0·44

 (d) 55·73 ÷ 6·3 (e) 8·116 ÷ 0·25 (f) 17·443 ÷ 4·6

5. (a) €97·16 ÷ 0·33 (b) €64·75 ÷ 3·8 (c) €19·96 ÷ 0·54

 (d) €36·21 ÷ 1·9 (e) €88·63 ÷ 4·7 (f) €73·46 ÷ 2·8

6. 148·4 is the product of 2·8 and what other number? _____

7. (a) What is the greatest number of stamps a lady can buy with €115 if each stamp costs €0·68? _____

 (b) How much change will she get? € _____

8. Cathal added 17·64 to 65·39 and then divided the answer by 1·1 What answer should he get, correct to two decimal places? _____

9. A delivery van is carrying cartons with a total weight of 88·96kg. If each carton weighs 0·64kg, how many cartons are there in the van? _____

10. How many times can I take 0·85 from the sum of 38·42, 5·37 and 13·16? _____

11. (a) Which is the better value and (b) by how much: 17 boxes of cereal for €60·52 or 19 boxes for €64·41? (a) _____ (b) _____

12. A syndicate of 17 office workers shared a small lotto win of €1,392 equally. How much did each receive? € _____

13. Gráinne spent €97·96 on coloured buttons for a dress she was entering in a design competition. Each button cost €0·62. How many buttons did she buy? _____

Challenge On the morning of November 1st, the gas meter reading was 1354·5. By the end of November 22nd, the reading was 2164·1.

 (a) What was the average daily unit use of gas by the user? _____

 (b) What was the daily cost to the user if each unit of gas cost 16·8c? € _____

Problem-solving

1. For how long is Dublin Castle open to the public: (a) Monday to Friday inclusive? ___
   (b) over the weekend? ___ (c) during a full week? ___

2. For how many minutes does the castle open on: (a) Wednesday? ___ (b) Sunday? ___

3. How many minutes less than 40 hours is the castle open over the week? ___

4. Dublin Castle was built between 1204 and 1230. Count each year as a full year and calculate how many days it took to build the castle. (Allow for a leap year every 4 years.) ___

5. Calculate what a family of 2 adults and 3 children under 12 would pay for a tour. € ___

6. A coach of tourists comes to do a tour of the castle. There are 47 tourists in total, all adults. (a) How much will they pay? € ___ (b) If they receive one free ticket for every 6 full price tickets, what will they pay then? € ___ (c) How much will they save? € ___

7. €981 was taken one day in full price adult ticket sales. How many adults visited? ___

8. How many adult tickets would have to be sold to yield €994·50? ___

9. Dublin Castle was handed back to Michael Collins and Irish control on January 16th, 1922. How many days was it from that day to St. Patrick's Day 1922, including both dates? (Note: 1922 was not a leap year.) ___

10. What was the average daily attendance for April if 6,360 people visited the castle? ___

11. How many cups of coffee were sold on one day when the takings for coffee were €383·60? ___

12. How much was taken in by the shop if 94 cups of tea, 48 cakes and 54 bowls of soup were sold one day? € ___

13. How much was taken in by the shop if 57 cups of coffee, 73 bowls of soup and 39 cakes were sold one day? € ___

Historic Dublin

Visit Dublin Castle

Opening hours:
Mon–Fri: 10:00–16:45
Sat & Sun: 14:00–16:45

Admission:
Adults: €4·50
Children under 12: €2
Discounts available for groups

Shop
Coffee €2·80
Tea €2·15
Cakes €2·65
Soup €4·55

Dublin Castle:
Started 1204
Completed 1230

1204 was a leap year

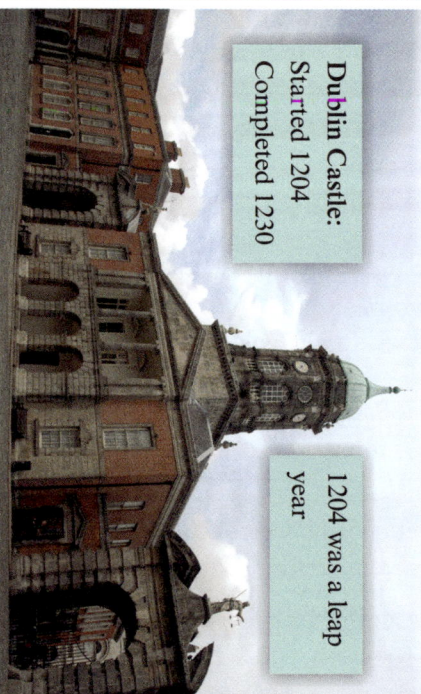

Maths Fact

The fantastic Chester Beatty Library Museum is housed in the grounds of Dublin Castle. It won European Museum of the Year in 2002.

Challenge

If 7,936 children visited the Chester Beatty Library in the month of March, what was the daily average number of child visitors? ___

84

Chapter 17: Length

1. We use **mm**, **cm**, **m** and **km** to measure **length**. Select the best instrument to measure each of these:

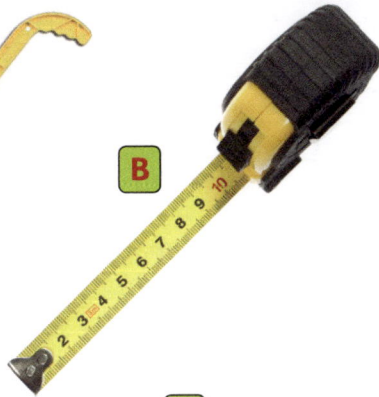

   (a) the length of a shirt sleeve.

   (b) the distance from Cork City to Midleton.

   (c) the length of a piece of guttering.

   (d) the depth of a tyre tread.

   (e) the perimeter of a sports field.

   (f) the thickness of *Busy at Maths 6*.

   (g) the height of a 12-year-old child.

   A   **B**   **C**   **D**   **E**

2. What **unit of measurement** is best to measure the length of each item in question 1 above?

   (a) _____   (b) _____   (c) _____   (d) _____   (e) _____   (f) _____   (g) _____

3.
   The width of this fingernail is almost 1cm.

   Estimate the length of each of the following lines. Then measure them with a ruler.

   (a) _____   (b) _____

   (c) _____   (d) _____

   (e) _____   (f) _____

   (g) _____   (h) ▬

4. Use your ruler to draw lines of the following lengths:

   (a) 4cm   (b) 11cm   (c) $8\frac{1}{2}$cm   (d) 3·5cm   (e) 13cm

   (f) 5·5cm   (g) 0·8cm   (h) 24mm   (i) 13mm   (j) 4·2cm

5. 120 seconds after take-off a space shuttle would be approximately 45km above the Earth. How many metres is this? _____ m

Maths Fact

4·2 metres is the length of the minute hand on London's Big Ben clock.

Challenge

Write the length of Big Ben's minute hand in:

(a) cm [____]   (b) mm [____]

STRAND **Measures**   STRAND UNIT/ELEMENT *Length*

LANGUAGE *Millimetres (mm), centimetres (cm), metres (m), kilometres (km), fractions, decimals, perimeter*

Length

A plumber needs to order lengths of pipe, each 87cm long.
He must submit his order in metres. How should he write this?

$87cm = \frac{87}{100}m = 0.87m$

$1cm = \frac{1}{100}m = 0.01m$

$10cm = \frac{1}{10}m = 0.1m$

$100cm = 1m = 1.0m$

$110cm = 1\frac{1}{10}m = 1.1m$

1. Write these **centimetres** as **metres**.

(a) 63cm = _____ m   (b) 25cm = _____ m   (c) 72cm = _____ m   (d) 14cm = _____ m

(e) 136cm = _____ m   (f) 245cm = _____ m   (g) 8cm = _____ m   (h) 60 cm = _____ m

2. Write these **metres** as **centimetres**.

(a) 0.34m = _____ cm   (b) 0.57m = _____ cm   (c) 0.18m = _____ cm   (d) 0.8m = _____ cm

(e) 1.29m = _____ cm   (f) 7.06m = _____ cm   (g) 5.5m = _____ cm   (h) 8.01m = _____ cm

3. 13cm is the width of the seed of a Climbing Gourd plant. Express this as metres. _____ m

$1m = \frac{1}{1000}km = 0.001km$

$100m = \frac{100}{1000}km = \frac{1}{10}km = 0.1km$

$1,000m = 1km = 1.0km$

$7m = \frac{7}{1000}km = 0.007km$

$637m = \frac{637}{1000}km = 0.637km$

$2,637m = 2\frac{637}{1000}km = 2.637km$

10s, 100s and 1000s – decimals are so easy to deal with!

4. Write these **metres** as **kilometres** using decimals.

(a) 542m = _____ km   (b) 6m = _____ km   (c) 73m = _____ km   (d) 270m = _____ km

(e) 90m = _____ km   (f) 11m = _____ km   (g) 1,430m = _____ km   (h) 3,472m = _____ km

5. Write these **metres** as **kilometres** using fractions or mixed numbers.

(a) 734m = _____ km   (b) 38m = _____ km   (c) 410m = _____ km   (d) 9m = _____ km

(e) 50m = _____ km   (f) 580m = _____ km   (g) 40m = _____ km   (h) 2,030m = _____ km

(i) 5,160m = _____ km   (j) 3,002m = _____ km   (k) 5,704m = _____ km   (l) 9,080m = _____ km

6. These distances are in **kilometres (km)**. Write the distances as **metres**.

(a) $\frac{3}{10}$ km = _____ m   (b) 0.4km = _____ m   (c) 0.59km = _____ m

(d) $\frac{7}{10}$ km = _____ m   (e) 0.316km = _____ m   (f) 5.7km = _____ m

(g) 0.007km = _____ m   (h) 6.2km = _____ m   (i) $4\frac{9}{10}$ km = _____ m

(j) $3\frac{5}{1000}$ km = _____ m   (k) 6.259km = _____ m   (l) $3\frac{13}{100}$ km = _____ m

(m) 9.01km = _____ m   (n) 0.45km = _____ m   (o) 0.309km = _____ m

Challenge   The Hubble Space Telescope orbits at 569km above the Earth's surface.
What height would the Hubble telescope orbit at if its orbit height was increased
by 50%. [_____] km

Length – Addition and subtraction

Ciarán increased his long jump record of 7·79m by 28cm.
What was his new record?

7·79m + 0·28cm = ☆   Estimate: 8m + 0m = 8m

I prefer to use decimals when doing this!

m	cm
7	79
+ 0	28
8	07

→

$$7 \cdot 79 \text{ m}$$
$$+ 0 \cdot 28 \text{ m}$$
$$8 \cdot 07 \text{ m}$$

Now try these.

1.
(a)
```
  m  cm
  2  37
+ 3  53
_____
```

(b)
```
  m  cm
  2  56
+ 2  78
_____
```

(c)
```
  6 · 35 m
+ 2 · 47 m
_____
        m
```

(d)
```
  5 · 69 m
+ 3 · 74 m
_____
        m
```

(e)
```
  8 · 17 m
+ 6 · 85 m
_____
        m
```

(f)
```
  7 · 06 m
+ 5 · 89 m
_____
        m
```

Now do the following.

2.
(a)
```
  cm  mm
   5   3
+  3   6
_____
```

(b)
```
  5 · 7 cm
+ 2 · 9 cm
_____
       cm
```

(c)
```
  35 · 4 cm
+ 17 · 8 cm
_____
        cm
```

(d)
```
  km   m
   3  36
+  4  975
_____
```

(e)
```
  7 · 208 km
+ 5 · 987 km
_____
         km
```

(f)
```
  43 · 728 km
+ 39 · 677 km
_____
          km
```

Elizabeth's best long jump was 58cm less than Kelly's
best jump of 6·45m. How far did Elizabeth jump?

6·45m − 0·58m = ☆   Estimate: 6m − 1m = 5m

m	cm
6	45
− 0	58
5	87

→

$$6 \cdot 45 \text{ m}$$
$$- 0 \cdot 58 \text{ m}$$
$$5 \cdot 87 \text{ m}$$

Now do the following.

3.
(a)
```
  m  cm
  7  42
− 2  56
_____
```

(b)
```
  4 · 39 m
− 2 · 58 m
_____
        m
```

(c)
```
  8 · 07 m
− 3 · 65 m
_____
        m
```

(d)
```
  cm  mm
   4   7
−  2   4
_____
```

(e)
```
  25 · 6 cm
− 15 · 7 cm
_____
        cm
```

(f)
```
  50 · 3 cm
− 35 · 6 cm
_____
        cm
```

4.
(a)
```
  km   m
  8  525
− 3   68
_____
```

(b)
```
  km   m
  4   36
− 1  359
_____
```

(c)
```
  7 · 324 km
− 3 · 425 km
_____
         km
```

(d)
```
  18 · 202 km
− 12 · 723 km
_____
          km
```

(e)
```
  35 · 110 km
− 17 · 427 km
_____
          km
```

(f)
```
  51 · 063 km
− 24 · 775 km
_____
          km
```

Maths Fact 91·5 metres of tubing carrying cooling water is needed in the spacesuit of an astronaut.

Challenge How much less than 300m is the total tubing required for 3 astronauts?

_____ m

87

Length – Multiplication and division

Sarah ordered 4 lengths of fencing each 2·53m long.
What was the total length of fencing ordered?

2·53m × 4 = ☆   Estimate: 3m × 4 = 12m

```
  m  cm
  2  53          2 · 53 m
×     4      →  ×      4
─────────       ─────────
 10  12         10 · 12 m
```

Now try these.

1. (a) cm mm
```
     3   4
×        4
─────────
```

(b)
```
    5 · 6 cm
×       3
──────────
       cm
```

(c)
```
    4 · 6 cm
×      7
──────────
      cm
```

(d) m cm
```
    7  24
×      6
─────────
```

(e)
```
    8 · 73 m
×       8
──────────
       m
```

(f)
```
   34 · 55 m
×        9
──────────
        m
```

2. (a) km m
```
    2  146
×       5
──────────
```

(b) km m
```
    7  316
×       3
──────────
```

(c)
```
    4 · 227 km
×       4
───────────
        km
```

(d)
```
    9 · 405 km
×       9
───────────
        km
```

(e)
```
   22 · 073 km
×        8
───────────
         km
```

(f)
```
   18 · 007 km
×        7
───────────
         km
```

A fibre optic cable of 14km 856m was cut into
4 equal lengths. What was the length of each piece?

14·856km ÷ 4 = ☆   Estimate: 15 ÷ 4 = 3¾ = 3·75

```
  km    m
4)14  856          4)14·856 km
   3  714      →      3·714 km
```

Now try these.

3. (a) cm mm   (b) cm mm   (c)   (d)   (e)   (f)
```
4)9   2          6)16   2          3)11·4 cm      7)40·6 cm      9)59·4 cm      8)98·4 cm
```

4. (a) $\frac{1}{6}$ of 93·72m   (b) $\frac{1}{9}$ of 55·89m   (c) $\frac{1}{3}$ of 11·52m   (d) $\frac{1}{5}$ of 40m 80cm

5. (a) 44km 280m ÷ 3   (b) 86km 100m ÷ 7   (c) 6)112·32 km

   (d) 65·056km ÷ 4   (e) $\frac{5}{6}$ of 43km 44m   (f) $\frac{3}{5}$ of 13km 35m

Convert these questions to decimal form before completing.

6. (a) (15m − 6·29m) × 4   (b) (826cm + 7m 9cm) ÷ 5   (c) (11cm 3mm − 5·7cm) × 7

   (d) (4½km − 272m) ÷ 7   (e) (7mm + 2·1cm + 35mm) × 9   (f) (8$\frac{7}{10}$m + 374m) ÷ 2

Maths Fact   254cm of rain falls (on average) in a rainforest each year.

Challenge   (a) Calculate how many cm less than 4m this rainfall is. ☐

(b) Then find what the difference should be over a six-year period. ☐

Length – Perimeter

Remember: Perimeter is the measure of the total length of the boundary of a shape. Patrick wants to fence off a small area for sheep. This drawing has a scale of 1cm = 1m (1:100). How much fencing does he need? Measure. Use the scale.

Width: $5\frac{1}{2}$cm = $5\frac{1}{2}$m.   Length: 4cm = 4m.

Perimeter = $5\frac{1}{2}$m + 4m + $5\frac{1}{2}$m + 4m = 19m.

This is a scale drawing of 2 pitches. The outer pitch is Croke Park. The inner is the Aviva Stadium. The side of each small square represents 10m. These are **close** to the exact measurements of the stadia.

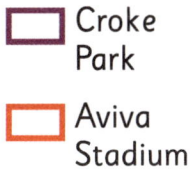

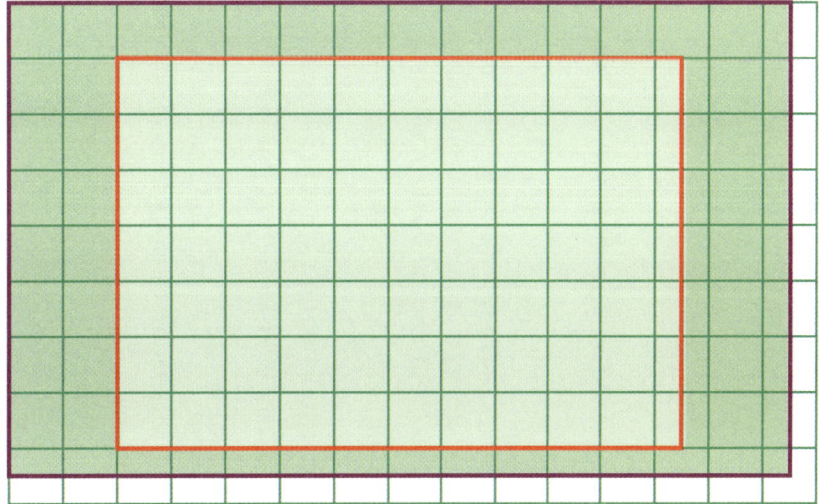

☐ Croke Park

☐ Aviva Stadium

1. (a) What is the length of the Croke Park pitch?
   (b) What is the length of the Aviva pitch?
   (c) How wide is the Aviva pitch?
   (d) How much wider is the Croke Park pitch?
   (e) Calculate the perimeter of the Aviva pitch.
   (f) Now find the perimeter of the Croke Park pitch.
   (g) What is the difference between the perimeters of the pitches?

2. **Estimate first. Then measure the perimeter of each shape.** Scale: ☐ = 1m²

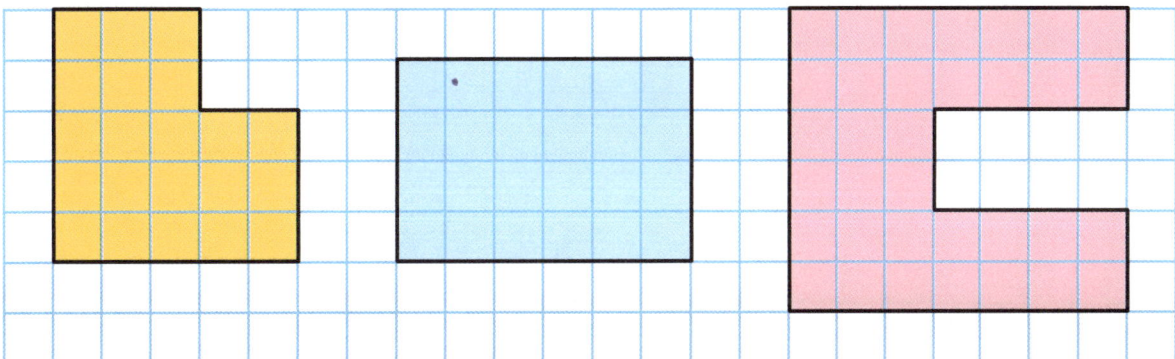

Maths Fact The moon moves about 3·8cm further away from Earth each year.

Challenge About how much further from Earth should the moon be after a quarter of a century? ☐

Length – Cruising through length

1. The low water depth at Cobh cruise berth is 9·1m. The low water depth in the channel is 11·2m. What is the difference between both of the depths in cm? ____

2. The maximum length that can be accommodated at Cork's cruise berth is 152m. At Cobh it is 350m. Express the difference between both lengths as a decimal fraction of a kilometre. ____

3. *MSC Magnifica* is a cruise ship 293·8m long. *Sea Cloud II* is an older ship 109·5m long. What is the total length of the two ships? ____

4. The *Titanic* called to Cobh (then Queenstown) in April 1912. It was 269m long. Write this in km. ____ km

5. There were four funnels on the *Titanic*, each rising 24·84m above the deck. What was the combined height of the four funnels? ____ m

6. The *Lusitania* was torpedoed off the Old Head of Kinsale in May 1915 and 1,198 people lost their lives. The *Lusitania* was 239·1m in length. How much shorter than the *Titanic* was this? ____ m

7. Cobh's best known athlete is Sonia O'Sullivan. Among many other successes, Sonia won World and European gold medals over 5,000m, 3,000m, 10,000m, 8km, and 4km. What total distance does this amount to in kilometres? ____ km

8. The marathon distance is 42·195km. How far would an athlete have run if she completed 9 marathons? ____ km

9. (a) How much longer than the *Titanic* is the *MSC Magnifica*? ____ m
   (b) How much shorter than the *Titanic* is *Sea Cloud II*? ____ m

10. What is the total length of the two longest vessels mentioned in the questions above? ____ m

11. The *Titanic* was almost 53·38 metres in height. That is the same height as a 17-storey building. Based on this information, find the height of one storey of the building if all storeys were of equal height? ____ m

12. 12·416km/h was the cruising speed of the *Titanic* just before it hit the iceberg. How far would it have travelled at this speed in the 9 hours before it struck the iceberg? ____ km

Maths Fact

The diameter of the moon is 3,474km.

Challenge

Earth's diameter is 12,742km. Which of these is the best estimate for how many times bigger than the moon's diameter the Earth's diameter is?

(a) $3\frac{1}{2}$ (b) 3·7   (c) 3·9   (d) 4·1. ____

A quick look back 5

1. Write the value of the underlined digit.

   <u>3</u>87,596 _____

2. 283 × 100 = _____

3. How many times can I take
   200 from 3,000? _____

4. What is the ratio of girls to boys?

   ___ : ___

5. Write $\frac{8}{36}$ in its lowest terms. ☐
                                           ☐

6. $\frac{2}{5}$ of the 60 children in a group are boys. How many girls are there in the group? _____

7. Write $7\frac{59}{1000}$ as a decimal number.

   _____

8. What is the value of 3^3? _____

9.  Andrew ran $6\frac{2}{5}$ km on Monday and 2,570m on Wednesday. How many km did he run altogether?

   _____ km

10. The ratio of pigs to sheep on a farm is 3:7.
    If there are 18 pigs, how many sheep are there?

    _____

11. What is the lowest common multiple of 12 and 9? _____

12. Is the number 56,898 divisible by 9 without having a remainder? Use the divisibility tests to check. _____

13. Write the value of 3^4. _____

14.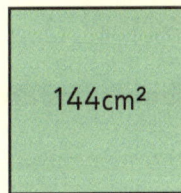

    144cm²

    What is the length of a side of this square if its area is 144cm²?

    _____

15. $\sqrt{121}$ = _____

16. 1·7 × 0·6 = _____

17. How many times can I take 0·7 from 6·3?

    _____

18. The perimeter of a rectangle is 50cm. If its longer side is 16cm, what is the length of its shorter side? _____

    ←————16cm————→

    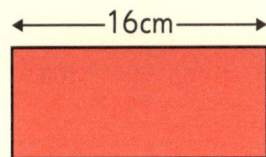

19. A plank of wood is 3m 25cm long. What is the length of 5 such planks?

    Answer in metres. _____ m

20. Alan cycled 5·9km. Alex cycled 7,450 metres. How many kilometres further did Alex cycle than Alan?

    _____ km.

Chapter 18: Fractions/Decimals/Percentages 1

A Quick Reminder:

1. Write the (i) fraction, (ii) decimal and (iii) percentage of the 100-square that is coloured:

1	2	3	4	5	6	7	8	9	10
11	12	13	14	15	16	17	18	19	20
21	22	23	24	25	26	27	28	29	30
31	32	33	34	35	36	37	38	39	40
41	42	43	44	45	46	47	48	49	50
51	52	53	54	55	56	57	58	59	60
61	62	63	64	65	66	67	68	69	70
71	72	73	74	75	76	77	78	79	80
81	82	83	84	85	86	87	88	89	90
91	92	93	94	95	96	97	98	99	100

(a) Yellow: (i) $\frac{1}{100}$, (ii) 0·01, (iii) 1%.

(b) Red: (i) _____, (ii) _____, (iii) _____.

(c) Blue: (i) _____, (ii) _____, (iii) _____.

(d) Green: (i) _____, (ii) _____, (iii) _____.

(e) Purple: (i) _____, (ii) _____, (iii) _____.

(f) Grey: (i) _____, (ii) _____, (iii) _____.

(g) What percentage of the 100-square is

(i) coloured? _____ (ii) not coloured? _____

Changing **fractions** and **decimals** to **percentages**.

A Change a **fraction** to a percentage.
Multiply by 100.

$$\frac{1}{4} \times \frac{100}{1} = \frac{100}{4} = 25\%$$

$$\frac{2}{5} \times \frac{100}{1} = \frac{200}{5} = 40\%$$

B Change a **decimal** to a percentage.
Multiply by 100.

$$0{\cdot}25 \times 100 = 25\%$$

$$0{\cdot}4 \times 100 = 40\%$$

> Move the digits two places to the left!

2. Now write each of the following as **percentages**.

(a) $\frac{1}{2}$ = _____   (b) $0{\cdot}09$ = _____   (c) $0{\cdot}5$ = _____   (d) $\frac{4}{5}$ = _____   (e) $0{\cdot}55$ = _____

(f) $\frac{3}{20}$ = _____   (g) $0{\cdot}63$ = _____   (h) $\frac{79}{100}$ = _____   (i) $\frac{9}{10}$ = _____   (j) $0{\cdot}98$ = _____

Changing **fractions** to **percentages**. Simplify first!

A $\frac{7}{\,20\,} \times \frac{\overset{5}{100}}{1} \longrightarrow \frac{35}{1} = 35\%$

B $\frac{19}{\,25\,} \times \frac{\overset{4}{100}}{1} \longrightarrow \frac{76}{1} = 76\%$

C $\frac{23}{\,50\,} \times \frac{\overset{2}{100}}{1} \longrightarrow \frac{46}{100} = 46\%$

3. Try simplifying first to change the **fractions** to **percentages**.

(a) $\frac{7}{50}$ (b) $\frac{11}{25}$ (c) $\frac{3}{5}$ (d) $\frac{13}{20}$ (e) $\frac{1}{2}$ (f) $\frac{9}{25}$ (g) $\frac{8}{20}$ (h) $\frac{13}{25}$ (i) $\frac{19}{20}$

Some fractions don't divide evenly and we have more than 2 decimal places.

$$\frac{7}{\,15\,} \times \frac{\overset{20}{100}}{1} = \frac{140}{3}$$

$$\frac{3)1\,4^2 0}{4\,6\,R\,2} = 46\tfrac{2}{3}\%$$

or

$$3\overline{)140{\cdot}0000} \quad 4\,6{\cdot}6\,6\,6\,6 \text{ etc.}$$

$0{\cdot}466666 \times 100 = 46{\cdot}66\%$ (stop after 2 decimal places)

4. Change these **fractions** to **percentages**. Stop after 2 decimal places.

(a) $\frac{2}{3}$ (b) $\frac{3}{7}$ (c) $\frac{4}{9}$ (d) $\frac{7}{30}$ (e) $\frac{1}{6}$ (f) $\frac{5}{12}$ (g) $\frac{5}{8}$ (h) $\frac{5}{6}$ (i) $\frac{7}{9}$ (j) $\frac{11}{12}$

5. Change these **decimals** to **percentages** (2 decimal places).

(a) $0{\cdot}6666$ (b) $0{\cdot}0378$ (c) $0{\cdot}4533$ (d) $0{\cdot}1666$ (e) $0{\cdot}7488$ (f) $0{\cdot}9327$

STRAND Number   **STRAND UNIT/ELEMENT** *Fractions, decimals and percentages*
LANGUAGE *Fractions, decimals and percentages, express, expressing, calculator, calculate, spent, amount*

Fractions/Decimals/Percentages 1

1. Write the coloured amounts as a **percentage** of the **full amounts** (2 decimal places).

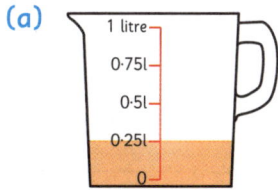

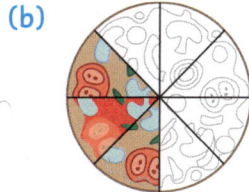

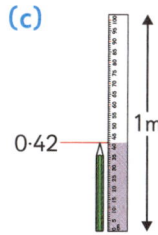

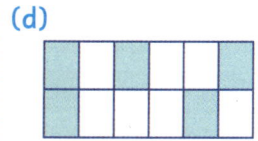

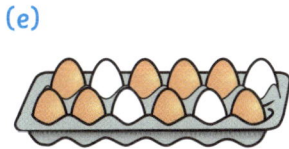

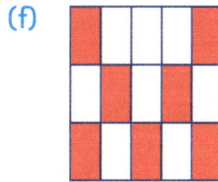

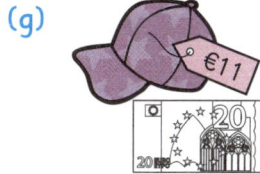

(a)

(b)

(c) 0·42

(d)

_____   _____   _____   _____

(e)

(f)

(g) €11

(h) 0·125kg

_____   _____   _____   _____

Changing percentages to fractions or decimals.

A Change a **percentage** to a **fraction**. **Divide by 100.**

(i) $60\% \rightarrow \dfrac{60}{100} \rightarrow \dfrac{6}{10} = \dfrac{3}{5}$

(ii) $15\% \rightarrow \dfrac{15}{100} = \dfrac{3}{20}$

B Change a **percentage** to a **decimal**. **Divide by 100.**

(i) $60\% \div 100 = 0·60$

(ii) $15\% \div 100 = 0·15$

> When dividing by 100, move the digits two places to the right!

2. Now change each of these **percentages** to **fractions** and **decimals**.

(a) 12% = _____ = 0·_____

(b) 70% = _____ = 0·_____

(c) 45% = _____ = 0·_____

(d) 4% = _____ = 0·_____

(e) 50% = _____ = 0·_____

(f) 5% = _____ = 0·_____

Changing more difficult **percentages** to **fractions** or **decimals**.

A

(i) $33\tfrac{1}{3}\% \rightarrow \dfrac{33\frac{1}{3}}{100} \times \dfrac{3}{3} \rightarrow \dfrac{100}{300} \rightarrow \dfrac{100}{300} = \dfrac{1}{3}$

(ii) $12\tfrac{1}{2}\% \rightarrow \dfrac{12\frac{1}{2}}{100} \times \dfrac{2}{2} \rightarrow \dfrac{25}{200} \rightarrow \dfrac{25}{200} = \dfrac{1}{8}$

B

(i) $33·33\% \div 100 = 0·3333$
(or 0·33 to two decimal places)

(ii) $12·5\% \div 100 = 0·125$

3. Now change each of these **percentages** to **fractions** and **decimals**.

(a) $37\tfrac{1}{2}\%$ = _____ = 0·_____

(b) $11\tfrac{1}{9}\%$ = _____ = 0·_____

(c) $66\tfrac{2}{3}\%$ = _____ = 0·_____

(d) $41\tfrac{2}{3}\%$ = _____ = 0·_____

(e) $83\tfrac{1}{3}\%$ = _____ = 0·_____

(f) $16\tfrac{2}{3}\%$ = _____ = 0·_____

Challenge 1 It is 05:00 . What percentage of a full day has already passed? (2 decimal places) _____

Challenge 2 A game lasts for 70 minutes. When 20 minutes have been played, what percentage has still to be played? (2 decimal places) _____

Fractions/Decimals/Percentages 1

1. Groups of three.
Find the matching sets of **fractions**, **decimals** and **percentages**. Colour the matching sets.

33·33%	0·2222	$\frac{2}{3}$	0·25	$\frac{2}{6}$	22·22%
$\frac{5}{8}$	$\frac{1}{4}$	58·333	62·5%	$\frac{7}{12}$	$58\frac{1}{3}$% 25%
0·6666	$\frac{2}{9}$	0·625	$66\frac{2}{3}$%	0·3333	

2. Write the next **three terms** in each of the following sequences.

(a) $\frac{3}{10}$, 40%, 0·5, _____, _____, _____.

(b) $\frac{4}{25}$, 0·24, 32%, _____, _____, _____.

(c) 15%, 0·3, $\frac{9}{20}$, _____, _____, _____.

(d) $12\frac{1}{2}$%, $\frac{1}{4}$, 0·375, _____, _____, _____.

(e) 0·06, 12%, $\frac{9}{50}$, _____, _____, _____.

(f) $\frac{2}{9}$, $33\frac{1}{3}$%, 44·44, _____, _____, _____.

3. What goes up but never comes down? Order from **biggest** to **smallest** to find the answer.

G $\frac{4}{6}$, **O** $\frac{6}{8}$, **Y** 75·5%, **E** $\frac{70}{1000}$, **U** $\frac{5}{7}$, **R** 0·705, **A** 70%.

Answer: ☐ ☐ ☐ ☐   ☐ ☐ ☐

4. Complete the table:

Fraction	$\frac{30}{100}$			$\frac{5}{12}$			
Percentage		9·5%			$24\frac{1}{2}$%		$16\frac{2}{3}$%
Decimal			0·625			0·723	

5. Write the following **fractions**, **decimals** and **percentages** on the number line.

$\frac{3}{8}$, $\frac{260}{1000}$, 77·7%, $\frac{1}{3}$, 0·050, $\frac{48}{50}$, 0·499, $\frac{9}{25}$, 14%

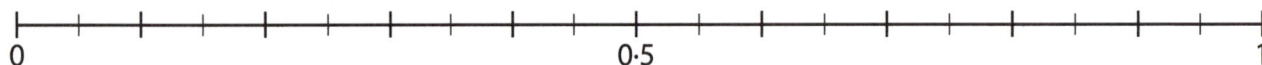

```
├──┼──┼──┼──┼──┼──┼──┼──┼──┼──┼──┼──┼──┼──┼──┼──┼──┼──┼──┤
0                             0·5                              1
```

Challenge

Write the missing amounts on the interlinking dominoes. The order should be percentage, fraction, decimal, percentage, fraction, decimal …

| 25% | $\frac{1}{8}$ | 0·125 | 12% | | | $16\frac{2}{3}$% | | 0·19 | $37\frac{1}{2}$% | | 0·625 |

| 0·28 | $\frac{1}{2}$ | | 0·48 | | 25% | | $\frac{33}{50}$ | | 0·39 | |

Fractions/Decimals/Percentages 1

Weather percentages.

A It was sunny for 27 days of June. What percentage was that?

$$\frac{27}{30} \times \frac{100}{1} \rightarrow \frac{270}{3} \rightarrow \frac{90}{1} = 90\%$$

B It rained for 18 days in April. What percentage was that?

$$\frac{18}{30} \times \frac{100}{1} \rightarrow \frac{180}{3} \rightarrow \frac{60}{1} = 60\%$$

1. Write each of the following as a **percentage**.

   (a) It snowed for 7 of the 28 days in February.

   (b) It rained for 21 days in September.

   (c) November had 9 days of sunshine.

   (d) June had rain on 24 days.

Expressing numbers as a percentage of each other. First write in fraction form.

C Aaron spent €7 of his €20 going to the cinema. That means he spent $\frac{7}{20}$ of his money.

$$\frac{7}{20} \times \frac{100^{5}}{1} = \frac{35}{1} = 35\%$$

D Sally spent €9 of her €25 buying a dress. That means she spent $\frac{9}{25}$ of her money.

$$\frac{9}{25} \times \frac{100^{4}}{1} = \frac{36}{1} = 36\%$$

2. **Work out what percentage of his €20 Aaron spent on each of the following:**

   (a)
   €4

   (b)
   €3·00

   (c)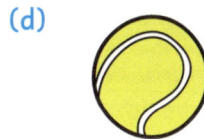
   €2·60

   (d)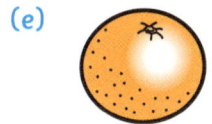
   €1·40

   (e)
   €0·20

   (f) What percentage of his money had Aaron left after buying one of each item? _____

---

3. Expressing numbers as **decimals** of each other. Use your calculator to 2 decimal places.

   (a)
   Free kicks: 37
   Goals scored: 6
   Success rate 0·16

   (b)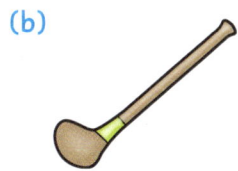
   Frees: 73
   Points: 65
   Success rate ____

   (c)
   Free shots: 25
   Scored: 19
   Success rate ____

   (d)
   Penalties: 7
   Scored: 5
   Success rate ____

   (e)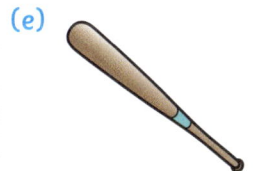
   Pitches: 127
   Strikes: 74
   Success rate ____

---

4. Sonia had €85. She spent 60% of it buying a dress. How much money had she left? €_____

5. 87·5% of Toni's money is €54·60. How much money has she altogether? € _____

Challenge Alex spent €9, Ava spent €11 and Amy spent €17. Calculate the amount each spent as a decimal fraction of the total amount spent (to 2 decimal places).

Alex _____, Ava _____, Amy _____

Chapter 19: Time

Family movies in a multiplex cinema

FILM	DENIS THE MENACE	Mrs. Doubtfire	CASPER	HOME ALONE	Harry Potter and the Philosopher's Stone
Duration	94 mins	125 mins	100 mins	103 mins	153 mins
Cinema times	14:30	16:50	17:40	20:50	21:10

Christmas Songs

SONG	Wonderful Christmastime	Joy to the World	CRAZY ELF DANCE	DRUMMER BOY	Santa Claus is Coming to Town
Duration	3 mins 37 secs	5 mins 34 secs	2 mins 30 secs	4 mins 35 secs	7 mins 22 secs

1. Write the duration of each film in hours and minutes.

2. Write the duration of each song in seconds.

3. What is the total duration of the films *Denis the Menace* and *Home Alone*?

4. What is the total duration of *Mrs. Doubtfire* and the *Harry Potter* film?

5. What is the difference in the duration of *Mrs. Doubtfire* and *Denis the Menace*?

6. Dara listened to the *Drummer Boy* six times. How long did he spend listening to it?

7. Pam listened to *Wonderful Christmastime* nine times. How long did she spend listening to it?

8. If all five Christmas songs were on the one CD and there were five seconds between the end of one song and the beginning of the next, what would the length of the CD be in minutes and seconds?

9. If you watched the *Harry Potter* film over three days and spent the same length of time watching it each day, how long would you spend watching it each day?

10. Write the finishing time of each film in (a) digital form and (b) as **am** or **pm** time.

11. How many hours and minutes are there between these film starting times:
    (a) *Casper* and *Harry Potter*? (b) *Mrs. Doubtfire* and *Casper*? (c) *Mrs. Doubtfire* and *Home Alone*?

12. Leo wants to see two films today. Which of the following options will allow him to see both films from start to finish without the times overlapping?

DENIS THE MENACE and Mrs. Doubtfire	Mrs. Doubtfire and CASPER	CASPER and HOME ALONE	HOME ALONE and Harry Potter

Challenge

Leo lives 44 minutes away from the cinema. (a) Write the time he should depart from his house to be just in time for each film. (b) Write the time he should arrive home after having watched each film if he left for home immediately.

	FILM	Denis the Menace	Mrs. Doubtfire	Casper	Home Alone	Harry Potter and the Philosopher's Stone
	Cinema Times	14:30	16:50	17:40	20:50	21:10
(a)	Depart					
(b)	Return					

STRAND Measures   STRAND UNIT/ELEMENT Time
LANGUAGE Hours, minutes, seconds, time, speed, distance, total, digital, analogue, depart, arrive, return, kilometres, average, rotates, bar chart, calculator, time zones, longitude, degrees, international date line

Time – Time, speed and distance

Time: Lily travelled 258km at an average speed of 86km/h. How long did it take her to complete the journey?

258km ÷ 86km/h = 3 hours

Speed: It took Lily 3 hours to drive 258km. What was her average speed for the journey?

258km ÷ 3 hours = 86km/h

Distance: Lily drove for 3 hours at an average speed of 86km/h. How far did she travel altogether?

86km/h × 3 hours = 258km

Time

1. Róisín rollerskates at an average speed of 12km/h. How long would it take her to travel:

   (a) 24km   (b) 48km   (c) 60km   (d) 18km   (e) 30km
   (f) 54km   (g) 28km   (h) 51km   (i) 57km?

2. Jack rides his horse at an average speed of 16km/h. How long would it take him to travel: (a) 32km   (b) 48km   (c) 64km
   (d) 72km   (e) 40km   (f) 56km   (g) 52km   (h) 76km   (i) 80km?

3. Gran set out in her car on a journey of 255km at 12:45. She travelled at an average speed of 85km/h.

   (a) How long did it take her to complete the journey?

   (b) At what time did she reach her destination?

4. A car travelled at an average speed of 64km/h. How long did it take to travel 240km?

Speed

5. The distance between a town in Galway and a town in Waterford is 270km. It takes Liz 2 hours and 30 minutes to drive there. What is her average speed in km/h?

6. The distance between a Carlow town and a Sligo town is 232km. If it takes 2 hours and 30 minutes to drive there, what is the average speed in km/h?

7. Joe cycled 42km in 1·75 hours. What was his average speed in km/h?

Distance

8. Luke rides his bicycle for 3 hours at an average speed of 28km/hour. How far does he travel?

9. Sam drove at an average speed of 100km/h for $3\frac{1}{4}$ hours. How far did he travel?

10. An aeroplane flies at an average speed of 850km/h. What distance will it have travelled in 3·5 hours?

11. The Shanghai Maglev, the world's fastest train, travels at an average speed of 251km/h. How far will it have travelled in $4\frac{1}{2}$ hours?

Challenge The zoo is 259km away from Ellie's home. It took 3 hours 30 minutes to get there without any stops. What was the average speed in km/h?

Speed in metres per second

1. This bar chart shows how many seconds it took Darragh and his friends to complete the 100-metre sack race.

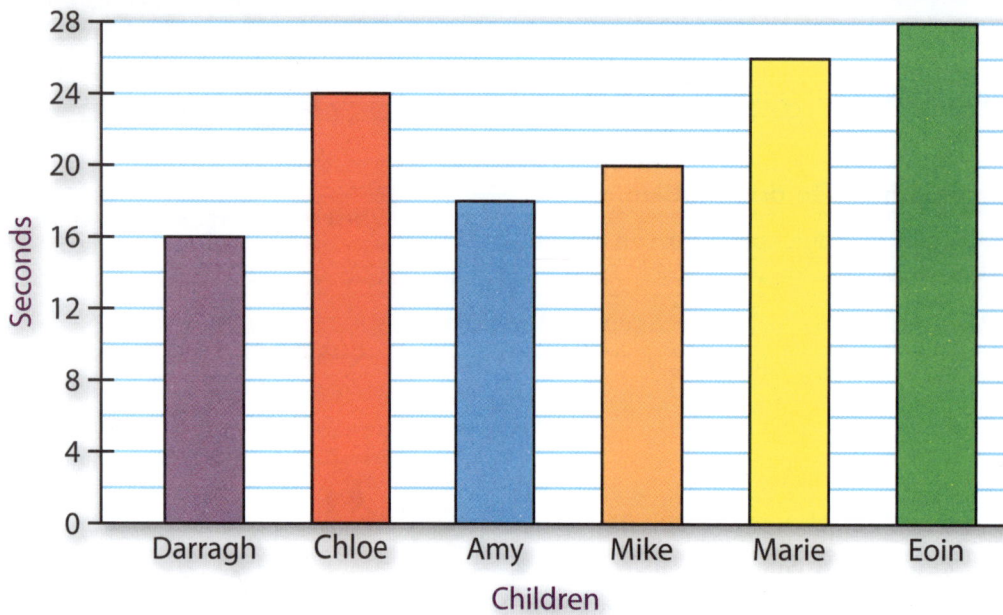

(a) Who was (i) the slowest and (ii) the fastest?

(b) What was the average time taken to complete the 100 metres?

(c) Which children went (i) faster than the average time and (ii) slower than the average time?

2. The famous Irish runner, Paul Hession, ran the 100 metre sprint in 10·18 seconds. To work out his average speed per second on the **calculator**, we divide the distance by the time taken: 100 ÷ 10·18 = 9·8231827. We round this to 9·82 metres per second (m/s).

Use your calculator to find the average speed per second of these famous athletes.

Athlete	Distance (metres)	Time (seconds)	Average speed in metres per second (m/s)	Round to 2 decimal places
Usain Bolt	100 metres	9·58		
Florence Griffith-Joyner	100 metres	10·49		
Usain Bolt	200 metres	19·19		
Florence Griffith-Joyner	200 metres	21·34		
Michael Johnson	400 metres	43·18		
Marita Koch	400 metres	47·60		

3. Calculate the average speed per second for each child in **Q.1** above. Round to 2 decimal places.

Challenge

It took Sophia 35 seconds to run from the Music Shop to the Sport Shop and 55 seconds to run from the Sport Shop to the Coffee Shop. What was her average speed for the total distance from the Music Shop to the Coffee Shop in metres per second?

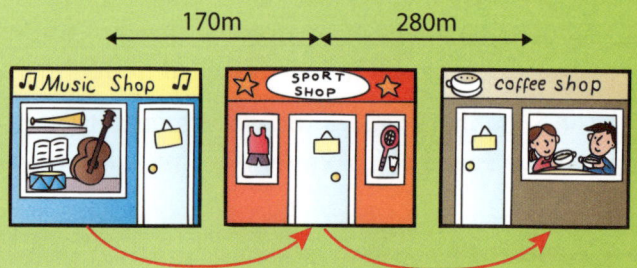

_____ m/s

International time zones

Did you ever wonder why children in Denver, U.S.A are eating breakfast, children in Helsinki are having their dinner, children in Sydney, Australia are asleep and you are finishing your school day all at the same time?

The Earth rotates 360° on its axis every 24 hours. As the Earth rotates, the Sun shines on only one half of it at any one time. The other half is dark. While the sun shines where you live, it's night-time somewhere else. The Earth has 24 different time zones. These time zones are measured in one-hour intervals along lines of longitude. Each 15° of longitude represents a one-hour time difference.

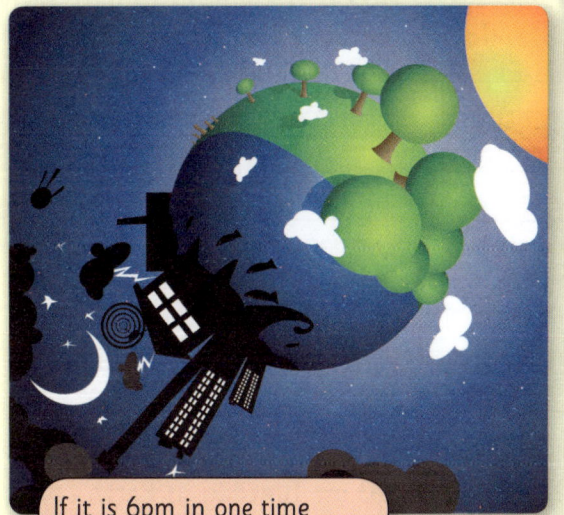

Greenwich Mean Time

The line of longitude through Greenwich (London) is 0°. All the time zones East and West are measured from Greenwich.

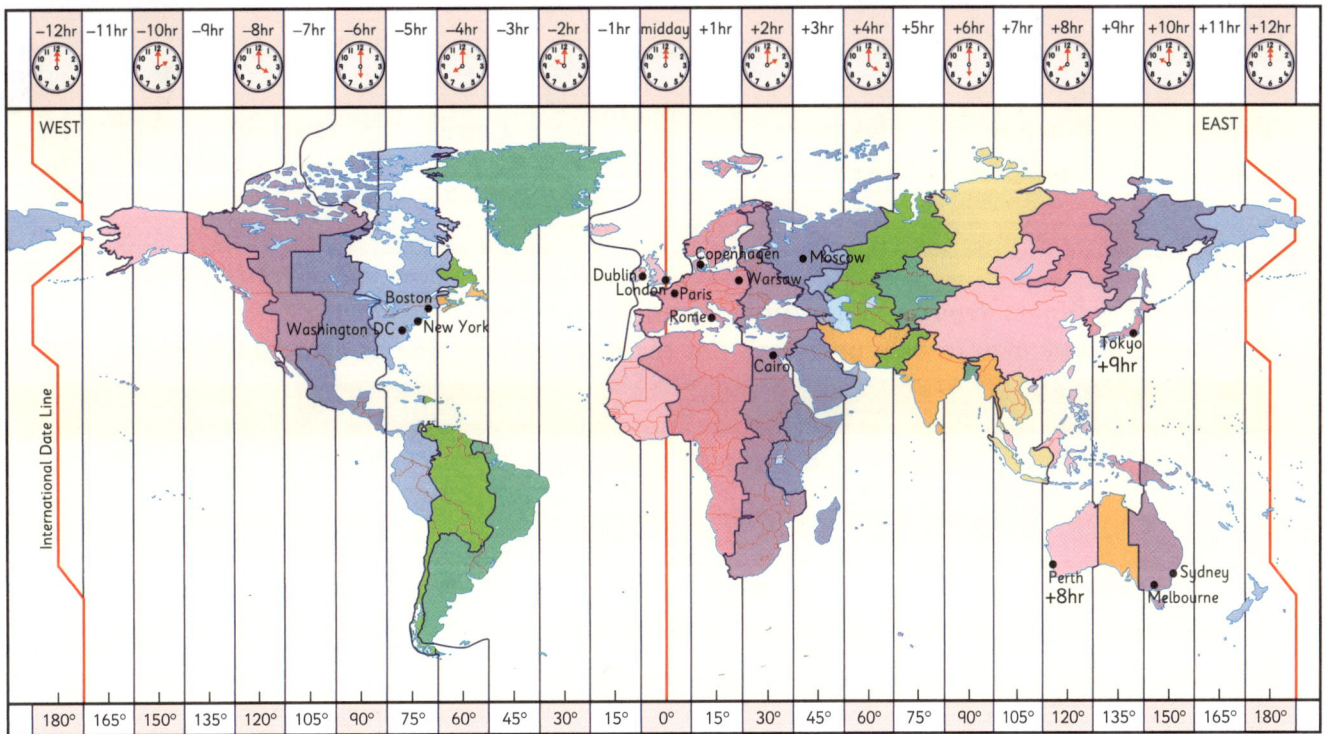

If it is 6pm in one time zone, 15° **west** would be 1 hour behind and 15° **east** would be 1 hour ahead.

1. **What time is it? Complete the table.**

Local time	15° West	30° East	60° West	75° East
14:00	13:00			19:00
19:00				
12:00				
05:00				
09:00				
08:30			04:30	

International time zones

1. If it is 17:00 on Tuesday in Dublin, draw the correct times on each clock for the following cities. Write whether it is am or pm. It may not be Tuesday in each city. Explain why. Use the time zone map on page 99 to help you.

New York 75°W	Tokyo 135°E	Sydney 150°E	Rome 15°E	London 0°	Perth 120°E
pm					

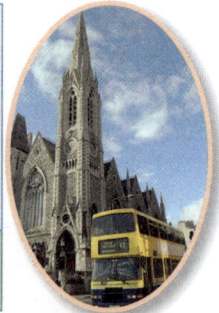

2. If it is 06:00 on Tuesday in Perth (Australia), draw the correct times on each clock for the following cities. Write whether it is am or pm.

Perth is 120° East.

Dublin 0°	Warsaw 15°E	Tokyo 135°E	Washington DC 75°W	Cairo 30°E	Moscow 45°E

Come fly with me!

3. The following flights depart Dublin Airport and fly non-stop to each city. Use the time zone map to help you work out the local arrival time at each destination.

Departure time	To	Flying Time	Time difference	Local arrival time
Monday 14:00	Boston	6 hours 30 minutes		15:30
Tuesday 13:00	Copenhagen	2 hours 3 minutes		:
Wednesday 09:00	Rome	3 hours 10 minutes		:
Thursday 10:00	Moscow	5 hours 15 minutes		:
Friday 08:00	Cairo	6 hours 52 miutes		:

Challenge

This table shows the local time in the cities of Dublin and New York.

(a) Use the time zone map to work out the time difference between the two cities.

(b) Work out the flight duration (i) from Dublin to New York (ii) New York to Dublin.

(c) Explain why you think the flight duration is different on both trips.

Outbound Flight	Departs Dublin 10:50	Arrives New York 13:20 (local time)	Time difference	Flight duration
Inbound Flight	Departs New York 17:30 (local time)	Arrives Dublin 05:10 (next day)	Time difference	Flight duration

Chapter 20: Equations and variables

A number sentence may have the following signs: **<**, **=** or **>**.

A	B	C
A snail travels 36m over 3 days. He travels 12m on average each day.	Ava is making pancakes. The recipe requires 300ml of milk. She has already put in 125ml. She adds in a further 250ml.	Darragh has €12. He buys 1 app for €1·99 and another for €3·99.
12m × 3 **=** 36m	125ml + 250ml **>** 300ml	€1·99 + €3·99 **<** €12

1. Are these number sentences **true** or **false**? Explain your answer.

   (a) 18 + 11 = 28   (b) 24 − 5 > 18   (c) 6 × 9 = 26 × 2   (d) 100 ÷ 4 > 11 × 3

   (e) 7 × 6 = 47 − 5   (f) 23 + 12 < 8 × 4   (g) 63 ÷ 7 < 54 ÷ 6   (h) 24 ÷ 8 = 9 ÷ 3

2. Put the correct sign (<, = or >) in each oval to make each number sentence true.

   (a) 15 + 8 ◯ 23   (b) 18 − 2 ◯ 10   (c) 4 × 9 ◯ 36   (d) 99 ÷ 9 ◯ 8 + 4

   (e) 6 × 9 ◯ 7 × 9   (f) 35 ÷ 5 ◯ 7 × 1   (g) 64 ÷ 8 ◯ 6 + 9   (h) 14 − 6 ◯ 3 + 5

A number sentence that has the equals sign (=) is called an **equation**.   7 + 5 = 10 + 2

(a) 6 × 4 = 24

(b) 48 ÷ 12 = 4 × 1

What is on the left (7 + 5) **has the same value** as what is on the right (10 + 2).

(c) 7 + 5 = 15 − 3

(d) 39 − 3 = 9 × 4

Both sides of the scales are equal so the scales balance!

---

3. Write the missing numbers to make each of the following into **equations**.

   (a) 7 + 6 = ____   (b) 8 + ____ = 12   (c) 14 − 6 = ____   (d) 11 − 7 = ____

   (e) 14 − 8 = ____   (f) 5 × 4 = ____   (g) 24 ÷ 8 = ____   (h) 7 × ____ = 35

   (i) 42 ÷ ____ = 6   (j) ____ × 6 = 54   (k) ____ ÷ 4 = 10   (l) ____ ÷ 9 = 8

   (m) ____ × 7 = 63   (n) 32 ÷ ____ = 4   (o) 5 × ____ = 45   (p) ____ ÷ 6 = 9

---

4. Now do these.

   (a) 7 + 9 = 8 + ____   (b) 6 + ____ = 4 + 7   (c) 18 − 9 = 1 + ____   (d) 19 − ____ = 7 + 8

   (e) 6 × 4 = 3 × ____   (f) 36 ÷ 9 = 20 ÷ ____   (g) ____ × 7 = 22 + 6   (h) 63 ÷ 9 = 1 × ____

STRAND Algebra   **STRAND UNIT/ELEMENT** Equations, variables
LANGUAGE Equation, number sentence, equals, balance, scales, variable, =, unknown part, represent

Equations and variables

1. Read each of the following **word problems**. Write the correct equations.

	Word problems	Equations
(a)	Jack had 19 stamps. He gave 12 to his friend. He has 7 left.	$19 - 12 =$ ____
(b)	Orla has 6 boxes of eggs. There are 12 eggs in each box. She has 72 eggs altogether.	
(c)	Derek shared 24 apples among his 3 friends. They each got 8 apples.	
(d)	Ellie bought 25 bones for her three dogs. Niall gave her 13 bones on Monday and 12 bones on Tuesday. Ellie has 50 bones now.	
(e)	Ronan had 23 cows. He sold 8 and bought 5 more. He has 20 cows now.	
(f)	Tim had 5 marbles. He won 8 in a game. He gave 4 to his friend. He had 9 marbles left.	$(5 + 8) - 4 =$ ____
(g)	Sandra had €8. She bought a pair of socks for €5. Her mother gave her €9. She then had €12.	
(h)	Each box of crayons has 8 crayons. Niamh bought 4 boxes. She had 32 crayons altogether.	
(i)	Pears are sold in nets of 7. A shopkeeper needed 6 nets to pack 42 pears.	
(j)	There are 8 apples in a net. A shopkeeper sold 7 nets of apples. He sold 56 apples altogether.	

2. Write or compose **word problems** for each of these **equations**.

   (a) $14 + 18 = 32$ (b) $25 - 7 = 18$ (c) $4 \times 12 = 48$ (d) $(36 - 12) - 9 = 15$

   (e) $48 \div 6 = 8$ (f) $(12 + 8) - 3 = 17$ (g) $(4 \times 9) + 4 = 40$ (h) $(7 \times 6) - 3 = 39$

3. Now write each of these **word problems** as **equations** and solve them.

	Word problems	Equations
(a)	Pat had 12 books. He bought 9 books. His friend gave him 8 books. How many books has he now?	$12 +$ ____ $+$ ____ $=$ ____
(b)	Yoghurt is sold in trays of 8. Cian bought 7 full trays and 5 loose cartons of yoghurt. How many cartons did he buy altogether?	
(c)	Terri had 75 chestnuts. She kept 3 and shared the rest equally among her 8 friends. How many chestnuts did each friend get?	
(d)	A florist had 9 trays of flowers. Each tray had 7 flowers. She kept 4 flowers and sold the rest. How many flowers did she sell?	

Rate your county!

To rate the counties, add the value of each letter in their names using the table below.

a	b	c	d	e	f	g	h	i	j	k	l	m
1	2	3	4	5	6	7	8	9	10	11	12	13

n	o	p	q	r	s	t	u	v	w	x	y	z
14	15	16	17	18	19	20	21	22	23	24	25	26

(a)
Clare	c	l	a	r	e	
Value	3	12	1	18	5	= 39

(b)
Limerick	l	i	m	e	r	i	c	k	
Value	12	9	13	5	18	9	3	11	= 80

Antrim 75	Cork 47	Donegal 58	Fermanagh 73	Galway 69	Kerry	
Armagh 48	Clare 39	Derry 70			Kilkenny 101	
	Cavan 41	Down 56			Kildare 60	
	Carlow 72	Dublin				

Limerick 80	Mayo	Offaly 65	Roscommon 125	Sligo 62	Tipperary 128	Waterford 110
Leitrim	Monaghan				Tyrone 97	Wicklow
Louth 76	Meath 47					Wexford 95
Laois 56						Westmeath 114
Longford 91						

1. Rate the value of the following counties using the table above.

   (a) Kerry   (b) Mayo   (c) Monaghan   (d) Wicklow   (e) Dublin   (f) Leitrim

---

Find the value of Clare + Clare or 2 Clare: 39 + 39 = 78   or   2 × 39 = 78 .

2. Now find the value of the following. Write an equation for each problem.

   (a) 3 Clare   (b) 2 Mayo   (c) 3 Louth   (d) Kerry + Mayo

   (e) 2 Monaghan   (f) 2 Monaghan + Wicklow   (g) 3 Mayo + 2 Kerry

   (h) 3 Cavan − Leitrim   (i) 6 Down − 2 Offaly   (j) 3 Carlow + 3 Donegal

---

3. Write the sum of the values of the groups of counties beginning with the letters:

   (i) C   (ii) D   (iii) K   (iv) W   (v) L   (vi) T

Now calculate the value of: Offaly + Sligo = ☆ → O + S = 65 + 62 = 127

4. Find the value of:

   (a) F + G   (b) R − S   (c) S + G   (d) F − S   (e) G + R

   How about O + T = ☆ ?   T can have two different values. Solve each equation.

Possibilities	Offaly + Tyrone = ☆	Offaly + Tipperary = ☆
O + T = ☆	65 + 97 = ____	65 + 128 = ____

5. Now work out the possible answers for C + G = ☆ . Write an equation for each and solve.

Possibilities	Cork + Galway	Clare + Galway	Cavan + Galway	Carlow + Galway
C + G = ☆	C + G = ____	C + G = ____	C + G = ____	C + G = ____

Busy B's Bistro

Noodles	€1·20
Pasta	€1·30
Vegetable salad	€1·10
Beef stew	€2·90
Fish pie	€2·70
Milk	€0·50
Water	€0·30

The staff at Busy B's only write down the first letter of each menu item when taking orders. If a customer orders pasta, beef stew and water, the waitress will record p + b + w in the order book.

If there is an order for 2 vegetable salads, the waitress just writes down 2v.

You are a waitress in Busy B's. Write down the following orders using only the first letter of each menu item.

1. Complete the orders for the tables below.

Order	Noodles/Milk	Pasta/Water	Vegetable salad/Milk	Beef stew/Noodles/Water	Fish pie/Milk/Vegetable Salad
Waitress	n + m				
Cashier	€1·20 + €0·50				
Equation	n + m = €1·70				

2. You are the cashier in the restaurant. Work out the cost of each bill.

Waitress	2v + b + w	p + n + m	f + 2n + 2w	3b + 3v + 2w + m
Cashier	(2 × €1·10) + €2·90 + €0·30			
Total	€5·40			

3. Now complete this table. (Remember the rule for brackets!)

Waitress	2(n + b) + 2m	(b + v) + 3n	(p + b) + 2m	3(f + v) + 2w + m
Cashier	2(€1·20 + €2·90) + 2 × €0·50			
Total				

4. Water was spilled on one order book. Some of the orders were illegible. Help the cashier work out the missing digit or letter in each order.

Cashier	n + f + ❈ = €4·20	2❈ + v + 2m = €7·90	b + p + 2❈ + m = €6·90
	❈(p + n) + 2w = €5·60	3v + ❈ + 2f = €11·60	❈w + 4m + 5v + 2b = €14·50
	3(b + f) + ❈ = €17·90	2❈ + 5(w + m) = €6·60	3n + 4b + 2❈ = €17·80

Challenge

A party of diners ordered the following: 2 vegetable salads, 3 beef stews, 4 fish pies, 3 noodles, 2 pastas, 4 milk and 8 water. You are taking the order. Write out the order as an equation and find the total cost.

Solving equations

When a symbol or letter is used in place of an unknown amount, it is called a variable.

To write 3 pens, we can write (**pen** × 3) or (3 × **pen**). We can also simply have the letter **p** represent the name pen so we have (3 × **p**) or (**p** × 3) ⟶ 3**p**.

A   If 5 pens cost €15, find the cost of 1 pen.

$$5p = €15$$
$$1p = €3$$
$$p = €3$$

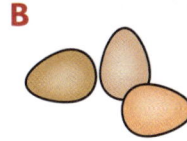

B   If 3 eggs cost 36 cent, find the cost of 1 egg.

$$3e = 36 \text{ cent}$$
$$1e = 12 \text{ cent}$$
$$e = 12 \text{ cent}$$

Find the value of the variable (unknown) letter in each of these.

1. (a) $2a = 8$ (b) $4b = 16$ (c) $5x = 30$ (d) $6y = 18$

   (e) $4p = 28$ (f) $5y = 40$ (g) $8f = 64$ (h) $9l = 72$

   (i) $5m = 60$ (j) $6l = 42$ (k) $7n = 56$ (l) $8h = 96$

2. (a) $3x = 25 - 1$ (b) $7y = 29 + 6$ (c) $5b = 61 - 6$ (d) $4m = 37 - 5$

   (e) $2f = 14 + 6$ (f) $6n = 52 - 4$ (g) $10d = 78 - 8$ (h) $9p = 70 - 7$

   (i) $5c = 10 \times 3$ (j) $8v = 12 \times 4$ (k) $6w = 9 \times 4$ (l) $4n = 8 \times 3$

$3m + 4$ 13	$3m + 4 - 4$ $13 - 4$	$3m$ 9
$3m + 4 = 13$	$3m + 4 - 4 = 13 - 4$	$3m = 9$ $m = 3$

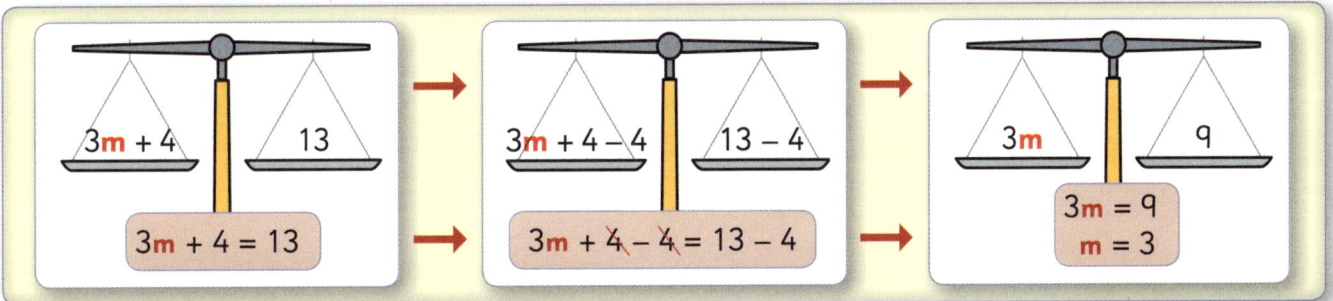

Find the value of the variable (unknown) amount in each of these.

1m is the same as **m**.

3. (a) $4a + 3 = 11$ (b) $5x + 2 = 22$ (c) $3l + 5 = 26$ (d) $6m + 4 = 40$

   (e) $5b + 6 = 41$ (f) $8c + 4 = 44$ (g) $6s + 7 = 55$ (h) $7d + 5 = 61$

   (i) $9t + 7 = 52$ (j) $7f + 8 = 64$ (k) $8k + 6 = 78$ (l) $9h + 7 = 88$

4. Write equations for the following. Use the letter **n** for the variable (unknown). Solve the equations.

(a)	Luke ate 12 apples and Carla ate some apples. All 18 apples were eaten. How many apples did Carla eat?	$12 + n = 18$	$n = \rule{2cm}{0.4pt}$
(b)	Mary has some money in her post office account and Denny has €3 more. Denny has €48. How much does Mary have?		$n = \rule{2cm}{0.4pt}$
(c)	3 boxes of cereal cost €4·80. Find the cost of one box.		$n = \rule{2cm}{0.4pt}$
(d)	Two times a number is 8. What is the number?		$n = \rule{2cm}{0.4pt}$
(e)	A number increased by 9 is 15. Find the number.		$n = \rule{2cm}{0.4pt}$
(f)	One half of a number is 8. Find the number.		$n = \rule{2cm}{0.4pt}$
(g)	The sum of a number and 8 equals 12. Find the number.		$n = \rule{2cm}{0.4pt}$
(h)	9 less than a number is 17. Find the number.		$n = \rule{2cm}{0.4pt}$
(i)	A number decreased by 12 is 14. Find the number.		$n = \rule{2cm}{0.4pt}$

More equations

$4m - 2 = 14$ → $4m - 2 + 2 = 14 + 2$ → $4m = 16$ \ $m = 4$

Find the value of the **variable** (unknown) amount in each of these equations.

1. (a) $3b - 2 = 10$
   (b) $4f - 5 = 11$
   (c) $5g - 4 = 26$
   (d) $6p - 5 = 43$

   (e) $4a - 3 = 29$
   (f) $7l - 5 = 44$
   (g) $8x - 2 = 70$
   (h) $9y - 4 = 50$

   (i) $8m - 2 = 86$
   (j) $6n - 4 = 62$
   (k) $7c - 6 = 57$
   (l) $8d - 4 = 76$

A Find the value of x.

$4x + 7 = 19 + 8$

$4x + 7 = 27$

$4x + 7 - 7 = 27 - 7$

$4x = 20$

$x = 5$

B Find the value of y.

$5y - 8 = 25 + 7$

$5y - 8 = 32$

$5y - 8 + 8 = 32 + 8$

$5y = 40$

$y = 8$

Now test yourself by doing these!

2. (a) $m + 16 = 20$
   (b) $12 + c = 18$
   (c) $14 - 8 = d$
   (d) $19 - w = 12$

   (e) $7 \times w = 28$
   (f) $5 \times 9 = r$
   (g) $6z = 48$
   (h) $7f = 63$

   (i) $13 + r = 26 - 3$
   (j) $5a + 7 = 4 \times 8$
   (k) $36 + 9 - 7 = v$
   (l) $4t = 30 - 2$

   (m) $8m = (70 - 9) + 3$
   (n) $0.8 + c = 1$
   (o) $g + 2.4 = 3.9$
   (p) $3d = 6.9$

Now find the value of the **variable** (unknown) amount in each of these equations.

3. (a) $3c + 5 = 16 + 4$
   (b) $4b + 3 = 19 - 4$
   (c) $2l - 4 = 12 + 6$
   (d) $5x - 6 = 18 - 4$

   (e) $6x - 3 = 29 - 2$
   (f) $5m + 2 = 8 + 9$
   (g) $7f - 1 = 28 + 6$
   (h) $9y + 5 = 52 + 7$

   (i) $8p - 2 = 9 \times 6$
   (j) $5r + 6 = 7 \times 8$
   (k) $5t - 4 = 9 \times 4$
   (l) $7n + 6 = 6 \times 8$

Write these challenges as equations and solve them.

Challenge 1: Paul thought of a number. He added 12 to it. The result was 23. What number did Paul think of?

$\boxed{} = 23$

Challenge 2: Livia thought of a number. She trebled it. She then added 3 to it. Her answer was 30. What number did she think of?

$\boxed{} = \boxed{}$

Equations – Fractions

Sometimes we can have a fraction of the **variable** (unknown) amount.

$\frac{1}{4}$ of a number is 6. What is the number?

Let the number be x.

$\frac{1}{4}$ of the number will be $\frac{1}{4}x$.

$\frac{1}{4}x$ can also be written as $\frac{x}{4}$.

$\frac{1}{4}x = 6$

$\frac{4}{4}x = 24$

$x = 24$

or

$\frac{x}{4} = 6$

$\frac{4x}{4} = 24$

$x = 24$

Solve these equations by finding the value of the variable (unknown) amount.

1. (a) $\frac{1}{2}x = 7$ (b) $\frac{1}{3}y = 4$ (c) $\frac{1}{5}l = 6$ (d) $\frac{1}{6}p = 7$ (e) $\frac{1}{4}m = 12$

2. (a) $\frac{1}{7}m = 8$ (b) $\frac{1}{9}s = 6$ (c) $\frac{1}{8}t = 9$ (d) $\frac{1}{10}y = 8$ (e) $\frac{1}{12}r = 10$

Laura spent $\frac{3}{5}$ of her money buying the ball. How much money had she at first?

€18

Let x represent her money.

$\frac{3}{5}x = €18$

$\frac{1}{5}x = €6$

$\frac{5}{5}x = €30$

$x = €30$

or

$\frac{3x}{5} = €18$

$\frac{x}{5} = €6$

$\frac{5x}{5} = €30$

$x = €30$

Now solve these equations by finding the value of the variable (unknown) amount.

3. (a) $\frac{2}{3}y = 10$ (b) $\frac{3}{4}m = 12$ (c) $\frac{2}{5}f = 16$ (d) $\frac{3}{7}p = 15$ (e) $\frac{4}{5}d = 32$

4. (a) $\frac{5}{8}z = 25$ (b) $\frac{5}{6}a = 35$ (c) $\frac{3}{8}c = 21$ (d) $\frac{7}{9}b = 28$ (e) $\frac{9}{10}z = 72$

Now solve these more difficult equations.

5. (a) $\frac{1}{4}x = 16$ (b) $\frac{1}{3}y = 24$ (c) $\frac{1}{6}b = 18$ (d) $\frac{1}{8}f = 32$ (e) $\frac{1}{5}x = 45$

6. (a) $\frac{1}{7}c = 47$ (b) $\frac{1}{5}l = 58$ (c) $\frac{1}{9}n = 75$ (d) $\frac{1}{10}p = 85$ (e) $\frac{1}{6}l = 94$

7. (a) $\frac{3}{4}f = 42$ (b) $\frac{2}{5}t = 48$ (c) $\frac{2}{3}y = 64$ (d) $\frac{3}{5}g = 39$ (e) $\frac{3}{8}m = 39$

8. (a) $\frac{7}{8}d = 56$ (b) $\frac{5}{9}q = 95$ (c) $\frac{5}{8}h = 120$ (d) $\frac{8}{9}l = 104$ (e) $\frac{5}{11}f = 85$

Challenge 1 Ariana has €48. This is $\frac{4}{7}$ of the cost of a dress.

What is the cost of the dress? € _____

Challenge 2 Pete gave 36 of his marbles to Laura. This was $\frac{3}{8}$ of all his marbles.

How many marbles had he at first? _____

Equations – More fractions

If $x = 4$, $y = 3$ and $z = 5$, find the value of each of these.

A

$3x + 4y + 5z =$ ☆

$(3 \times 4) + (4 \times 3) + (5 \times 5) =$ ☆

$12 + 12 + 25 = 49$

B

$2x \times 3y =$ ☆

$(2 \times 4) \times (3 \times 3) =$ ☆

$8 \times 9 = 72$

C

$\dfrac{2xy}{z} =$ ☆

$\dfrac{2 \times (4 \times 3)}{5} = \dfrac{24}{5} = 4\dfrac{4}{5}$

If $x = 2$, $y = 3$ and $z = 4$, find the value of the following.

1. (a) $x + y + z$
   (b) $x + y - z$
   (c) $y + z - x$
   (d) $z + x - y$

2. (a) $2x + 3y + z$
   (b) $3x + 2y + 2z$
   (c) $2z + 3z - x$
   (d) $4z + 5y - 2x$

3. (a) $3y \times 2x$
   (b) $4x \times 2z \times y$
   (c) $(4y \times 3z) + x$
   (d) $6x \div z$

4. (a) $8z \div 4x$
   (b) $(3x \div y) + 3z$
   (c) $5x \times y + 4z$
   (d) $(6y + 4z) \times 2y$

5. (a) $x^2 + 4y \times 2z$
   (b) $y^2 + 3y - 4y$
   (c) $x^3 + y^2 - x^2$
   (d) $z^2 + 4z - 2z$

6. (a) $y^3 + z^2 - x^2$
   (b) $z^2 + x^3 - y^2$
   (c) $(y^2 - x^2) + z$
   (d) $(x^2 + y^3) - z^2$

Solve these problems. Write the equation first.

7. The sum of two numbers is 24. One of the numbers is 13.
   What is the other number?

   24?

8. The difference between two numbers is 12. The bigger number is 64.
   What is the smaller number?

   64?

9. The difference between two numbers is 34.
   If the smaller number is 29, what is the bigger number?

   29?

10. Tim spent $\dfrac{3}{8}$ of his money buying a hurley for €9.
    How much money had he at the beginning?

11. Lucy spent $\dfrac{5}{9}$ of her money buying the coat and scarf.
    How much money had she at first?

    €12   €33

Challenge The perimeter of a rectangle is 36cm.
The width is twice as long as the length.
Find (a) the length, and (b) the width of
the rectangle.

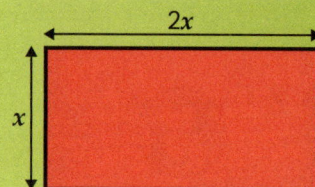

$2x$

x

Chapter 21: Data 2

The following sales were recorded at **Movie Magic** cinema last week.

	Wed	Thurs	Fri	Sat	Sun
Cinema tickets	140	240	570	420	250
Popcorn	10	25	60	45	35
Nachos	5	5	20	30	15

1. Represent the data for the sales of cinema tickets on a **bar chart**.

Copy and complete this bar chart in your copybook.

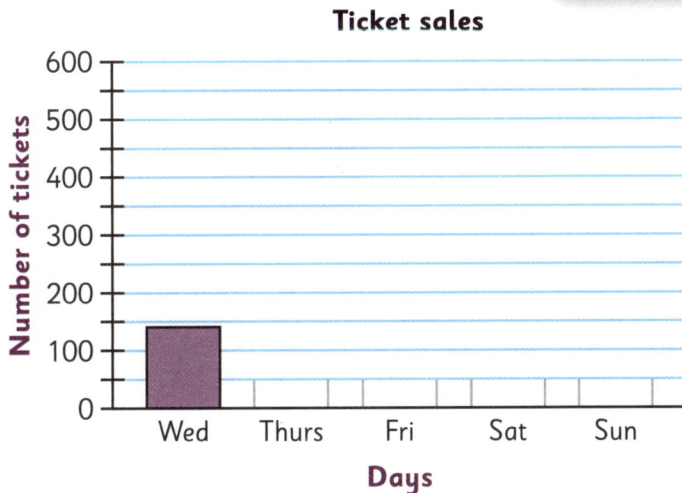

Ticket sales

(a) What was the total number of tickets sold over the five days?

(b) Calculate the average number of tickets sold daily.

(c) What was the difference in ticket sales between the busiest and quietest days?

(d) If all tickets on Wednesdays were sold at a special price of €3·28 each, how much money was made in ticket sales last Wednesday?

2. Represent the data for the sales of popcorn and nachos on a **multiple bar chart**.

Copy and complete this multiple bar chart in your copybook.

Food sales

(a) What was the average number of food items sold on Sunday?

(b) Calculate the average number of popcorn bags sold each night.

(c) Calculate the average number of nachos sold each night.

(d) How many nachos below average were sold on Thursday night?

(e) Were more food items sold on Saturday and Sunday combined or on Thursday and Friday combined?

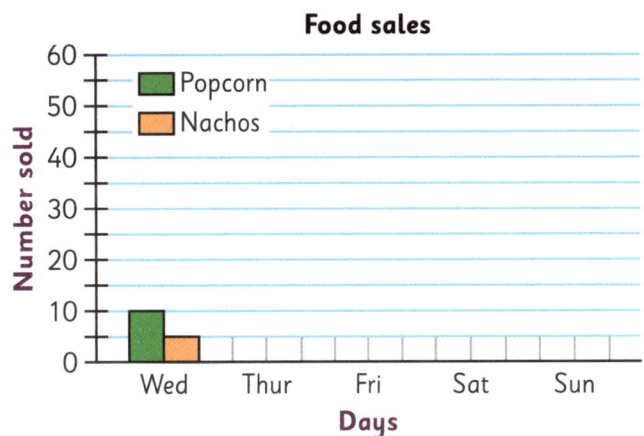

Challenge

These are the prices charged by Movie Magic.

€2·30   €4·60   €7·85   €3·40

Calculate the total amount of money collected by Movie Magic cinema on Friday night, if **79** of the tickets sold were for children. € _____

STRAND Data   **STRAND UNIT/ELEMENT** *Representing and interpreting data*
LANGUAGE *Represent, bar chart, multiple bar chart, total, difference, data, average, bar-line graph, more, less, above, below, trend graph, increase, greatest, fewest, between, more, decrease, plot, rounded*

Data 2

1. This **bar-line graph** shows the number of visitors to the Cliffs of Moher over six months.

Visitors to the Cliffs of Moher

(a) How many people visited the cliffs in (i) July? (ii) April? (iii) September?

(b) How many more people visited the cliffs in August than in May?

(c) What was the average monthly number of visitors to the cliffs?

(d) On which months did the cliffs receive above the average number of visitors?

2. We can also represent the above information on a **trend graph**.

(i) Using straight lines, we join the top of each bar to the next bar.

(ii) We then remove the bar lines.

Visitors to the Cliffs of Moher

The flow of the lines shows us whether the trend is increasing or decreasing.

(a) In which month did the tourist season peak (was busiest)?

(b) In which months did the number of tourists increase over the previous month?

(c) In which month was there a decrease in the number of visitors over the previous month?

(d) Which month showed the biggest increase in visitors?

(e) How many fewer visitors were there in September than in August?

(f) From looking at the trend, do you think October will have an increase or decrease?

Data 2

1. Sam and his family hosted a barbecue last summer and friends were invited to come any time between 12pm and 6pm. The following **trend graph** shows the attendance on the day.

Barbecue attendance

(a) Between what times was the greatest number of people at the barbecue?

(b) How many more people were at the barbecue at 2pm than at 6pm?

(c) What was the average number of people at the barbecue at any one hour (noon – 6pm)?

(d) If the first people to leave the barbecue left between 4pm and 5pm, and no one else arrived, how many people in total attended the barbecue?

(e) If Sam cooked an average of 3·5 sausages per person, how many sausages did he cook altogether?

2. Amy's uncle bought her a new book. The following data shows the number of pages she read each night for a week.

Mon	Tue	Wed	Thurs	Fri	Sat	Sun
7	15	12	17	5	36	41

(a) Represent the above data on a trend graph.

(b) On which days did she read: (i) most pages? (ii) fewest pages?

(c) On which days did she read more pages than on the previous day?

(d) Calculate the average number of pages she read per day.

(e) If there are 187 pages in the book, how many pages has she still to read?

Discuss possible reasons why Amy's reading increased at the weekend.

Challenge If this reading trend continues over the next week, on which day would Amy expect to finish to book? _____

Data 2

1. The following data shows the sales of **Jolly Umbrellas** last year. The sales have also been rounded to the nearest 10, making the numbers easier to plot on the trend graph.

Month	Jan	Feb	Mar	Apr	May	Jun	Jul	Aug	Sept	Oct	Nov	Dec
Actual Sales	516	506	689	431	193	85	70	43	148	307	530	682
Sales rounded to nearest 10	520	510	690	430	190	90	70	40	150	310	530	680

Umbrella Sales

(a) In which months were: (i) most umbrellas sold? (ii) least umbrellas sold?

Use the **actual** sales figures when answering these questions.

(b) Which months showed an increase in sales over the previous month?

(c) Which month showed the greatest increase in sales over the previous month?

(d) Which months showed a decrease in sales over the previous month?

(e) What was the average number of umbrellas sold in each month of (i) spring, (ii) summer, (iii) autumn, (iv) winter? (Remember, in Ireland, spring starts on February 1st.)

(f) What was the average monthly number of umbrellas sold over the year?

(g) If the shop buys an umbrella for €3·20 and sells it to the customers for €7·85, how much profit is made on each umbrella?

(h) In November the shop ran out of umbrellas. 87 people wanted to buy an umbrella but were turned away. How much **profit** did the shop lose by not having enough umbrellas?

2. The following data shows Lee's scores on a new computer game over 5 attempts.

Game 1	Game 2	Game 3	Game 4	Game 5
2,416	2,921	3,786	4,093	4,864

(a) Round each of the scores to the nearest hundred.

(b) Record the data on a trend graph. (Write the actual scores in brackets).

A quick look back 6

1. Write the value of the underlined digit.

   1,9̱34,875 _____

2. A shopkeeper buys a jar of honey for €2·30 and sells it for €3·90. How much profit would she make if she sold ten jars?

   € _____

3. 8·4 ÷ 1·2 = _____

4. Kieran spent 25% of his €24 buying the ball. How much did it cost?

   € _____

5. Write $\frac{4}{5}$ as a percentage. _____ %

6. Agatha spent 75% of her €80 buying a jacket. How much money had she left?

   € _____

7. Write 73% in decimal form. _____

8. A farmer had 360 hens. She sold 50% of them. How many hens had she left? _____

9. Anthony cycled for 3 hours at an average speed of 12·5km/h. What distance did he travel? _____

10. It takes mum $2\frac{1}{2}$ hours to travel a distance of 200km. What is her average speed in km/h? _____

11. The time difference between London and New York is 5 hours. When it is `14:45` in London, what time is it in New York?

    ☐ : ☐

12. The time difference between two cities is 7 hours. How many degrees apart are they (from East to West)? _____ degrees.

13. If it is `15:30` at Dublin zoo, what time is it at Moscow zoo (45° East)?

    ☐ : ☐

14. If a flight from Cairo (30° East) to Dublin took 4 hours and you left at `13:00`, at what time would you arrive in Dublin (Irish time)?

    ☐ : ☐

15. There are 23 apples in a box. Write an equation to show how many apples there are in 4 boxes.

    _____

16. Write the value of the variable to make an equation. 7 + ☐ = 31.

17. 15 less than a number is 24. Write an equation to find the variable.

    ☐ ◯ ☐ = ☐

18. The following numbers of tickets were sold for a raffle. Pat sold 24, Pam sold 16, Paul sold 25 and Penny sold 15. What was: (i) the total number of tickets sold? _____ , (ii) the average number of tickets sold? _____

19. 5^3 = _____

20. What answer should I get if I multiply 3·12 by 0·1? _____

Chapter 22: Fractions/Decimals/Percentages 2

Calculating a decimal of a number.

To find a decimal fraction of a number, we simply multiply by the decimal.

A Find 0·04 of 175

$$\begin{array}{r} 175 \\ \times\ 0·04 \\ \hline 7·00 \end{array}$$

B Find 0·11 of 220

$$\begin{array}{r} 220 \\ \times\ 0·11 \\ \hline 24·20 \end{array}$$

1. Now do the following. Find:
   (a) 0·3 of 230
   (b) 0·25 of 356
   (c) 0·06 of 50
   (d) 0·37 of 600

Calculating a percentage of a number.

We can find a percentage of a number by changing the **percentage** to a **fraction** or a **decimal**.

A Fraction Method

Find 75% of 60

$75\% \longrightarrow \frac{75}{100} = \frac{3}{4}$

$\frac{4}{4} = 60$

$\frac{1}{4} = 15$

$\frac{3}{4} = 45$

B Decimal Method

Find 75% of 60

$75\% \longrightarrow \frac{75}{100} = 0·75$

$$\begin{array}{r} 60 \\ \times\ 0·75 \\ \hline 45·00 \end{array}$$

Both methods will give the same answer.

2. Have a go at using both methods.
   (a) **Fraction method**
       (i) Find 40% of 50
       (ii) Find 7% of 200
       (iii) Find $66\frac{2}{3}$% of 12
       (iv) Find $37\frac{1}{2}$ % of 40

   (b) **Decimal method**
       (i) What is 60% of 50?
       (ii) What is 13% of 50?
       (iii) What is 50% of 35?
       (iv) What is 8% of 75?
       (v) What is 15% of 60?
       (vi) What is 35% of 80?

3. Find.
   (a) $33\frac{1}{3}$% of €12
   (b) 40% of 230g
   (c) 50% of 3km
   (d) $37\frac{1}{2}$% or 37·5% of 80cm
   (e) 8% of €4·50
   (f) 16·66% or $16\frac{2}{3}$% of 6cm
   (g) 75% of 28l
   (h) 80% of 330m
   (i) $87\frac{1}{2}$% of 208m

4. 1,800 people picked their favourite pets. Work out how many picked each one.
   (You can round to the nearest whole number if you use the **decimal** method.)

Dog	Cat	Budgie	Hamster	Goldfish	Snake
$33\frac{1}{3}$% or 33·33%	21·5%	$16\frac{2}{3}$% or 16·66%	15%	9·5%	4%

STRAND Number   **STRAND UNIT/ELEMENT** *Fractions, decimals and percentages*
LANGUAGE *Calculating, calculate, find, fraction, decimal, percentage, method, calculator, cost, bought, puzzles, increasing, decreasing, original amount, average, multiple bar chart*

Fractions/Decimals/Percentages 2 – The calculator

1. (a) Work out how much each child grew to the nearest centimetre (cm).

   (b) Order the children from the one who grew **most** to the one who grew **least**.

(i) Barry	(ii) Jenny	(iii) Adam	(iv) Helen	(v) Tom
Barry was 135cm. He grew 4%	Jenny was 128cm. She grew 12·5%.	Adam was 130cm. He grew 6%.	Helen was 126cm. She grew 10%.	Tom was 117cm. He grew $11\frac{1}{9}$%.

Calculating percentages using a calculator.
What is 56% of €15?

> You don't have to press the ⬜= sign for % method (on most calculators).

A Calculate using a decimal.

Press ①⑤✕⓪·⑤⑥＝

8·4

B Calculate using a percentage.

Press ①⑤✕⑤⑥％

8·4

Either way, 56% of €15 = €8·40!

2. Calculate the following using **decimals**. (Round the answer to the nearest whole number.)

   (a) 10% of 30   (b) 25% of 400   (c) 12·5% of 88   (d) 77% of 200   (e) 66·66% of 30

3. Calculate the following using **percentages**. (Round the answer to the nearest whole number.)

   (a) 75% of 40   (b) 80% of 45   (c) $37\frac{1}{2}$% of 72   (d) 49% of 10   (e) 16·66% of 30

4. Which one from each pair ate or drank more? Use your calculator to find out.

   (a)
seal	dolphin
Ate 59% of 3kg of fish	Ate 87% of 2kg of fish

   (b)
crocodile	lion
Ate 62·5% of 5kg of meat	Ate 66·66% of 4·5kg of meat

   (c)
elephant	giraffe
Drank 49% of 20l of water	Drank 87·5% of 11l of water

   (d)
parrot	goose
Ate 72% of 350g of seed	Ate 56·5% of 500g of seed

   (e)
lion cub	tiger cub
Drank 75% of 450ml of milk	Drank $37\frac{1}{2}$% of 888ml of milk

   (f)
monkey	chimpanzee
Ate 83·33% of 18 bananas	Ate 75% of 21 bananas

5. Trudy brought €48 with her on her holiday. Calculate how much she spent on each item.

   (a) $8\frac{1}{3}$% of her money

   (b) 5% of her money

   (c) $16\frac{2}{3}$% of her money

   (d) 17% of her money

   (e) 20% of her money

Challenge   What percentage of her money had Trudy left? ⬜%

Fractions/Decimals/Percentages 2 – Puzzles

It may help to find 100% first!

1. Solve these puzzles.

(a) Mary spent $66\frac{2}{3}$% of her money on a present and 10% on postage. If the postage cost €1·20, how much did the present cost?

(b) Kristin scored 35% of her team's goals this year. If the rest of the team scored 52 goals, how many did Kristin score?

(c) If it rained for $83\frac{1}{3}$% of the days in April, how many dry days were there?

(d) Jack had Maths, English and Irish homework. He spent 90 mins altogether at it. He spent 45% of the time at Maths and 30·5 mins at English. How long did he spend at Irish?

2. Increasing and decreasing by a fraction.

A

Increase 25 by $\frac{1}{5}$

We must find $\frac{5}{5} + \frac{1}{5} = \frac{6}{5}$

Short way

$\frac{5}{5} = 25$

$\frac{1}{5} = 5$

$\frac{6}{5} = 30$

B

Decrease 27 by $\frac{4}{9}$

We must find $\frac{9}{9} - \frac{4}{9} = \frac{5}{9}$

Short way

$\frac{9}{9} = 27$

$\frac{1}{9} = 3$

$\frac{5}{9} = 15$

Now try these.

(a) Increase 12 by $\frac{1}{3}$

(b) Decrease 24 by $\frac{1}{6}$

(c) Increase 18 by $\frac{2}{3}$

(d) Increase 20 by $\frac{3}{5}$

(e) Decrease 40 by $\frac{3}{4}$

(f) Decrease 56 by $\frac{3}{8}$

(g) Decrease 55 by $\frac{4}{5}$

(h) Increase 14 by $\frac{5}{7}$

(i) Decrease 36 by $\frac{2}{9}$

3. Increasing and decreasing by a percentage. (Hint: change to fractions first.)

C

Increase 21 by $33\frac{1}{3}$%

$33\frac{1}{3}\% \rightarrow \frac{33\frac{1}{3}}{100} \times \frac{3}{3} \rightarrow \frac{100}{300} = \frac{1}{3}$

We must find $\frac{3}{3} + \frac{1}{3} = \frac{4}{3}$

Short way

$\frac{3}{3} = 21$

$\frac{1}{3} = 7$

$\frac{4}{3} = 28$

D

Decrease 50 by 40%

$40\% \rightarrow \frac{40}{100} \rightarrow \frac{4}{10} = \frac{2}{5}$

We must find $\frac{5}{5} - \frac{2}{5} = \frac{3}{5}$

Short way

$\frac{5}{5} = 50$

$\frac{1}{5} = 10$

$\frac{3}{5} = 30$

Now do these.

(a) Increase 10 by 60%.

(b) Decrease 88 by $37\frac{1}{2}$%.

(c) Decrease 90 by $66\frac{2}{3}$%.

(d) Increase 18 by 50%.

(e) Decrease 40 by $62\frac{1}{2}$%.

(f) Increase 200 by 45%.

(g) Decrease 88 by $12\frac{1}{2}$%.

(h) Increase 48 by 75%.

(i) Decrease 120 by 15%.

Challenge A farmer had 96 cows. He increased his herd by $37\frac{1}{2}$%. How many cows had the farmer then? _____

Fractions/Decimals/Percentages 2 – Problem-solving

1. **Use fractions to help you solve these problems.**

   (a) During spring a farmer's flock of 45 sheep increased by 40%. How many sheep has she now?

   (b) Janine got 72 out of 100 in her last Math's test. What score did she get this time if she increased the result by $37\frac{1}{2}$%?

   (c) A typical day in June will have about 16 hours of daylight. By December this will have decreased by $56\frac{1}{4}$%. How many hours of daylight would you get then?

   (d) Eoin has saved €21 towards buying a concert ticket. He needs to increase his savings by $33\frac{1}{3}$% to buy one. What is the cost of a ticket?

2. **Increasing or decreasing by a percentage using a calculator.**

A Decimal method	B Percentage method

   A Decimal method

   Increase €7 by 13%

   We must find 100% + 13% = 113%

   113% = 1·13

   Press: 7 × 1 · 1 3 =

   → 7·91 or €7·91

   B Percentage method

   Decrease 184 by 8%

   We must find 100% − 8% = 92%

   Press: 1 8 4 × 9 2 %

   → 169·28

   You don't have to press the = key when using the percentage method (on most calculators)!

   Now try these using the decimal method.

   (a) Increase €12 by 14%

   (b) Decrease €24 by 18%

   (c) Increase €18 by 24%

   (d) Increase €20 by 60%

   (e) Decrease €40 by 75%

   (f) Decrease €56 by 37·5%

3. **Now try these using your calculator. (Answer to the nearest whole number.)**

   (a) Increase 99 by 47%

   (b) Increase 45 by 25%

   (c) Decrease 88 by 87·5%

   (d) Decrease 90 by 33·33%

   (e) Decrease 100 by 71%

   (f) Increase 50 by 80%

4. **Increasing and decreasing problems – use your calculator.**

   (a) Nick's journey to Primary School was 1·5km long. The distance he has to travel to Secondary School is a 76% increase. What is the length of his journey to secondary school?

   (b) When Digital World began selling the latest tablet, they decreased its price by 37·5%. If the original price was €210, how much does it now cost?

   (c) Sarah paid €12,700 for a car two years ago. Its value has fallen by 48%. How much is her car worth now?

   (d) The price of a cinema ticket increased by 25% this year. If the new price is €9·40, how much did the ticket cost last year?

Fractions/Decimals/Percentages 2 – Problem-solving

A The temperature today is 21°C. This is an increase of 40% on yesterday. What was yesterday's temperature?

Original amount + increase = new amount
100% + 40% = 140%
140% $\rightarrow \frac{140}{100} \rightarrow \frac{14}{10} = \frac{7}{5}$

We now have $\frac{7}{5}$. We must find $\frac{5}{5}$.

$\frac{7}{5} = 21°C \rightarrow$ (today's temperature)

$\frac{1}{5} = 3°C$

$\frac{5}{5} = 15°C \rightarrow$ (yesterday's temperature)

B A smartphone was reduced by €40. This was a reduction of 8% on the original price. What was the new price?

Original price − reduction = new price
100% − 8% = 92%
92% $\rightarrow \frac{92}{100} = \frac{23}{25}$

We have $\frac{2}{25}$ (8%). We must find $\frac{23}{25}$.

$\frac{2}{25} = €40 \rightarrow$ (reduction)

$\frac{1}{25} = €20$

$\frac{23}{25} = €460 \rightarrow$ (new price)

1. Write the missing amounts. Decreases are shown in brackets.

New amount	66kg	45cm			56km
Increase/decrease	kg	cm	(€8)	18l	
Original amount	kg	cm			
% increase/decrease	10%	50%	(40%)	$66\frac{2}{3}$%	75%

Expressing an increase or decrease as a percentage.

Aaron usually jogs 5km each Saturday. Last Saturday he only jogged 3km. What was the percentage decrease in the distance he jogged?

5km − 3km = 2km (decrease)
Fraction decrease = $\frac{2}{5}$

$\rightarrow$

Percentage decrease $\rightarrow \frac{2}{5} \times \frac{100}{1} = 40\%$

2. Express these increases/decreases as a percentage of the original:
   (a) 5kg increased to 8kg
   (b) €20 decreased to €12
   (c) 18l increased to 24l
   (d) 45m decreased to 40m

3. If there were 8cm of rain in April and 5cm of rain in May, what was the percentage decrease from April to May?

4. A lion cub increased in weight by $33\frac{1}{3}$% in its first six months of life. If it now weighs 36·8kg, what did it weigh when it was born?

5. When the cook finished making breakfast there were 140 eggs left. If that was a 30% decrease, how many eggs had he at the start?

6. Jack drank 270ml from a 1 litre bottle and still had 730ml left. What percentage did he drink?

Challenge What was Alex's height at his last birthday if the 165cm he is at his present birthday is a 5% increase on last year? _____ cm (2 places of decimals.)

Fractions/Decimals/Percentages 2 – Check-up

1. Use the **fraction method** to find the answers to these.

   (a) 40% of 350   (b) $62\frac{1}{2}$% of 96   (c) $8\frac{1}{3}$% of 72   (d) $87\frac{1}{2}$% of 56

2. Use the **decimal method** to find these.

   (a) 8% of 175   (b) 35% of 120   (c) 17·5% of 160   (d) 42·5% of 240

3. When a kestrel increased its speed by 20%, it was travelling at 75km/h. What speed was it flying at originally?

4. Find a match! Match an answer in the first box to its equivalent in the second box.

   If $\frac{7}{4}$ is €8·75, the original amount is … •

   80% is €1·80, so 100% is … •

   $\frac{6}{5}$ is €2·88, so 50% is … •

   €1 increased by 25% is … •

   A 10% increase is 20c, the original amount is … •

   • €5 decreased by 75%

   • 8% of €62·50

   • 4% of €50

   • Decrease €6·75 by $66\frac{2}{3}$%

   • Increase €1 by $\frac{200}{1000}$

5. True ☑ or false ☒! Work out the answer for each of these statements:

   Aoife's class recorded the temperature in the school yard over the last two years.

   Check if their statements are correct.

   (a) The lowest monthly temperature this year was $33\frac{1}{3}$% of the highest. ☐

   (b) November's average temperature this year was 50% higher than last year's. ☐

   (c) This year the temperature decreased by 40% from June's average to September's average. ☐

   (d) March's temperature this year decreased by 12·5% compared to last year's. ☐

   (e) January's average temperature over the last two years is 80% of November's average. ☐

   (f) Last year the temperature in January was $33\frac{1}{3}$% of that in March. ☐

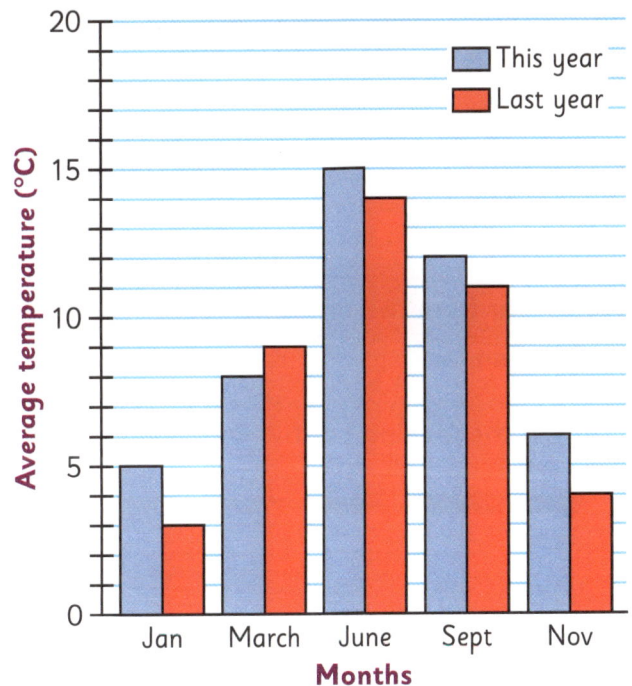

Challenge   The more you take the more you leave behind. What are they?
Put the answers to these in **descending** order to find out.

S 20% of 7.

T $\frac{2015}{1000}$

O 4% of 87·5

P Decrease 2·45 by 40%

T 6% of 50

E Reduce 100 by 98·5%

O Increase 2·5 by 50%

F $66\frac{2}{3}$% = 4, 100% = ?

S 11% of 22

Answer: ___ ___ ___ ___ ___ ___ ___ ___ ___

119

Chapter 23: Directed numbers

A **positive** number is more than zero.
A **negative** number is less than zero.

Use (+) positive and (−) negative numbers to complete these.

1. **On which level is the:**
   (a) red bird?   (b) green bird?
   (c) blue fish?   (d) red fish?
   (e) pink fish?   (f) yellow fish?

2. **What is the distance in levels between:**
   (a) the blue and red birds?
   (b) the green and red birds?
   (c) the blue bird and the blue fish?
   (d) the green bird and the green fish?
   (e) the yellow bird and the yellow fish?
   (f) the green bird and the orange fish?
   (g) the yellow bird and the green fish?
   (h) the red bird and the pink fish?

3. How many levels are there **above** sea level?

4. How many levels are there **below** sea level?

5. How far from the surface is the:
   (a) green fish?   (b) red bird?   (c) yellow bird?   (d) pink fish?   (e) blue bird?

6. Fill in the missing positive and negative numbers on the number line below.

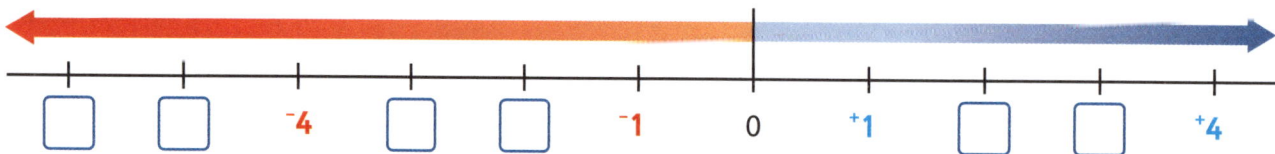

   ☐   ☐   ⁻4   ☐   ☐   ⁻1   0   ⁺1   ☐   ☐   ⁺4

7. Use the number line to help you work out how many steps the diver passes.
   (a) He goes from the blue fish to the blue bird. He passes __2__ steps.
   (b) He climbs from the blue bird to the yellow bird. He passes _____ steps.
   (c) He swims from sea level to the orange fish. He passes _____ steps.
   (d) He swims from the green fish to the pink fish. He passes _____ steps.
   (e) He swims from the orange fish to the surface. He passes _____ steps.
   (f) He dives from the red bird to the red fish. He passes _____ steps.
   (g) He dives from the green bird to the red fish. He passes _____ steps.

STRAND **Algebra**   STRAND UNIT/ELEMENT *Directed numbers*
LANGUAGE *Positive, negative, plus, minus, locate, number line, directed numbers, thermometer, Celsius, temperatures, increase, decrease, speed limits, kilometres, credit union, lodge, withdraw, transaction, before, after, Anno Domini, timelines*

Directed numbers on the thermometer

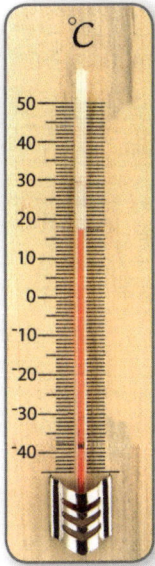

- Water freezes at 0°C (Celsius).
- Water boils at 100°C.
- Our average body temperature is 37°C.
- Negative temperatures are below freezing (0°C).
  Positive temperatures are above freezing.

The following are the average temperatures in major cities one day in January (in °C).

Barcelona +15	Dublin +3	Kiev −5	Glasgow −1
Helsinki −6	Miami +26	Lisbon +10	Volgograd −9
Prague −3	Vilnius +1	Warsaw −4	Athens +22
Chicago −9	Minneapolis −11	Shanghai +15	Hong Kong +20

1. Which city has: (a) the highest temperature? (b) the lowest temperature?

2. Which two cities have the same positive temperature?

3. Which two cities have the same negative temperature?

4. What is the difference between the temperatures in Barcelona and Hong Kong?

5. By how many degrees is it hotter in Lisbon than in Dublin?

6. By how many degrees is it colder in Shanghai than in Miami?

7. What is the difference in temperature between: (a) Glasgow and Vilnius? (b) Prague and Dublin?

8. Which city is warmer: (a) Chicago or Minneapolis? and (b) by how many degrees?

9. Which city is colder: (a) Glasgow or Volgograd? and (b) by how many degrees?

10. By how many degrees is Shanghai warmer than Chicago?

11. By how many degrees is Prague colder than Athens?

12. What is the difference between the highest and lowest temperatures listed?

13. Complete the following table. Use the temperatures above as your starting point.

City	Barcelona	Helsinki	Vilnius	Prague	Minneapolis
Increase each temperature by 5°C					
Decrease each temperature by 3°C					
Increase each temperature by 9°C					
Decrease each temperature by 8°C					

Keep to the speed limit!

(100) (80) (60)

If a driver drives at 90km/h where the speed limit is (80)k, s/he is **over** the limit by 10 km/h ➡ +10km/h.

If a driver drives at 70km/h where the speed limit is (80)k, s/he is **under** the limit by 10km/h ➡ ⁻10km/h.

> Driving over the speed limit can cause accidents and even death! It is also illegal.

1. Ciara, Ronan and Maria were travelling to a concert. The following speed limits were in place en route. Work out whether each driver was over or under the speed limit at the different speed checks. Complete the table.

(a)
Speed limit	100km/h	
Ciara	80km/h	⁻20km/h
Ronan	110km/h	
Maria	95km/h	

(b)
80km/h	
82km/h	+2km/h
75km/h	
90km/h	

(c)
60km/h	
65km/h	
70km/h	
55km/h	

2. Which driver was guilty of driving most km/h **over** the speed limit at **each** speed check?

3. Which driver drove most km/h **under** the speed limit at **each** speed check?

The music charts

If a song moves up the charts, it gains places (positive). If it moves down the charts, it loses places (negative). Work out whether each song below gained or lost places this week when compared with last week.

4. Complete the table.

Official Singles Chart Top 10 on April 1st.

	Title	Position this week	Last week	Gained or lost? ⁺ or ⁻?
(a)	Let It Go	1	3	+2
(b)	Boom Boom	2	6	
(c)	Dancing Prince	3	1	
(d)	Curly Teeth	4	4	
(e)	Red Canoe	5	24	
(f)	Night Fall	6	17	
(g)	Magic	7	5	
(h)	Chilly Chilly	8	12	
(i)	Funky Monkey	9	2	
(j)	Help Me Out	10	7	

Directed numbers – Addition and subtraction

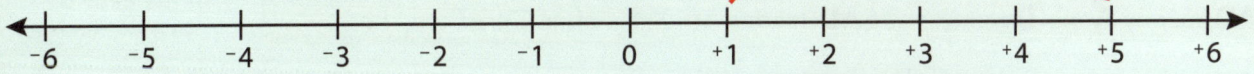

If you start at $^+1$ and jump forward 4, you will land on $^+5$. $^+1 + {}^+4 = {}^+5$

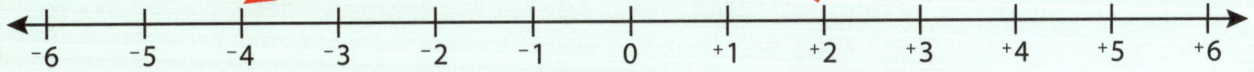

If you start at $^+2$ and jump back 6, you will land on $^-4$. $^+2 + {}^-6 = {}^-4$

1. **Solve the following. Use the numberline to help you.**

   (a) $^+2 + {}^+4$ (b) $^-3 + {}^-2$ (c) $^+2 + {}^-2$ (d) $^+3 + {}^-4$ (e) $^-5 + {}^+1$

   (f) $0 + {}^+5$ (g) $^-1 + {}^+3$ (h) $^-6 + {}^+3$ (i) $^+5 + {}^-4$ (j) $^+6 + {}^-6$

2. **Now do these.**

   (a) $^+4 + {}^-3 + {}^-2$ (b) $^-3 + {}^+6 + {}^+4$ (c) $^-5 + {}^+7 + {}^-2$ (d) $^-8 + {}^+3 + {}^+4$ (e) $^+1 + {}^+4 + {}^+1$

   (f) $^+3 + {}^-7 + {}^+2$ (g) $^+6 + 0 + {}^-8$ (h) $^+9 + {}^-3 + {}^-4$ (i) $^+9 + {}^-1 + {}^-2$ (j) $^+3 + {}^-3 + {}^-3$

3. Seán and Róisín went scuba diving. Seán dived $^-9$ metres. Róisín dived 3 metres deeper. How far did Róisín dive?

4. Mary joined her local Credit Union on March 1st. She can lodge or withdraw money. If she withdraws more money than she has in her account, she is overdrawn or in the red. It is not good business sense to be overdrawn, as she would have to pay interest on that money. Complete the following table showing Mary's transactions for the month of March.

	Date	Transaction	Amount	Balance
(a)	March 1st	Lodged the €90 she got for her birthday.	$^+90$	$^+90$
(b)	March 5th	Withdrew €15 to buy a pair of jeans.	$^-15$	$^+75$
(c)	March 12th	Lodged €10 she received for doing some jobs.	$^+10$	
(d)	March 14th	Withdrew €30 to buy a dress.		
(e)	March 21st	Withdrew €50 to buy 2 tickets for a concert.		
(f)	March 23rd	Lodged €25 she received from her Gran.		
(g)	March 28th	Withdrew €40 to buy a pair of shoes.		
(h)	March 31st	Lodged €20.		

   (i) How much money had Mary in her account at the end of March 31st?

   (j) Do you think that Mary's last transaction was a wise one? Explain.

Directed numbers – BC and AD

BC means **B**efore **C**hrist.   432**BC** means 432 years before Christ was born.

AD means **A**nno **D**omini.   36**AD** means 36 years after Christ was born.

> Christ was born in the year 0.

Interesting dates in history

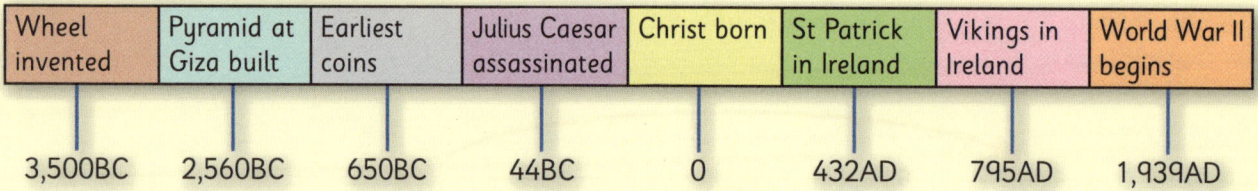

Wheel invented	Pyramid at Giza built	Earliest coins	Julius Caesar assassinated	Christ born	St Patrick in Ireland	Vikings in Ireland	World War II begins
3,500BC	2,560BC	650BC	44BC	0	432AD	795AD	1,939AD

Now answer these questions about the timeline.

1. Which of the historical events was the (a) earliest and (b) latest?

2. How many years were there between the assassination of Caesar and St Patrick coming to Ireland?

3. How many years were there between these events:
   (a) Invention of the wheel and the building of the pyramid at Giza in Egypt?
   (b) The Vikings coming to Ireland and the beginning of World War II?
   (c) The earliest use of coins and the birth of Christ?
   (d) The earliest use of coins and the Vikings coming to Ireland?
   (e) The assassination of Caesar and the invention of the wheel?

4. What is the time difference between the earliest and latest events shown on the timeline?

5. Decide if the following structures were built before or after the birth of Christ. Complete the table.

	structure	story	directed date
(a)		Newgrange passage tomb Co. Meath, built about 3,200BC.	‾3,200
(b)		Colosseum in Rome, built around 80AD.	
(c)		Eiffel Tower in Paris, built in 1,889AD.	
(d)		Taj Mahal, India, completed in 1,659AD.	

	structure	story	directed date
(e)		Great Wall of China, begun in 214BC.	
(f)		Statue of Liberty in New York, erected 1,886AD.	
(g)		Leaning Tower of Piza, begun in 1,173AD.	
(h)		Pyramid of Giza, completed in 2,560BC.	

6. How many years were there between:
   (a) The building of the Colosseum and the erection of the Statue of Liberty?
   (b) The Taj Mahal being completed and the erection of the Eiffel Tower?
   (c) The start of the Great Wall of China and the completion of the Pyramid at Giza?
   (d) The completion of the Pyramid at Giza and the building of Newgrange, Co. Meath?

Chapter 24: Area

A   **Area** is ...
the space covered by a 2-D shape.

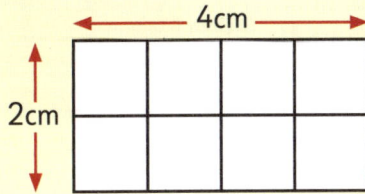

←——— 4cm ———→

2cm

Length × width = area
2cm × 4cm = **8cm²**

B   **Perimeter** is ...
the distance around a 2-D shape.

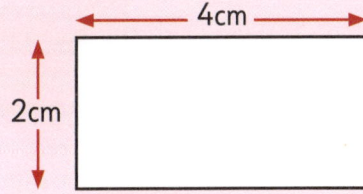

←——— 4cm ———→

2cm

Add all sides = perimeter
4cm + 2cm + 4cm + 2cm = **12cm**

1.   Calculate the following:

Use a ruler to measure the sides!

(a)

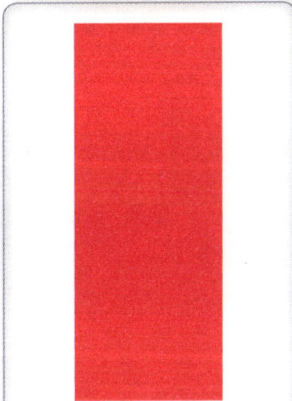

length = _____ cm
width = _____ cm
area = _____ cm²
perimeter = _____ cm

(b)

length = _____ cm
width = _____ cm
area = _____ cm²
perimeter = _____ cm

(c)

length = _____ cm   width = _____ cm
area = _____ cm²   perimeter = _____ cm

(d)

length = _____ cm
width = _____ cm
area = _____ cm²
perimeter = _____ cm

2.   Calculate the (i) **area** and (ii) **perimeter** of the following rectangles.

Estimate first!

	length	width
(a)	7cm	3cm
(b)	6cm	5cm
(c)	8cm	4cm

	length	width
(d)	18cm	3cm
(e)	16cm	13cm
(f)	24cm	19cm

	length	width
(g)	13cm	3·5cm
(h)	19cm	7·2cm
(i)	36cm	9·8cm

3.   Calculate the (i) **perimeter** and (ii) **area** of each shape. (Note: These are not exact measurements.)

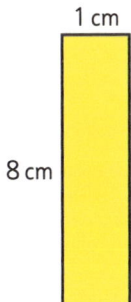

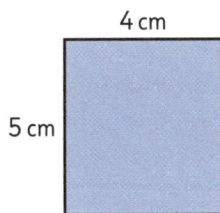

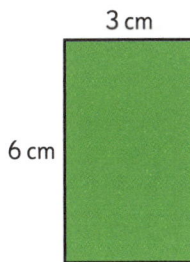

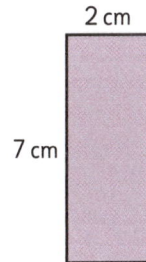

1 cm

8 cm

4 cm

5 cm

3 cm

6 cm

2 cm

7 cm

Do rectangles with the same perimeter always have the same area? Explain!

STRAND Measures   **STRAND UNIT/ELEMENT** Area

LANGUAGE *Area, space, 2-D shape, perimeter, distance, length, width, height, add, shapes, rectangles, squares, measure, surface, calculate, total cuboids, grid, ares, hectares*

125

Area – Finding the area of 'trickier' shapes

Step 1
Divide the shape into rectangles/squares.

4cm 2cm
3cm 3cm
8cm

Step 2
Calculate the length of any missing sides that you will need.

4cm 2cm
3cm 3cm
8cm 8cm
5cm

Step 3
Calculate the area of each rectangle/square.

32cm² 16cm²
15cm²

Step 4
Add the areas to find the total.

32cm²
15cm²
16cm²
‾‾‾‾‾
63cm²

1. Calculate the area of the following shapes. Note: they are not exact measurements!

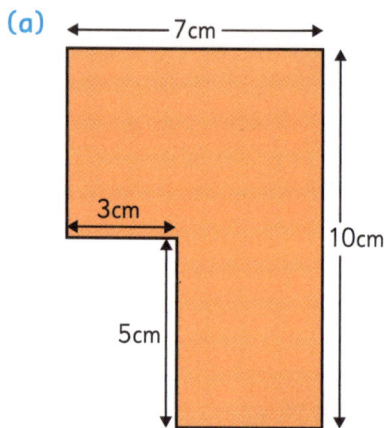

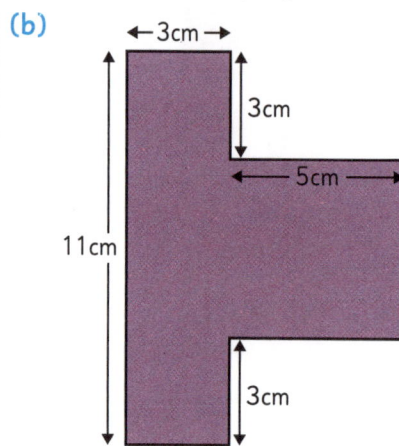

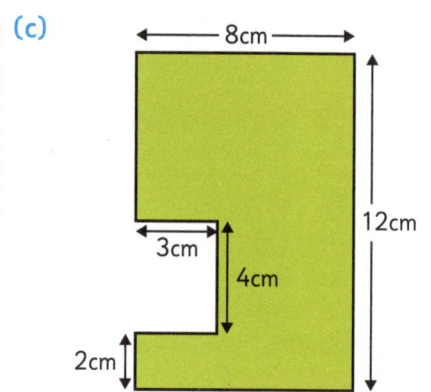

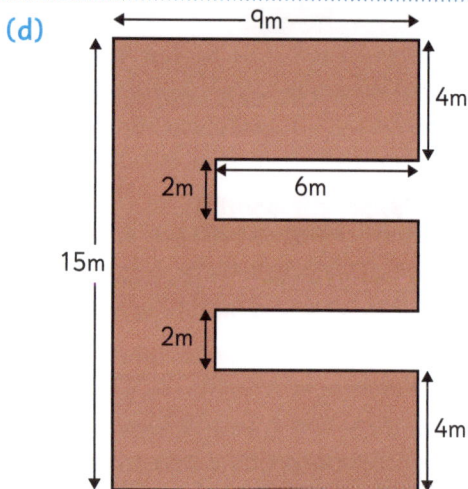

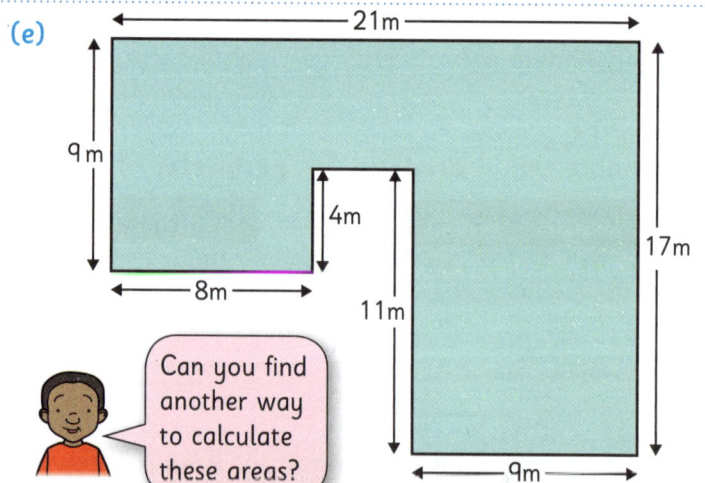

(a)
7cm
3cm
8cm (not labelled)
5cm
10cm

(b)
3cm
3cm
5cm
11cm
3cm

(c)
8cm
3cm
4cm
2cm
12cm

(d)
9m
4m
2m 6m
15m
2m
4m

(e)
21m
9m
4m
8m
11m
17m
9m

Can you find another way to calculate these areas?

Challenge

26m
Oldtown Park
21m 14m
12m

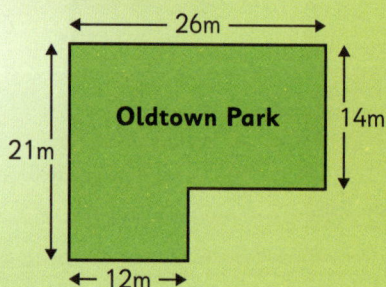

A bag of grass seed costs €7·24. Each bag has enough seed to sow 16m² of land. How much will it cost to sow the whole of Oldtown Park? €ㅤㅤ

Area

Measuring the surface area of 3-D shapes.

(i) Calculate the area of each face.

(ii) Combine the areas to find the total.

Looking at the net of the shape helps!

Cubes

1.

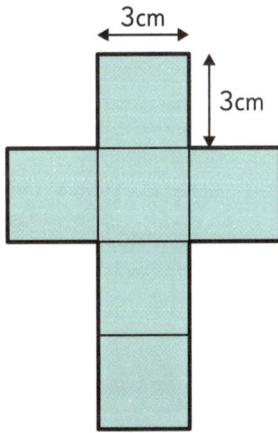

3cm

3cm

(a) Number of faces = _____

(b) Area of each face = _____

(c) Total area of cube = _____

2. Calculate the total surface area of this cube.

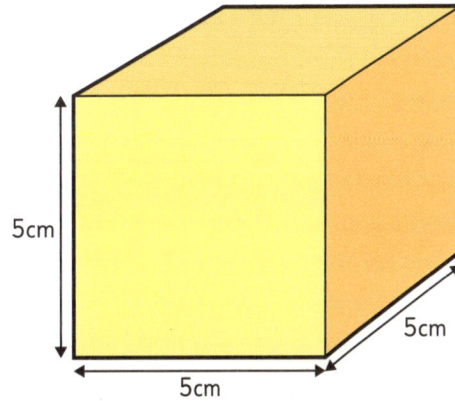

5cm

5cm

5cm

3. Calculate the surface area of cubes with sides of:

(a) 2cm   (b) 4cm   (c) 7cm   (d) 9cm   (e) 2·5cm.

Cuboids

Cuboids are trickier than cubes!

4.

2cm   2cm

5cm

2cm

3cm

(a) Number of faces = _____

(b) Area of blue face = _____ cm × _____ cm = _____ cm^2

(c) Area of yellow face = _____ cm × _____ cm = _____ cm^2

(d) Area of green face = _____ cm × _____ cm = _____ cm^2

(e) Total area of all 6 faces = _____ cm^2

5. Calculate the total surface area of these cuboids.

(a)

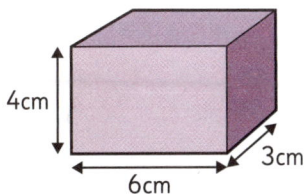

4cm

6cm

3cm

(b)

4cm

7cm

5cm

6. Calculate the surface area of the following cuboids.

	length	width	height
(a)	5cm	2cm	6cm
(b)	4cm	5cm	7cm
(c)	6cm	1·5cm	2cm

Challenge

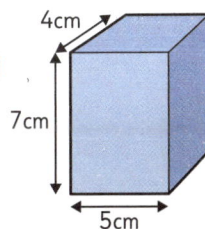

surface area = 216cm^2

This cube has a surface area of 216cm^2.

Calculate the length of one side. _____

Area

This is a plan of Adrenaline Outdoor Adventure Centre.
It is drawn to a scale of 1cm = 1metre (1:100). Use your ruler to find all the measurements.

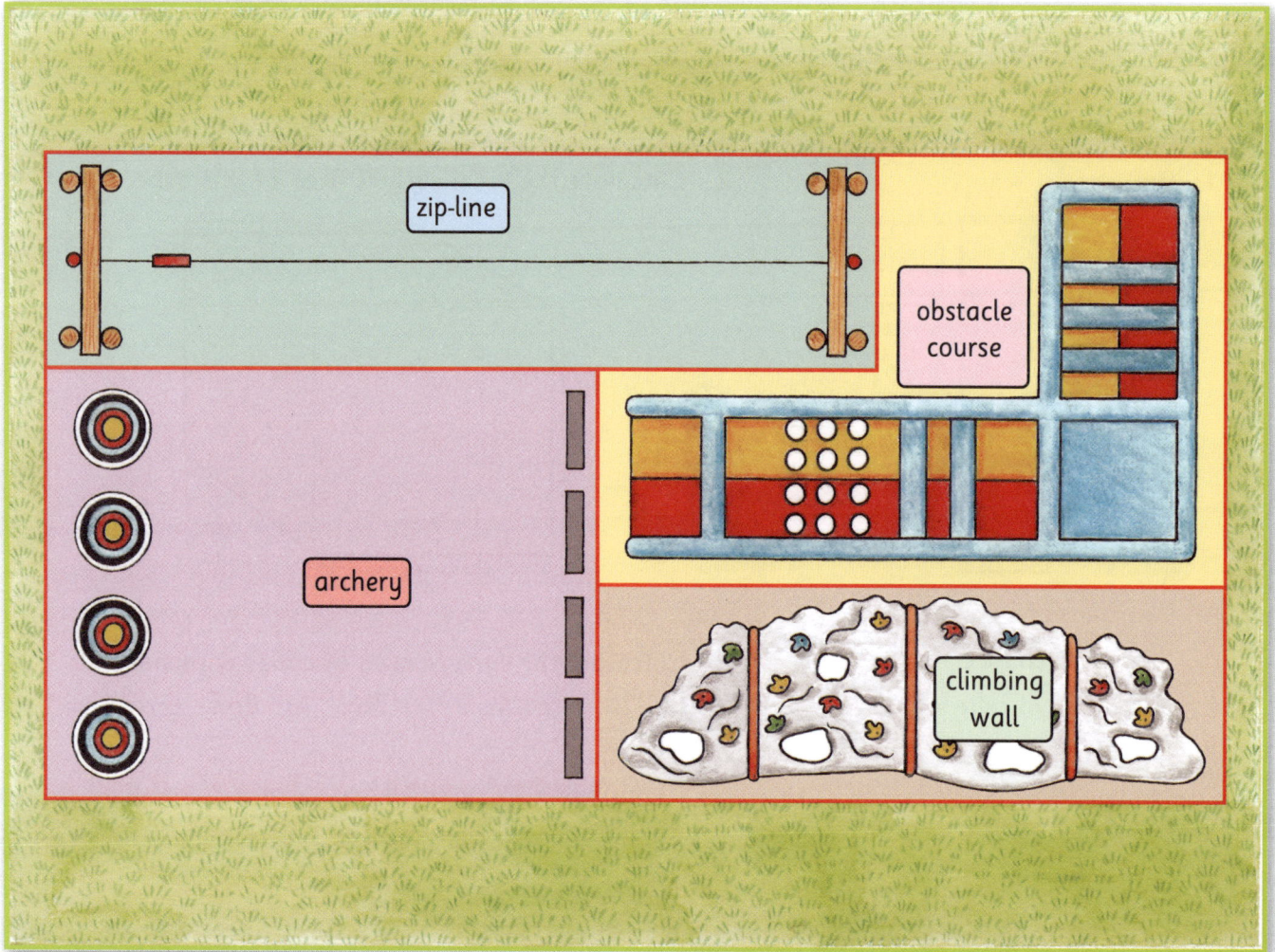

1. Complete the tables for each activity zone.

	zone	perimeter	area
(a)	zip-line	_____ m	_____ m²
(b)	archery	_____ m	_____ m²

	zone	perimeter	area
(c)	obstacle course	_____ m	_____ m²
(d)	climbing wall	_____ m	_____ m²

2. Calculate the total (a) area and (b) perimeter of Adrenaline Outdoor Activity Centre.

   There is more than one way of doing this!

3. An adult ticket into Adrenaline costs €12·75 . A child's ticket costs €9·85 . Calculate the cost of entry for a group of 3 adults and 14 children.

4. The safety fence around the archery zone needs replacing. A new fence costs €23·40 per metre . Labour costs will be €260 . What will be the total cost of fitting a new fence?

5. The complete climbing wall zone needs to be fitted with soft tiles that cost €13·92 per square metre . Calculate the total cost of the tiles needed.

Area – m², ares, hectares 1

The following pictures show different areas of the same park.

Can you find this section of the park in the other sections?

1.

1m²

100 cm

100 cm

100cm × 100cm = 10,000cm²

1m² = 10,000cm²

(a) Write as **m²**:
(i) 20,000cm² (ii) 87,000cm² (iii) 69,000cm²
(iv) 38,600cm² (v) 17,650cm² (vi) 23,490cm²

(b) Write as **cm²**:
(i) 3m² (ii) 7m² (iii) 9m² (iv) 1·3m²
(v) 2·6m² (vi) 6·4m² (vii) 3·98m² (viii) 7·61m²

Challenge A vegetable patch is 3·5m long and 2·5m wide. What is the area of the patch in
(i) _____ cm² and
(ii) _____ m²?

2.

1 are

10 m

10 m

10m × 10m = 100m²

1 are = 100m²

An **are** is 100 times bigger than 1m²! or **100m² = 1 are** .

(a) Write as **ares**:
(i) 300m² (ii) 700m² (iii) 130m²
(iv) 1,000m² (v) 1,900m² (vi) 1,740m²
(vii) 2,878m² (viii) 3,781 m² (ix) 5,085 m²

(b) Write as **m²**:
(i) 2 ares (ii) 5 ares (iii) 9 ares
(iv) 13 ares (v) 24 ares (vi) 6·9 ares
(vii) 7·32 ares (viii) 16·92 ares (ix) 20·73 ares

3.

1 hectare

100 m

100 m

100m × 100m = 10,000m²

1 hectare = 10,000m²

1 hectare = 100 ares

A **hectare** is 100 times bigger than an **are** or **100 ares = 1 hectare** .

(a) Write as **m²**:
(i) 2 hectares (ii) 6 hectares (iii) 2·5 hectares
(iv) 3·26 hectares (v) 4·93 hectares (vi) 3·976 hectares

(b) Write as **hectares**:
(i) 200 ares (ii) 800 ares (iii) 1,000 ares
(iv) 1,100 ares (v) 1,950 ares (vi) 2,360 ares
(vii) 2,820 ares (viii) 2,947 ares (ix) 3,762 ares

(c) Write as **ares**:
(i) 3 hectares (ii) 7 hectares (iii) 14 hectares
(iv) 4·2 hectares (v) 19·3 hectares (vi) 22·43 hectares

Area – m², ares, hectares 2

1. Which of the following objects are most likely to cover an area of:
   (i) **1m²**, (ii) **an are** or (iii) **a hectare**?

(a)   (b)   (c)   (d)   (e)

(f)   (g)   (h)   (i)   (j)

2. Complete the following tables of rectangles.

	length	width	area in m²	area in ares
(a)	20m	10m		
(b)	30m	50m		
(c)	20m	70m		
(d)	40m	85m		

	length	width	area in m²	area in ares
(e)	20m		600m²	
(f)		20m		14 ares
(g)		30m	750m²	
(h)	40m			32 ares

3. Calculate the area of the following floor plans in: (i) **m²**, (ii) **ares** and (iii) **hectares**.

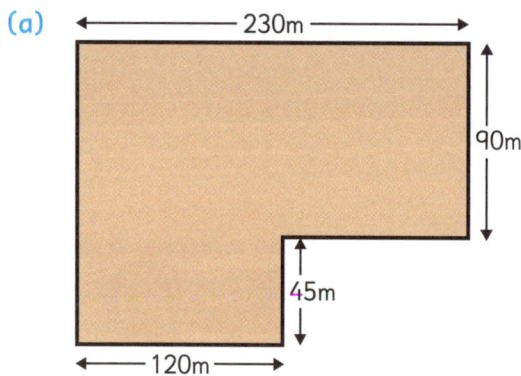

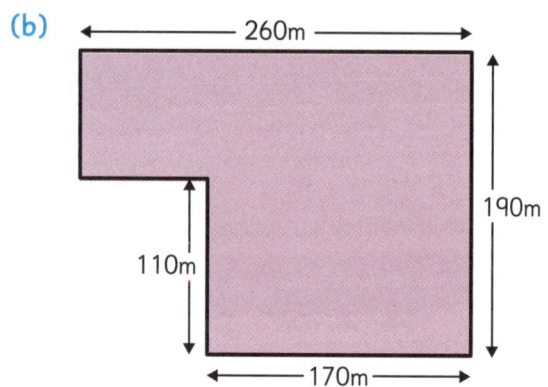

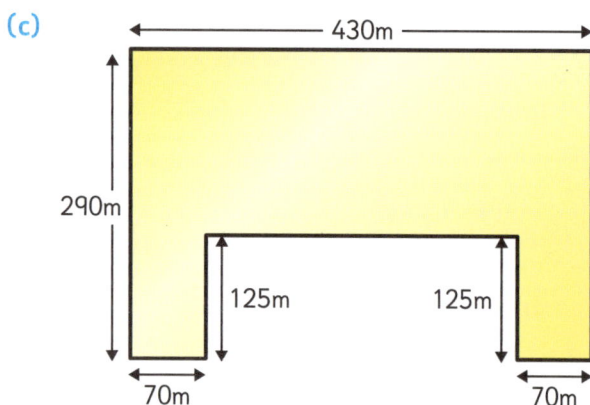

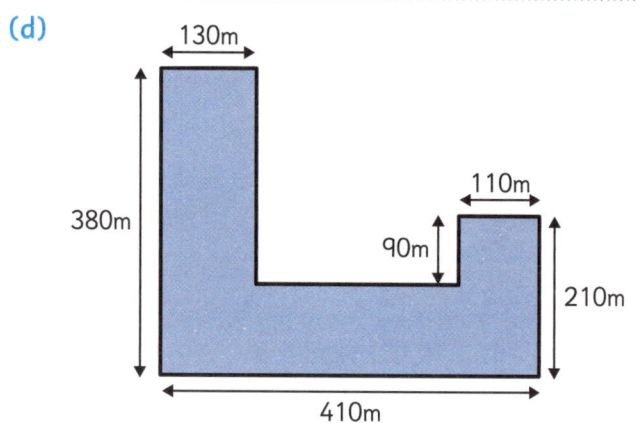

(a)
230m
90m
45m
120m

(b)
260m
190m
110m
170m

(c)
430m
290m
125m   125m
70m   70m

(d)
130m
380m
110m
90m
210m
410m

130

A quick look back 7

1. What is 75% of 80? _____

2. There are 300 children in Bridgetown Primary School. One day 9% of them were absent. How many were absent? _____

3. A farmer had 64 cows. He sold $37\frac{1}{2}$% of them. How many cows did he sell? _____

4. What is 12·5% of 96? _____

5. Elaine spent 0·77 of her €200 buying a coat. The coat cost € _____.

6. Increase 36 by $33\frac{1}{3}$%. _____

7. Decrease 72 by $37\frac{1}{2}$%. _____

8. Brian has €2·50. John has 0·8 of Brian's amount. How much money have they between them? € _____

9. The increased price of a pair of football boots is €36. If the percentage increase was 20%, what was the old price? € _____

10. A scooter that usually costs €110 was decreased in price by 10%. What is the new price? € _____

Special offer 10% off

11. Jake lost 0·3 of his 70 marbles. How many marbles had he left? _____

12. Jenny's apartment is on the 5th floor of the building. Her car is parked 2 floors below the 1st floor. How many floors above her car is her apartment? _____

13. The temperature was ⁺13°C one day. It was ⁻6°C that night. What was the difference in degrees between the two temperatures? _____ °C

14. In a soccer league, Kilkee had scored 43 goals and conceded 19 goals. Bansha had scored 18, but had conceded 25. By how many goals was Kilkee's goal difference better than Bansha's? _____

15. How many degrees are there in the angle marked A? _____

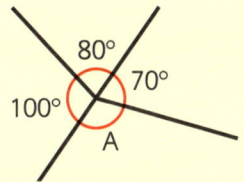

    80° 70° 100° A

16. Write the value of 4³ _____

17. 3·4 × 0·09 = _____

18. Tara walked 7·7km. Terry walked 8,955m. How many km further did Terry walk? _____ km

19. It took Mam 4 hours to travel a distance of 260km. What was her average speed? _____ km/h

20. A rectangle has a perimeter of 70cm. If its longer side measures 26cm, what is the area of the rectangle? _____ cm²

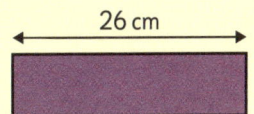

    26 cm

Chapter 25: Fractions/Decimals/Percentages 3

We make a profit when we sell something for more than it cost us to buy.

sale price €50 { €10 profit / €40 cost paid }

Sale price = cost price + profit
€50 = €40 + €10

profit = €10

1. Calculate the **profit** for each of these.

   (a) Cost: €275. Sold for €399·99.

   (b) Selling price: €12,750. Cost price: €8,900.

   (c) 8 footballs cost €99. They were sold for €15 each.

   (d) A hat and a scarf cost €7·50 each. Sold for a total of €19·85.

We make a loss when we sell something for less than it cost us to buy.

cost price €75 { €25 loss / €50 sale price }

Sale price = cost price – loss
€50 = €75 – €25

loss = €25

2. Calculate the **loss** for each of these.

   (a) A television was bought by a shop for €250, and sold for €189·99.

   (b) Cost price: €125·50. Sold for €79.

   (c) Cost: €1·99 each. Sold altogether for €8.

   (d) Sold for €159·95, cost €247.

   (e) 7 bought at €8·75 each. Sold for a total of €47·50.

   (f) Watches were sold for €11·90 each. They were bought at €119·70 for 9 watches.

   (g) 36 apples were bought for €15. They were sold for 35c each.

   (h) Oranges were sold at 45c each. 68 oranges cost the shopkeeper €35·70.

3. Write the missing amounts. A loss is written with a **minus** sign.

Cost Price	€59	€25		€53	€247	€89·49		
Profit/Loss	€19		–€29·50	–€17·01		€37·53	–€36·59	–€101·99
Sale Price		€49·99	€100		€149·99		€199·01	€247·50

4. Solve these **profit** or **loss** problems.

   (a) A bookshop bought a box of 50 books for €299. If each book was sold for €9·99, calculate how much profit or loss the bookshop made.

   (b) Al's Autos sold a car for €23,499. If they had paid €18,750 for it, calculate the profit or loss made.

Challenge A dealer bought 6 microwaves for a total of €1,176. She sold them at €179·50 each. Calculate her profit or loss on the microwaves.

STRAND **Number**   STRAND UNIT/ELEMENT *Fractions, decimals and percentages*
LANGUAGE *Fraction, decimal, percentage, profit, loss, less, smaller, bigger, money, bought, sold, cost/selling price, survey, pie chart, express, write, sale*

Profit or loss percentages

A A dealer paid €150 for a bike. He sold it for €180. What percentage profit did he make?

Cost price = €150
Sale price = €180

Profit = €30

Fraction profit $\rightarrow \dfrac{30}{150} \rightarrow \dfrac{3}{15} = \dfrac{1}{5}$

% profit $\rightarrow \dfrac{1}{5} \times \dfrac{100}{1} \rightarrow \dfrac{100}{5} = 20\%$

B Tina bought a tablet for €240. She sold it for €200. What percentage loss did she make?

Cost price = €240
Sale price = €200

Loss = €40

Fraction loss $\rightarrow \dfrac{40}{240} \rightarrow \dfrac{4}{24} = \dfrac{1}{6}$

% loss $\rightarrow \dfrac{1}{6} \times \dfrac{100}{1} \rightarrow \dfrac{100}{6} \rightarrow \dfrac{50}{3} = 16\frac{2}{3}\%$

1. Complete the chart. Calculate the percentage profit/loss for each of these. Losses are shown in brackets ( ).

Joe's Hardware Shop

	tool	selling price	cost price	profit/loss	percentage profit/loss
(a)		€15	€20	(€5)	$\dfrac{5}{20} \rightarrow$ _____ % loss
(b)		€21		€3	
(c)			€12·50	(€2·50)	
(d)		€17·50	€14		
(e)		€38·50	€35		
(f)		€4·50		€1·50	

2. Solve these problems.

(a) **Pro Surf** bought ten surfboards for a total of €1,500. The surfboards were sold for €200 each. What percentage profit was made on each surfboard?

(b) **Classic Cars** paid €9,000 for a vintage Ferrari and sold it for €11,250. What percentage profit did they make?

(c) **Harry's Holiday Store** bought 40 pairs of sunglasses for €500. They had to sell them for €10 each due to a wet summer. Calculate the overall percentage profit/loss.

(d) Find the percentage profit/loss on a skateboard bought for €36 and sold for €45.

(e) **Super Sports** bought 20 jerseys for €390 and 20 pairs of shorts for €350. They were sold in sets for €40·70 per set. What was the overall percentage profit/loss made by **Super Sports**?

Challenge   **Fred's Fruit and Veg** bought a box of 50 pineapples for €40. Half of them were bad. The rest of them were sold for €2·20 each. Find the percentage profit or loss.

Cost price and selling price

A By selling a bed for €600, a shop made a profit of 20%. What was the original cost of the bed?

Profit = 20%

Fraction profit → $\frac{20}{100}$ → $\frac{2}{10} = \frac{1}{5}$

Sale price = cost price + profit = $\frac{6}{5}$

$\frac{6}{5}$ = €600 → (sale price)

$\frac{1}{5}$ = €100

$\frac{5}{5}$ = €500 → (cost price)

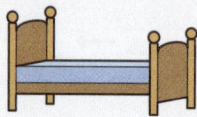

B A football was sold for a profit of 75%. The actual profit was €15. What were the cost and selling prices?

Profit → 75% = $\frac{3}{4}$ and Actual profit = €15

$\frac{3}{4}$ = €15

$\frac{1}{4}$ = €5

$\frac{4}{4}$ = €20 → (cost price)

$\frac{7}{4}$ = €35 → (sale price)

1. **Abbie's Antiques** bought and sold these items. How well did they do? Losses are in **brackets**.

Abbie's Antiques

	item	selling price	cost price	profit/loss	percentage profit/loss
(a)		€80		€16	
(b)			€60	(€15)	
(c)				(€21)	(30%)
(d)		€280			40%
(e)			€80		45%
(f)		€168			(16%)

2. Now solve these **profit** or **loss** problems.

(a) *Skate and Surf* made a 25% profit on all skateboards they sold. If they made €15 profit on one of them, what was the cost price?

(b) *The Fright Factory* bought ten Hallowe'en masks for a total of €25. They want to make a 10% profit. At what price must they sell each mask?

(c) *Crazy Price Cars* made a 15% profit on a van they sold. If their profit was €690, what were the cost and selling prices of the van?

(d) Pam bought an old bicycle for €27. She spent €48 fixing it. She then sold it for a 12% profit. What was the selling price?

(e) *Whatever the Weather* bought 100 umbrellas for €500. If they sold 60 of them for a 20% profit and the rest for a $12\frac{1}{2}$% profit, what was their total profit?

Challenge Glen's Garage bought a damaged car for €2,369. It cost the garage €2,131 to repair the car. At what price must they sell the car to make a profit of 18%?

Fractions/Decimals/Percentages 3 – Shopping

1. Sunny Days Fruit and Veg

30c each	€1·80 each	€1·65 each	€1·20 each	60c each
apples	mangos	pineapples	coconuts	peaches

(a) If the shopkeeper bought a box of 25 apples for €5·00 and sold them all, what percentage profit did the shopkeeper make?

(b) The shopkeeper made a 20% profit on each coconut sold. How many coconuts did the shopkeeper sell yesterday if she made a profit of €6?

(c) How much did **Sunny Days** pay for a peach if they are selling them at a 25% profit?

(d) The shipping costs for the mangos were €50 for a crate of 100. If the mangos cost another €100 per crate to buy, what was the profit or loss on each mango?

(e) **Sunny Days** makes a $22\frac{2}{9}$% profit on each pineapple it sells. How much does a pineapple cost them?

(f) The following week, coconuts were on sale at a discount of $7\frac{1}{2}$%. What was the new selling price?

2. Adrenaline Sports – Sale Now On!

Mountain Bikes $16\frac{2}{3}$% off

All Karts 40% off

All Skateboards 25% off

All BMX Bikes $37\frac{1}{2}$ % off

(a) If a mountain bike originally sold for €300, what is the sale price?

(b) A kart now costs €270. What was the old price?

(c) If a skateboard has been reduced in price by €25·50, how much was it originally?

(d) A BMX originally sold for €480. What is the sale price?

(e) Which of the four items was reduced by the least amount of money?

(f) Express the sale price of a skateboard as a percentage of the sale price of a kart. (Round to the nearest full per cent.)

Challenge (a) A downhill mountain bike cost the shop €300 to buy and they were making a 10% profit at the old selling price. How much of a loss are they now making?

(b) If a kart was sold in the sale for €267, what was the original selling price?

Fractions/Decimals/Percentages 3

Cappuccino	€3·00
Regular Coffee	€2·50
Tea	€1·50
Scone	€2·00
Carrot Cake	€3·50
Toast	€0·50

$12\frac{1}{2}$% service charge on orders over €10

Study the menu. Answer the questions.

1. Cake and Coffee Café

(a) If Maria bought four cappuccinos, what would the service charge be?

(b) Barry bought two regular coffees and two carrot cake slices. How much did he pay in total including service charge?

(c) If Eanna wants to leave an $11\frac{1}{9}$% tip for his regular coffee and scone, how much should he leave?

(d) The Café buys its loaves of bread for €3 each. If it makes 10 slices of toast per loaf, what is the percentage profit on each slice of toast it sells?

(e) If a customer bought two of everything, how much would they have to pay including service charge?

(f) Richard bought 4 regular coffees, 8 toast and 4 scones. What change had he from €30?

2. Everything Electric

(a) The shop paid €3,000 for 10 laptops. How much must they sell each of them for to make a profit of $66\frac{2}{3}$%?

(b) *Everything Electric* reduced the price of a speaker system from €250 to €150. What percentage discount is that?

(c) A television is on sale at 40% off. The sale price is €465. What was the television selling for before the sale?

(d) A washing machine costs €299 and a drier costs €199. If you buy both of them together, you get a $33\frac{1}{3}$% discount. What would you pay for both together?

(e) An X-Box costing €255 now has a 4% discount. A Playstation that used to cost €299 is now discounted by 12%. Which item is (a) cheaper and (b) by how much?

(f) *Everything Electric* makes a $37\frac{1}{2}$% profit on sales of its most expensive smartphone. If their profit is €196·50, what does it sell for?

(g) An American style fridge-freezer is on sale for €1,375. If this is a discount of $16\frac{2}{3}$%, how much was it selling for before the sale?

Challenge

A tablet costs the shop €200 to buy and was on sale for €300. By what percentage will they have to increase the sale price if they want to make a 75% profit on it?

Fractions/Decimals/Percentages 3

Check what you have learned!

1. Use your head! Find:

   (a) $\frac{7}{8}$ of 112   (b) 0·04 of 8   (c) 80% of 2,000   (d) 0·55 of 280

   (e) What % of 40 is 16   (f) Decrease 24 by $37\frac{1}{2}$%   (g) Increase 80 by 75%   (h) $\frac{79}{1000}$ = ____ %

2. Complete each row so that it adds up to the given **target** number:

   (a)

				target
(i)	0·25	%	$\frac{2}{5}$	
(ii)		0·45	15%	→ 95%
(iii)	%	$\frac{3}{4}$	0·05	

   (b)

				target
(i)	0·7	%	$\frac{1}{4}$	
(ii)	21%		0·64	→ 1·25
(iii)	$\frac{3}{5}$	0·	43%	

3. What kind of coat can only be put on when it is wet? Order the amounts of the following from the **smallest** to the **biggest** to find out (round to 2 decimal places).

T	$66\frac{2}{3}$% of 14	A	$4\frac{5}{8}$ + 3·095	C	$4\frac{5}{9}$ + $3\frac{5}{6}$	P	$10\frac{1}{4}$ − 0·7
I	increase 6 by 75%	N	Find 0·11 of 99	O	15 reduced by 44%	A	$\frac{10}{4}$ × 4
O	$9\frac{5}{11}$	F	50% of 19	A	35% is 3·5 so 90% = ____	T	2 ÷ $\frac{1}{6}$

   □   □ □ □ □   □ □   □ □ □ □ □

4. Birthday presents!

   A survey was carried out by the 240 boys and girls in a school to see what presents they would like for their birthdays.

   (a) Study this pie-chart and find out how many children picked:

   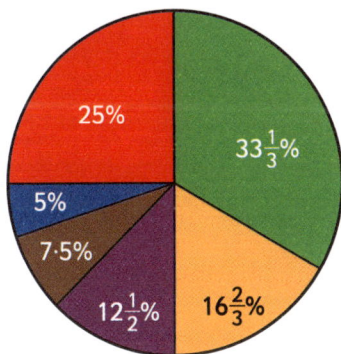

   Pie-chart sections: 25%, $33\frac{1}{3}$%, 5%, 7·5%, $12\frac{1}{2}$%, $16\frac{2}{3}$%

   (1) **Bicycle** = ____ children

   (2) **Tablet** = ____ children

   (3) **Books** = ____ children

   (4) **Runners** = ____ children

   (5) **Clothes** = ____ children

   (6) **Money** = ____ children

   (b) Express the number of children who picked money as a percentage of the number who picked a tablet.

   (c) What percentage of the children picked either a bicycle or runners? (Round your answer to 2 decimal places.)

Challenge   A football was normally priced at €15. In the summer sale the price was reduced by 50%. After the sale was over the price was increased by 50%.

How much does the football cost now? (Be careful!) € _____

Chapter 26: Puzzles 1

1. Write the missing **operation signs** to make each of the following true.

   (a) 57 ◯ (16 ◯ 5) = 137

   (b) (29 ◯ 8) ◯ 17 = 215

2. Find the area of each **square** in **square centimetres** (cm^2).

   (a) ← 5cm →
   (b) ← 7cm →
   (c) ← 9cm →
   (d) ← 6cm →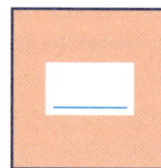
   (e) ← 11cm →

3. Now find the length of each side of these squares.

   (a) ← ___ → 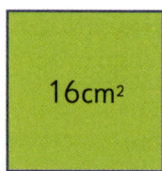 16cm²
   (b) ← ___ →  64cm²
   (c) ← ___ →  144cm²
   (d) ← ___ →  400cm²
   (e) ← ___ →  900cm²

4. Write the answers to these questions.

   (a) 2 × 2 × 2 = ____   (b) 3 × 3 × 3 = ____   (c) 4 × 4 × 4 = ____

   We could have asked the questions like this: $2^3 = $ ____ , $3^3 = $ ____ , $4^3 = $ ____ .

   (d) $5^3 = $ ____   (e) $6^3 = $ ____   (f) $7^3 = $ ____   (g) $8^3 = $ ____   (h) $9^3 = $ ____   (i) $10^3 = $ ____

5. Now try these.

   (a) 2^4 (b) 3^4 (c) 5^4 (d) 6^4 (e) 10^4 (f) 2^5 (g) 3^5 (h) 10^5

6.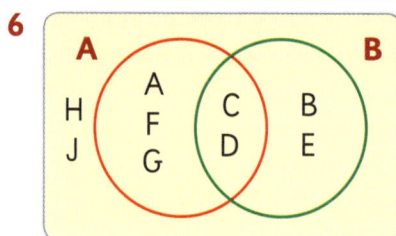

   Write the letters that are in:
   (i)   circle **A**
   (ii) circle **B**
   (iii) both circles
   (iv) circle **A** only
   (v)   circle **B** only
   (vi) no circle

   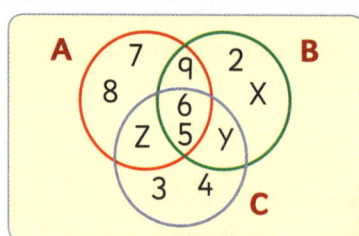

   Write the digits/letters in:
   (i)   circle **A**
   (ii) circle **B**
   (iii) circle **C**
   (iv) all 3 circles
   (v)   **A** and **B** but not in **C**
   (vi) **B** and **C** but not in **A**

   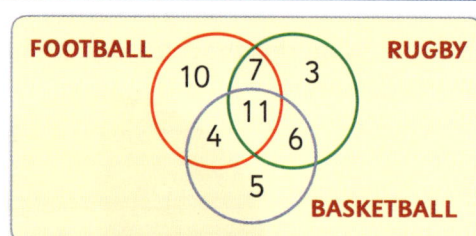

   Sports liked by a class:
   (i)   all 3 sports
   (ii) football
   (iii) rugby
   (iv) basketball
   (v)   1 sport only
   (vi) at least 2 sports

7. A prize was shared between Zach, Zoe and Zeth in the ratio 11:8:7. If Zoe got €384. How much did **(i)** Zach and **(ii)** Zeth get?

Challenge   If Audrey gave two of her books to Ben, they would then have the same number of books each. If Ben had given two of his books to Audrey, she would have had nine times as many as him. What is the least number of books each could have?

138

Puzzles 2

1. Complete these magic squares. Write the **magic number**. All rows, columns and diagonals must add up to the same number.

(a)

17		4	14
	12		9
	8	7	
5			2

Magic number: ☐

(b)

16		15	
6	13	9	18
	14	10	
19			

Magic number: ☐

(c)

	11	5	24	18
19		7		
26	20	14	8	2
3	22			9
10			17	16

Magic number: ☐

2. Jeremy gave one-third of his chestnuts to Leo. Leo gave half of the chestnuts he got from Jeremy to Victoria. Victoria kept nine of the chestnuts and gave seven to Lucy. How many chestnuts had Jeremy in the beginning?

3. Write the missing numbers:

(a) _____ × 9 + 14 = 797

(b) _____ × 7 − 19 = 457

(c) _____ × 8 − 55 = 385

(d) _____ ÷ 4 + 17 = 41

(e) _____ ÷ 7 − 18 = 75.

(f) _____ ÷ 5 + 925 = 941

4. What number am I?

> I am a four-digit number. My first digit is a square number.
> My last digit is five less than my first. My second digit is half my last digit. My third digit is three times my second digit.

I am _____

5. Complete the Sudoku puzzles. Each row and column must have the digits 1 to 9.

(a)

	1	4	5		9	7		6
6		2		3		4	9	8
	7	3		6	4			
7			1	8	5	3	6	2
5	6			7	2			4
3		8	9		6	5	7	1
	9	7	2	5			4	3
4				1		8		
2		6	4	9	3		5	

(b)

9		8	6		3		2	5
5	3		4			1	6	7
		4	1		5	2		8
3	2			7	5		4	1
7			9	3		1		6
		5	4	2	8		3	9
2	1	3			4	7	9	8
		6	7	8		9		
8		5	1		7		3	4

> Each box of 9 squares should also have the digits 1–9.

6. Can you fit these numbers across or down on the grid?

5 digits	4 digits	3 digits	2 digits
25937	3296	167	42
46819	9275	436	19
	5468	683	13
	7243	293	96
	6384	985	

Grid values: 7, 2, 4, 3

Chapter 27: Money

A Value for money!

Super Savers

€1·50 — Now two litres for the same price!

Eggs: 6 pack €2

Sausages: 200g for €1·50

Yoghurt: €1·60 each

Value Town

Eggs: €2·40 for six

Milk 1 litre: €0·80

Now two extra eggs free!

Sausages: 400g for €2·80

Yoghurt: €1·80 each — Now 4 for the price of 3!

Super Prices

Milk 2 litres: €1·80

Eggs €0·35 each

Sausages: €5·50 per kg

Yoghurt: €1·70 each

or €3 for 2!

(a) If you wanted 4 litres of milk, which shop would give you the best value?

(b) A baker bought 24 of the cheapest eggs. How much did she pay?

(c) If you want to buy 12 yoghurts, which shop gives the best value?

(d) Shane bought 6 yoghurts in *Super Prices*. He misread the sign and thought it was 3 for €2. How much extra did he have to pay?

(e) What is the cost of 500g of sausages in each shop?

(f) The owner of a bed and breakfast needs 48 eggs and 3kg of sausages. She has time to go to one shop only. Which should she choose to get the best value?

B Broadband and TV offer!

SPEED NET

Television: €30 per month

Broadband: 6 months free with television package. €40 per month thereafter.

Home Entertainment

Television: €40 per month
Broadband: €30 per month

Order both and get a $37\frac{1}{2}$% discount on television price

Direct TV

Television and broadband: €72 per month

Special offer: 25% off per month, if you order today!

(a) (i) Work out how much you would pay for a television and broadband package with each company for one year. (ii) Which shop offers the best value?

(b) If you had to sign a two-year contract, is the same package the best value?

(c) Why might a company offer a discount for six months only?

C Special Offers!

Work out the percentage saving for each of these:

Hint: The % saving is the same no matter what the price for one item is, but it might help you to work it out if you pick a price of €1.

(a) Buy one get one free!

(b) 3 for the price of 2!

(c) Buy 4 and get 1 extra free!

(d) Buy one and get the second one for half price!

STRAND Measures   STRAND UNIT/ELEMENT Money
LANGUAGE Euro, cent, Value Added Tax (VAT), interest, foreign currency/exchange, Dollar, Yen, Sterling, Krone, Franc, Rand, household budget, bank accounts

Money – Value Added Tax (VAT)

VAT (or **Value Added Tax**) is a tax added to the price of goods and services we buy. A business charges VAT as a percentage of the selling price and then pays the money to the government. The VAT charged varies for different items. This book uses the following rates.

0% VAT: Children's clothes, books and comics, uncooked food, milk, fruit/veg.

13% VAT: Café, restaurant food, hotels, cinema, hairdressers/barbers.

23% VAT: Sweets and soft drinks, electrical goods, toys, cakes and muffins.

1. **VAT in the Superstore** – fill in the boxes (use the VAT rates from above).

   (a) Television €350·00
   VAT @ 23% € _____
   Price incl. VAT € _____

   (b) Five bananas €1·37
   VAT @ _____ % € _____
   Price incl. VAT € _____

   (c) Book € _____
   VAT @ _____ % € _____
   Price incl. VAT €11·99

   (d) Superstore Café €6·00
   VAT @ _____ % € _____
   Price incl. VAT € _____

   (e) Microwave € _____
   VAT @ _____ % € _____
   Price incl. VAT €123·00

   (f) Bottle of Cola € _____
   VAT @ _____ % € _____
   Price incl. VAT €2·46

2. **A shopping trip** – calculate the prices including VAT.

   (a) Eve went to the hairdressers as soon as she got into town. What did she pay for a haircut, if the price before VAT was €50?

   (b) After that, she bought two apples from a fruit stall for €0·39 each before VAT.

   (c) Next, she met two of her friends and they went to the cinema. The tickets cost €7 each before VAT and Eve paid for all three tickets.

   (d) After the film, she met her younger brother for dinner and she paid the bill. Before VAT the total of the bill was €27.

   (e) After leaving the restaurant, she called into a shop and bought a litre of milk costing €1·19 and a packet of sweets for €2 (both prices before VAT).

   (f) Eve then went to an electronics shop and bought headphones that cost €34 before VAT.

   (g) Lastly, she bought a book for €9·99 and a blueberry muffin costing €3 for the journey home (both prices before VAT).

   (h) How much in total did Eve spend on her shopping trip?

   (i) How much money had she left from €200?

Challenge Express the amount of money Eve spent on her shopping trip as a percentage of her original €200. (Round to 2 decimal places.) _____

Money – Interest

Borrowing and saving

A

Simona bought a new television costing €500. She didn't have to pay for it until a year later but it cost her an extra 4% in **interest**. How much altogether did she have to pay for the television?

| Price: 100% = €500 |
| Interest: 4% = €20 |
| Total: 104% = €520 |

Short way

| 100% = €500 |
| 1% = €5 |
| 104% = €520 |

B

Tony deposited €2,500 in a bank, at an interest rate of 3% for a year. How much was his money worth at the end of the year?

| Deposit: €2,500 |
| Interest: 3%: = €75 |
| Total: €2,575 |

Short way

| 100% = €2,500 |
| 1% = €25 |
| 103% = €2,575 |

Now try these problems involving **simple interest**. You may use a calculator to check answers!

1. Joanne bought a car that costs €7,000. She borrows the money for a year at a rate of 6% interest. How much will she pay in total for the car?

2. Mark took out a loan of €1,750 for a year at an interest rate of 11% to upgrade his kitchen. How much did he have to pay back at the end of the year?

3. Joe invested €760 in a post office savings account for one year at an interest rate of 3·5%. What was his investment worth at the end of the year?

4. Conor borrowed €3,400 from the Credit Union. The interest rate was 6·25% per year. How much interest did he owe after 6 months?

5. Frankie had €1,350. He put it on deposit in a bank for two years where he was paid 3·5% interest per year (per annum). He spent €1,379 of his money two years later buying a racing bicycle. How much money had he left?

6. Work out the interest for these after (i) 3 years and (ii) 6 months.

   (a) €1,800 at 7% per year
   (b) €1,350 at 5·8% per year
   (c) €1,950 at 6% per annum
   (d) €1,760 at 6·5% per annum
   (e) €2,580 at 9·5% p.a.
   (f) €3,240 at $8\frac{1}{2}$% p.a.

7. Sofia borrowed €1,660 for two years at an interest rate of 8·45% per annum. How much, in total, had she to pay back at the end of the two year period?

Challenge 1 Kay wants to get a new television and pay for it in a year's time. *Electric City* will sell it for €350 and charge 5% interest. *Total Television* charges €300 and 7·5% interest. How much will Kay save by choosing the better value deal?

Challenge 2 Alex put €1,580 on deposit for 2 years at a rate of 4·25% p.a. When the 2 years were up, he took his money from the bank and bought a computer for €978 and the latest iphone for €565. How much money had he left?

Money – Foreign exchange

Foreign Exchange Rates	
🇪🇺	€1·00
🇺🇸	US$1·25
🇦🇺	AUD$1·45
🇿🇦	R13·92
🇬🇧	£0·78
🇩🇰	Kr 7·44
🇨🇭	CHF 1·21
🇯🇵	¥143·02

US Dollar ($) · **South African Rand (R)** · **Danish Krone (Kr)** · **Australian Dollar ($)**

Japanese Yen (¥) · **Swiss Franc (CHF)** · **Pound Sterling (£)** · **Euro (€)**

Countries all over the world use different currencies.

1. Name the currencies and their countries shown in the table.

> The **€/US $** exchange rate is 1·25. This means that if you exchanged €1 for dollars, you would get $1·25 for it.

2. Which is worth more: €1 or US $1? Explain.

> The **€/£** exchange rate is 0·78. This means that if you exchanged €1 for sterling, you would get £0·78 for it.

3. Which is worth more: €1 or £1? Explain.

4. List the 8 currencies from the table in order of the value of 1 unit of each currency. Start with the unit of highest value.

Converting currencies using foreign exchange rates.

> To convert euro to other currencies, we multiply.
>
> Convert €20 to US $
>
> €20 × 1·25 = US $25

> To convert other currencies to euro, we divide.
>
> Convert Kr200 to Euro
>
> Kr200 ÷ 7·44 = €26·88

5. Convert these amounts using your calculator.

   (a) €50 → US $
   (b) R100 → €
   (c) €10 → ¥
   (d) £100 → €
   (e) ¥3,510 → €
   (f) €49·50 → CHF
   (g) AUD $200 → €
   (h) €99 → Kr

6. Trip around the world.
   Robert and Sasha have been travelling around the world. Find the **euro** cost of the following:
   Each cost is for two adults.

   (a) Statue of Liberty tour US $15·50
   (b) Ice hockey game Kr 1,488
   (c) Hollywood tour US $21
   (d) Sushi restaurant ¥7,150
   (e) Sydney Opera House concert AUD $55
   (f) Great Barrier Reef scuba dive AUD $145
   (g) Safari R5,140
   (h) Ski pass CHF149·99
   (i) Legoland resort Kr125·50
   (j) London Eye £19·00
   (k) Football match £85·98
   (l) Table Mountain R2,088

7. Robert and Sasha brought these amounts of foreign currency home.
   How much are they worth in **€**?

   (a) ¥4,219
   (b) US $2·21
   (c) CHF 24·53
   (d) AUD $9·45
   (e) Kr 8·95
   (f) R20
   (g) £0·59

Money – Household budget and bank accounts

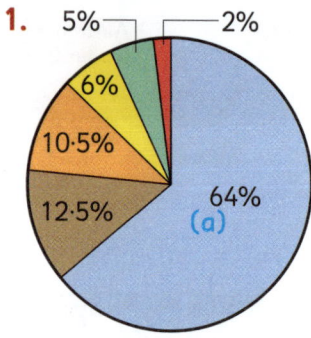

1. 5%—⌐ ⌐—2%

6%

10·5%

12·5%

64%
(a)

The Kenny family's bills for January are shown on this pie chart. If all the bills added up to €1,750, work out how much they spent on each. They are colour coded.

(a) **Mortgage** € _____   (b) **Electricity** € _____

(c) **Gas** € _____   (d) **Annual bin charges** € _____

(e) **Television and Broadband** € _____

(f) **Phone** € _____

2. Using the information above, fill the following transactions into the Kenny's household account. All spending transactions were paid for by debit card.

	Date	Details	Amount	Balance
	1st Jan	Opening Balance		– €450·00
Jan 3rd: Ms Kenny lodged her salary of €1,145·50; paid the gas bill; paid the phone bill.	3rd Jan	Salary Gas bill Phone bill	+ €1,145·50	+ €695·50
Jan 5th: Mr Kenny lodged US $120 left over from a holiday at a €/US $ exchange rate of 1·25 and paid the television and broadband bill.	5th Jan			
Jan 9th: Made mortgage repayment; paid electricity bill and annual bin charges. (See **Q1.** above)	9th Jan			
Jan 11th: Bought a new fridge, normally €234, at a discount of $12\frac{1}{2}$%.	11th Jan			
Jan 12th: Mr Kenny's salary of €1,100 lodged; paid butcher for a 1·5kg chicken at €5·98 per kg; spent €147·95 at the supermarket.	12th Jan			
Jan 14th: Ms Kenny lodged salary of €1,095; spent €96 in a restaurant plus a tip of $12\frac{1}{2}$%.	14th Jan			
Jan 16th: Bought a games console for the children costing €199 before VAT at 23%.	16th Jan			
Jan 20th: Repaid loan to *Everything Electric* for a €250 washing machine plus 6% interest for one year; took out €350 cash.	20th Jan			
Jan 26th: Paid house insurance for a full year. Got a deal on the €360 bill whereby they only had to pay for 11 months instead of 12.	26th Jan			

Money

1. School tour

Work out the cost of this tour for 32 children and 2 teachers.

(a) Bus: €3 per child, €5 per adult.

(b) Entry to zoo: Adult €5·00, child €4·00.
10% discount for groups over 20.

(c) Lunch: €5·35 per person, service charge 10%.

(d) Adventure park: €1·50 per go. Teachers arranged a deal where each person (including teachers) got five 'goes' for the price of four on the **Big Dipper**.

(e) Total cost of the tour: _____

Gifts 'R' Us

Use your calculator!   Round to 2 decimal places where necessary.

2. (a) The shop imported 60 televisions from Japan costing ¥35,640 each. If the €/¥ exchange rate was 148·50, how much did one television cost in Euro?

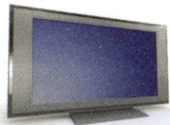

(b) A customer could pay €375 for a television, or get a loan at 6% interest per year. How much would a customer pay in total if she got a loan for 6 months?

3. A box of 200 packets of batteries cost the shop €270. They put them on sale as a special offer of 2 packets for the price of 1. If one packet was on sale for €3·30, what was the overall percentage profit?

4. The shop sold a toy car for €15 and a remote control car for €27·50. They sold 200 cars altogether in the ratio 3:2 (toy cars:remote control cars). How much money did they take in altogether on the sale of the cars?

5. The ratio of skateboards to snowboards sold in a shop over one month was 9:4. If the combined sales were 325, how many of each were sold?

6. Gifts 'R' Us included a 10% profit on each doll's house. They then added VAT at 23% to get the sale price. If the sale price was €184·50, how much did the doll's house cost Gifts 'R' Us?

7. Below are three limited edition comics on sale, including the profit for each one.

€12
(25% profit)

€9
(12½% profit)

€12·96
(33⅓% profit)

(a) What did each comic cost the shop to buy?

(b) If they reduced the price of each comic by 10% during a sale, what would the new price for each comic be?

8. Mary bought three books with list prices of €9·71, €5·47 and €6·93. (i) If she got a discount of $33\frac{1}{3}$% off her total bill, how much did she pay? (ii) The three books cost the shop €4 each. What overall percentage profit did the shopkeeper make?

Challenge There was a $16\frac{2}{3}$% profit made by a jeweller selling earrings at €24 per pair. At what price per pair should they be sold to make a profit of 20%? € _____ (Give answer to the nearest cent.)

Chapter 28: The circle – A quick revision

1. **What part of the circle is represented by each letter?**

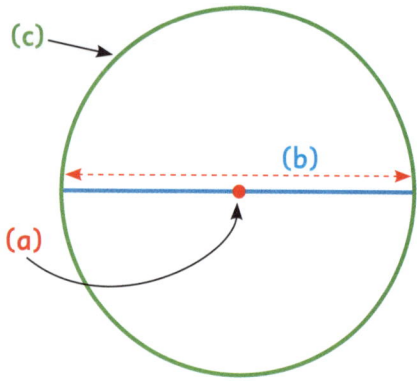

circumference

arc

diameter

centre point

sector

radius

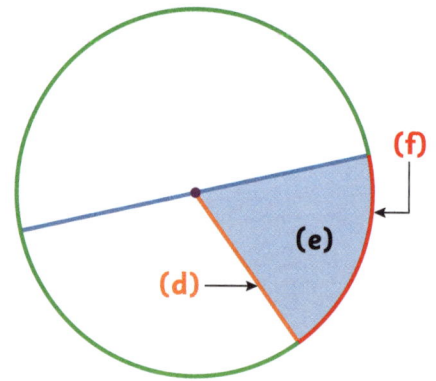

2. (a) What special name is given to the perimeter of a circle?

(b) What is another name for half a diameter?

(c) What is another name for a line of symmetry on a circle?

3. **Measure each line on this circle.**

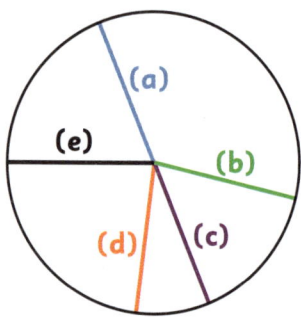

(a) What is the length of each line?

(b) What part of the circle is each line?

(c) What do the radii of a circle have in common?

4. **List all the co-ordinates marked on (i) the blue circle and (ii) the orange circle.**

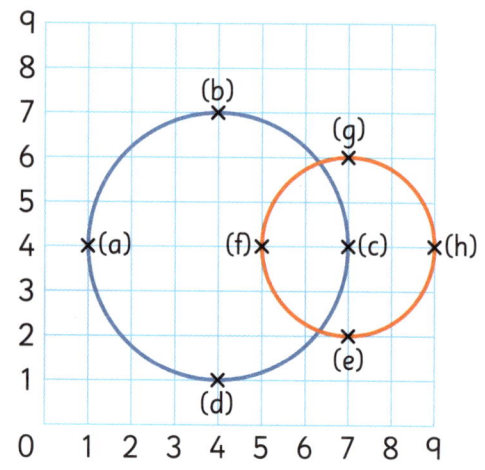

5. **Complete this grid.**

circle	radius	diameter
A	3cm	
B		24cm
C		63cm
D	17·2cm	
E		65·2cm
F	14·32cm	

6. **Use your protractor to measure the angle of each sector.**

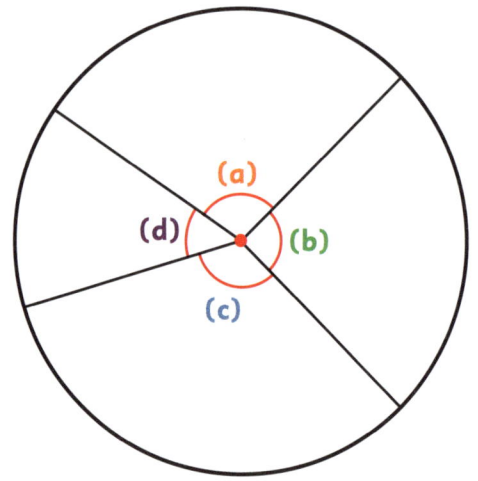

STRAND **Shape and space**   STRAND UNIT/ELEMENT *2-D shapes*

LANGUAGE *Circle, circumference, radius, radii, diameter, centre, sector, arc lines, co-ordinates*

The circle – Drawing circles

Draw a circle with a radius of 4cm.

Step 1	Step 2	Step 3
Stretch your compass to 4cm.	Mark a centrepoint.	Swivel compass around.
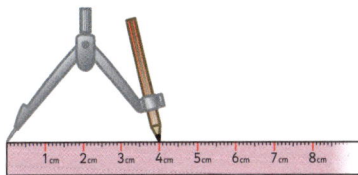	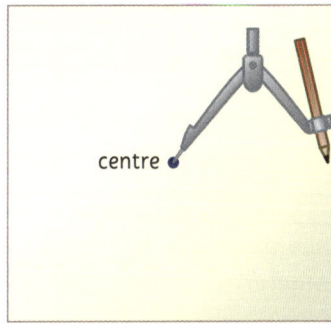	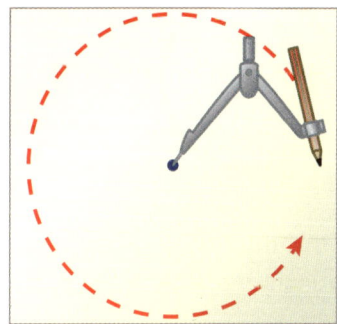

1. Construct circles that have a **radius** of:

   (a) 3cm   (b) $2\frac{1}{2}$cm   (c) 6cm

   (d) $6\frac{1}{2}$cm   (e) 2cm   (f) 1cm

   (g) 1·6cm   (h) 3·9cm   (i) $4\frac{4}{5}$cm

2. Construct circles that have a **diameter** of:

   (a) 10cm   (b) 5cm   (c) 7cm

   (d) 9cm   (e) 3cm   (f) 11cm

   (g) 6·2cm   (h) 4·8cm   (i) 8·6cm

3. Using the same centrepoint each time, draw circles with the following **radii**:

   (a) 2cm   (b) 3cm   (c) 4cm

4. (i) Draw a circle of **radius** 6cm.

   (ii) Label the following parts of the circle:

   (a) circumference (b) radius (c) diameter

   (d) centrepoint (e) sector (f) arc.

5. Three hula hoops, each with a radius of 39cm, were placed on a gym mat. (Measurement is from the centre to the **outside** of each hoop).

   (a) Calculate the length of the mat.

   (b) Calculate the width of the mat.

   (c) What is the surface area of the mat?

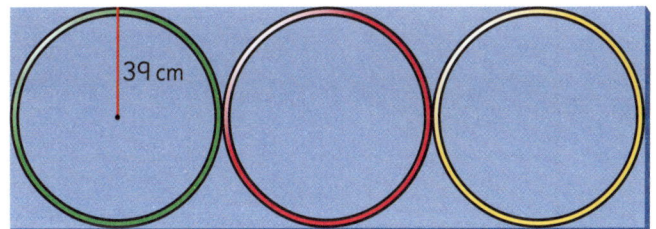

Challenge   Draw these designs into your copybook. Start each by drawing the square.

A

B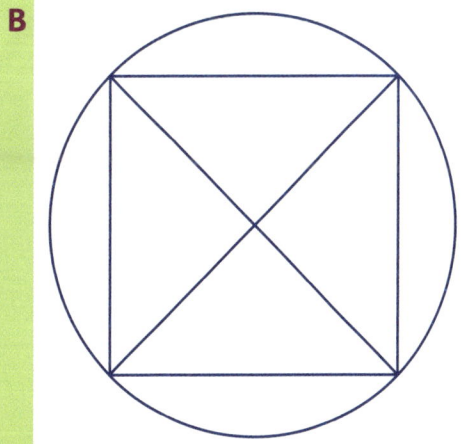

The diagonals will give you the centrepoint.

The circle – Measuring the circumference

Step 1: Using string, measure the circumference of a paper plate.

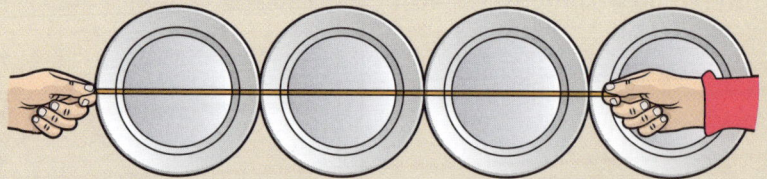

Step 2: Unravel the measured piece of string and stretch it across four such paper plates.

Findings: The circumference of a circle measures a little more than three times the diameter.

Rule: circumference = diameter × 3·14

1. Calculate the **circumference** of the following circles. Use the rule!

(a) 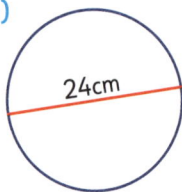 24cm

(b) 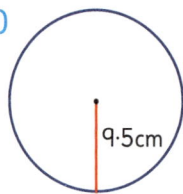 9·5cm

(c) 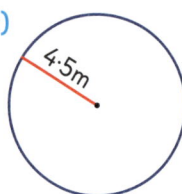 4·5m

(d) 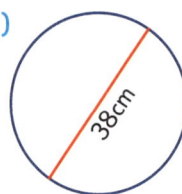 38cm

(e) 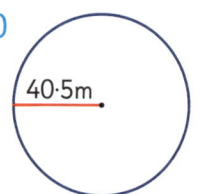 40·5m

2. Complete the following grids.

	radius	diameter	circumference
(a)	7cm		
(b)		18cm	
(c)	4·5cm		
(d)		46cm	

	radius	diameter	circumference
(e)	35·5cm		
(f)		56cm	
(g)			15·7m
(h)			26·69m

3. Calculate the **perimeter** of each of the following:

Remember: a semi-circle is half of a circle!

(a) 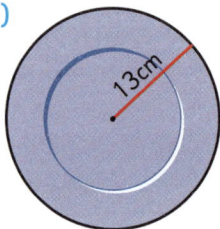 13cm

(b)  WELCOME 64cm

(c) 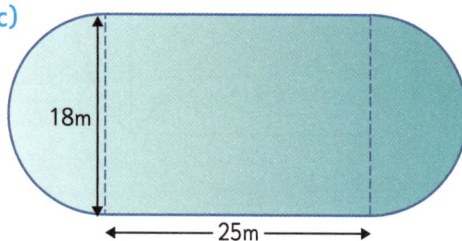 18m 25m

(d) 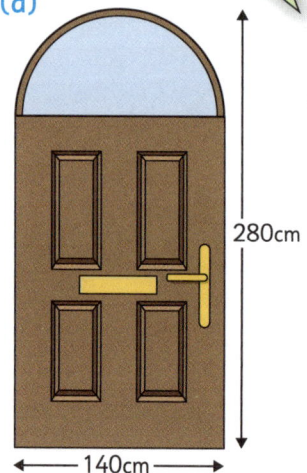 280cm 140cm

The circle – Approximate area

1. Calculate the approximate area of each circle.
   Each square on the grid represents **1cm square** or **1cm²**.

Count all the squares in the circle that are at least half a 1cm² as a full cm².

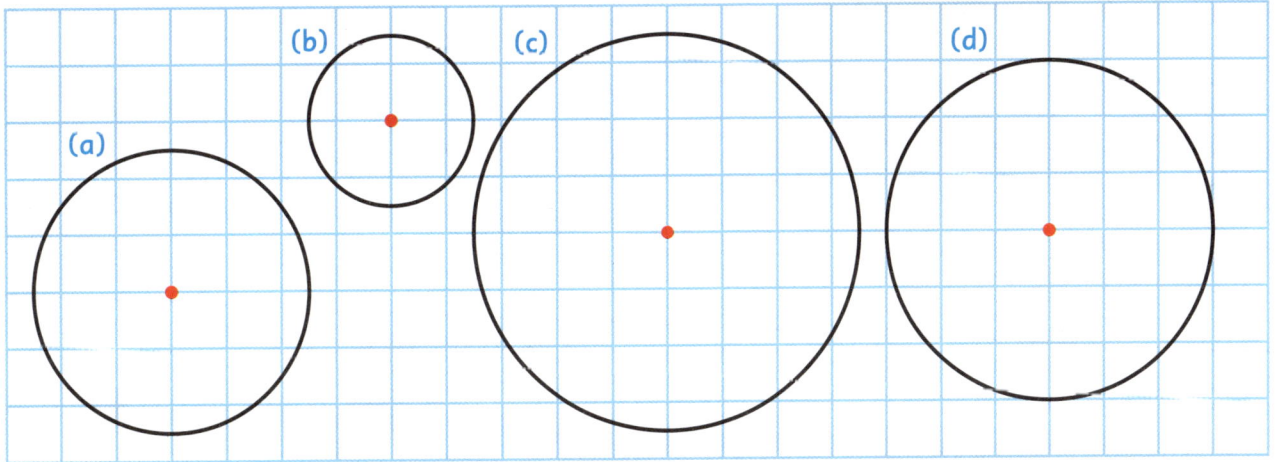

(a) (b) (c) (d)

We can find the approximate area of a circle by drawing a square around it as shown.

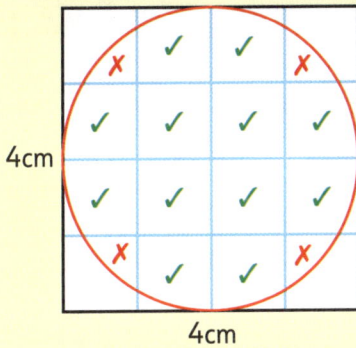

4cm

4cm

(a) Area of square = 16cm²

(b) Approximate area of circle = 12cm²

We can see that the approximate area of this circle is $\frac{3}{4}$ of its own square. → $\frac{12cm^2}{16cm^2} = \frac{3}{4}$

Rule: The area of a circle is approximately $\frac{3}{4}$ of its own square.

2. (i) Calculate the **area** of each square. (ii) Use this information to calculate the approximate area of the circle **inside** each square.

(a)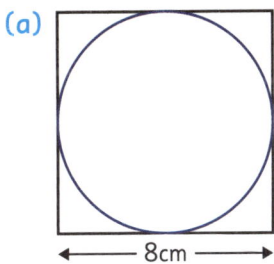
8cm

(b)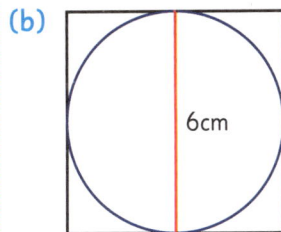
6cm

(c)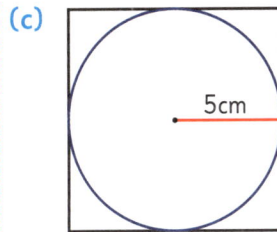
5cm

(d)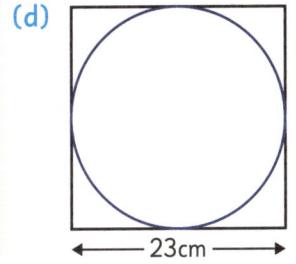
23cm

Hint: Find the area of each circle's own square first.

---

3. Find the approximate area of circles that have **diameters** of:

   (a) 7cm (b) 2cm (c) 11cm (d) 6·4cm (e) 9·6cm (f) 58cm

---

4. Find the approximate area of circles that have **radii** of:

   (a) 4·5cm (b) 10cm (c) 15cm (d) 3·8cm (e) 9·5cm (f) 28cm

---

5. Find the approximate area of the **largest** circle that can be drawn **inside** squares of side:

   (a) 10cm (b) 25cm (c) 36cm (d) 40cm (e) 50cm

   (f) 12m (g) 16m (h) 6·8m (i) 14·6m (j) 18·4m

The circle – Area and circumference

The following wheels are on display in *The Wheel Outlet*. Each display wheel is mounted on a square shaped piece of wood as shown.

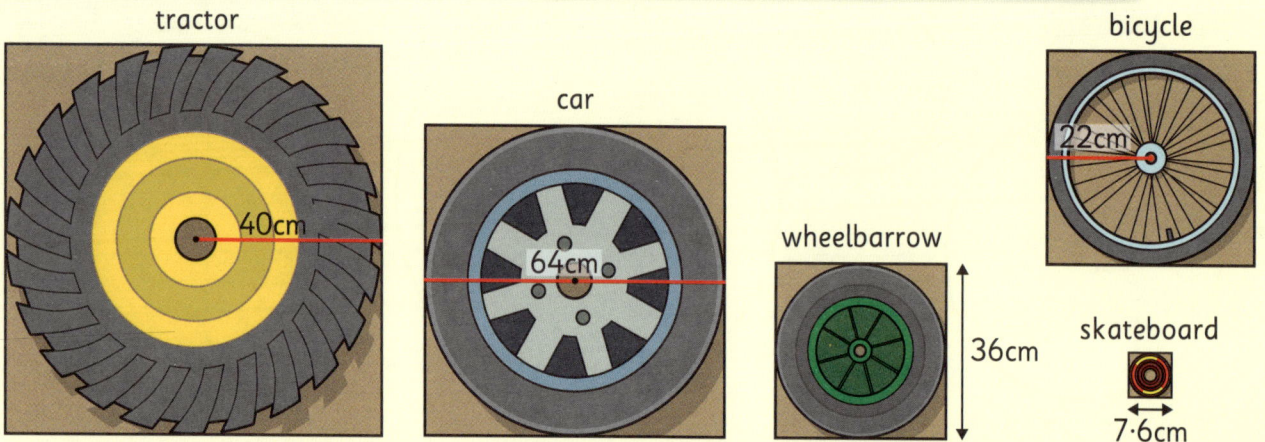

tractor

40cm

car

64cm

wheelbarrow

36cm

bicycle

22cm

skateboard

7·6cm

1. Copy and complete this grid.

Wheel	Circumference	Area of wooden mount	Approx. area of wheel
(a) car			
(b) tractor			
(c) wheelbarrow			
(d) bicycle			
(e) skateboard			

2. What distance would the car wheel travel in 12 full revolutions? (Answer in metres rounded to two decimal places). _____

3. What distance will a tractor wheel travel in 15 full revolutions? _____

4. A wheelbarrow wheel and a skateboard wheel both rolled for 23 full revolutions. How much further did the wheelbarrow wheel travel? _____

5. What is the total approximate area of 16 such bicycle wheels? _____

Challenge

Six wheelbarrow wheels were placed on a piece of board (as in diagram).

(a) Calculate the area of the board. _____

(b) Approximately what area of the board is **not** covered by the wheels? _____

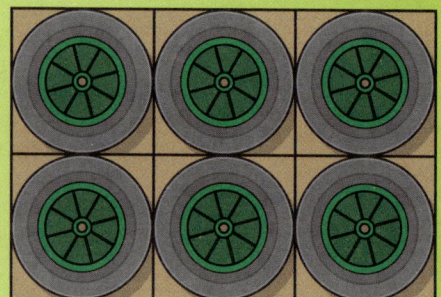

Chapter 29: Rules and properties – Pattern

The Italian mathematician Fibonacci wrote a book, Liber Abaci, in 1202. In this book he describes his now famous number sequence. The rule is that each number is equal to the sum of the preceding two numbers. He always used the first number twice.

1. Write the next **five terms** of his sequence. 1, 1, 2, 3, 5, 8, _____ , _____ , _____ , _____ , _____ .

2. Write the next **three terms** in the following Fibonacci type sequences:
    (a) 2, 2, 4, 6, 10, _____ , _____ , _____ .
    (b) 4, 4, 8, 12, 20, _____ , _____ , _____ .
    (c) 7, 7, 14, 21, 35, _____ , _____ , _____ .
    (d) 9, 9, 18, 27, 45, _____ , _____ , _____ .
    (e) 12, 12, 24, 36, 60, _____ , _____ , _____ .
    (f) 15, 15, 30, 45, 75, _____ , _____ , _____ .

A Fibonacci poem (or Fib) is based on the Fibonacci sequence. The number of **syllables** in each line equals the total number of syllables in the preceding two lines.

Raul, Haiku Painter
His
Words
Flow with
Elegance
To create paintings
On a canvas filled with white light,
Bursting with everlasting imagery of nature
By Lena Townsend

The word imagery is pronounced here as im – age – ry .

3. (a) Write the number of syllables in each line.
    (b) Check that the poem keeps to the Fibonacci sequence.
    (c) Write a Fibonacci poem of your own.
    (d) Ask your partner to check that your poem keeps to the Fibonacci sequence.

The Twelve Days of Christmas

On the first day of Christmas my true love sent to me: A Partridge in a Pear Tree.	On the second day of Christmas my true love sent to me: 2 Turtle Doves and a Partridge in a Pear Tree.	On the third day of Christmas my true love sent to me: 3 French Hens, 2 Turtle Doves and a Partridge in a Pear Tree.	On the fourth day of Christmas my true love sent to me: 4 Calling Birds 3, French Hens, 2 Turtle Doves and a Partridge in a Pear Tree.

4. Now complete the following table for each of the 12 verses of this Christmas carol. They are called **triangular** numbers.

(a)

Day	1	2	3	4	5	6	7	8	9	10	11	12
Number of Gifts	1	3	6	10								
Pattern		+2	+3	+4	+5							

(b) If this pattern continued, how many gifts would have been given by the 13th day?

(c) Now work out how many gifts would have been given by the 20th day.

STRAND **Algebra**   STRAND UNIT/ELEMENT *Rules and properties, Place value, Number theory*
LANGUAGE *Next, first, second, third, fourth, pattern, sequence, Fibonacci, brackets, of, multiply, division, addition, subtraction, rules of operations*

Fun with pattern

D. R. Kaprekar (1905–1986) was an Indian schoolteacher. He loved maths and discovered what has become known as the **Kaprekar number**.

When a number is squared, if the answer can be split into two parts that add up to the original number again, it is a **Kaprekar number**.

Examples:

$9^2 = 81$ and $(8 + 1) = 9$

$999^2 = 998{,}001$ and $(998 + 1) = 999$

$2{,}728^2 = 7{,}441{,}984$ and $(744 + 1{,}984) = 2{,}728$

1. Use your calculator to work out which of the following are **Kaprekar numbers**.

   (a) 45   (b) 50   (c) 55   (d) 78   (e) 99

   (f) 106   (g) 297   (h) 703   (i) 998   (j) 2,223

2. Follow the steps to find an interesting pattern.

   Step 1: Write down a two-digit number. → 46

   Step 2: Reverse the digits of the number. → 64

   Step 3: Subtract the smaller number from the bigger number. 64 − 46 = 18

   Step 4: Now use the answer 18 and start again. → 18

   Step 5: Reverse the digits of the number. → 81

   Step 6: Subtract the smaller number from the bigger number. 81 − 18 = 63

   Step 7: Continue this way until you can't go any further. What do you notice?

   (a) Now try this with another two-digit number and proceed as above.

   (b) Now try this using a three-digit number. You may use a calculator.

3. Write the next 3 terms in the square number sequence: 1, 4, 9, 16, 25, _____, _____, _____.

4. Write the next 3 terms in the prime number sequence: 2, 3, 5, 7, 11, _____, _____, _____.

5. Write the next 3 terms for each of these sequences.

   (a) 3, 6, 9, 12, 15, _____, _____, _____.   (b) 4, 8, 12, 16, 20, _____, _____, _____.

   (c) 5, 10, 15, 20, 25, _____, _____, _____.   (d) 6, 12, 18, 24, 30, _____, _____, _____.

   (e) 7, 14, 21, 28, 35, _____, _____, _____.   (f) 8, 16, 24, 32, 40, _____, _____, _____.

   (g) 9, 18, 27, 36, 45, _____, _____, _____.   (h) 10, 20, 30, 40, 50, _____, _____, _____.

   (i) 11, 22, 33, 44, 55, _____, _____, _____.   (j) 12, 24, 36, 48, 60, _____, _____, _____.

6. Now complete these.

   (a) 55, 52, 49, 46, _____, _____, _____.   (b) 50, 46, 42, 38, _____, _____, _____.

   (c) 69, 63, 57, 51, _____, _____, _____.   (d) 81, 74, 67, 60, _____, _____, _____.

   (e) 93, 84, 75, 66, _____, _____, _____.   (f) 97, 85, 73, 61, _____, _____, _____.

   (g) 225, 210, 195, 180, _____, _____, _____.   (h) 176, 162, 148, 134, _____, _____, _____.

Sequences

Observe the relationship between the numbers in each sequence.

A

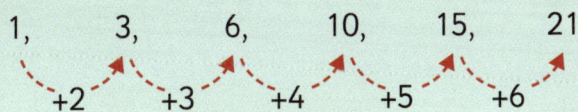

B

Work out the pattern in each sequence. Write the next **4 terms** in each one.

1. (a) 2, 3, 5, 8, 12, ____, ____, ____, ____.

    (b) 4, 6, 10, 16, 24, ____, ____, ____, ____.

    (c) 3, 4, 6, 9, 13, ____, ____, ____, ____.

    (d) 46, 45, 43, 40, 36, ____, ____, ____, ____.

    (e) 78, 76, 72, 66, 58, ____, ____, ____, ____.

    (f) 97, 96, 93, 88, 81, ____, ____, ____, ____.

    (g) 5, 8, 14, 23, 35, ____, ____, ____, ____.

    (h) 7, 11, 19, 31, 47, ____, ____, ____, ____.

2. Write the next **4 terms** in these sequences. You may use your **calculator** to check your answers.

    (a) 2·1, 2·3, 2·5, 2·7, ____, ____, ____, ____.

    (b) 4·3, 4·6, 4·9, 5·2, ____, ____, ____, ____.

    (c) 6·4, 6·9, 7·4, 7·9, ____, ____, ____, ____.

    (d) 8·6, 9·2, 9·8, 10·4, ____, ____, ____, ____.

    (e) 17·2, 18·4, 19·6, 20·8, ____, ____, ____, ____.

    (f) 25·3, 27·9, 30·5, 33·1, ____, ____, ____, ____.

    (g) 42·7, 46·0, 49·3, 52·6, ____, ____, ____, ____.

    (h) 97·2, 92·7, 88·2, 83·7, ____, ____, ____, ____.

3. Now complete these **fraction** sequences by adding 4 terms.

    (a) $\frac{2}{3}, \frac{4}{6}, \frac{8}{12}, \frac{16}{24},$ ____, ____, ____, ____.

    (b) $\frac{1}{4}, \frac{2}{8}, \frac{4}{16}, \frac{8}{32},$ ____, ____, ____, ____.

    (c) $\frac{3}{5}, \frac{6}{10}, \frac{9}{15}, \frac{12}{20},$ ____, ____, ____, ____.

    (d) $\frac{3}{2}, \frac{6}{4}, \frac{9}{6}, \frac{12}{8},$ ____, ____, ____, ____.

    (e) $\frac{9}{10}, \frac{18}{20}, \frac{27}{30}, \frac{36}{40},$ ____, ____, ____, ____.

    (f) $\frac{7}{9}, \frac{14}{18}, \frac{21}{27}, \frac{28}{36},$ ____, ____, ____, ____.

    (g) $\frac{7}{8}, \frac{14}{16}, \frac{21}{24}, \frac{28}{32},$ ____, ____, ____, ____.

    (h) $\frac{6}{11}, \frac{12}{22}, \frac{18}{33}, \frac{24}{44},$ ____, ____, ____, ____.

4. Write the **missing numbers** to complete these sequences.

    (a) 21, 27, 33, ____, 45, ____, 57.

    (b) ____, 44, ____, ____, 56, 60, 64, ____.

    (c) ____, ____, 42, 48, 54, ____, 66.

    (d) 88, 84, ____, 76, ____, 68, ____.

    (e) 131, ____, ____, 119, 115, ____, 107.

    (f) 248, 245, ____, 239, ____, ____, 230.

    (g) 420, 435, ____, ____, 480, 495, ____.

    (h) 573, 564, ____, 546, ____, ____, 519.

    (i) 876, 869, ____, 855, ____, 841.

    (j) 938, 949, ____, 971, ____, 993.

Challenge   Complete these more difficult sequences.

(a) 3, 2, 6, 5, 9, 8, 12, 11, 15, ____, ____, ____, ____.

(b) 7, 13, 9, 15, 11, 17, 13, 19, 15, ____, ____, ____, ____.

(c) 23, 26, 22, 25, 21, 24, 20, 23, 19, ____, ____, ____, ____.

Order of operations

When adding 3 or more numbers, the order of addition doesn't matter.

1. (a) 2 + 6 + 8 = _____
   (b) 6 + 8 + 2 = _____
   (c) 8 + 2 + 6 = _____
   (d) 12 + 9 + 11 = _____
   (e) 11 + 9 + 12 = _____
   (f) 9 + 12 + 11 = _____
   (g) 24 + 25 + 26 = _____
   (h) 25 + 26 + 24 = _____
   (i) 26 + 24 + 25 = _____
   (j) 42 + 12 + 18 = _____
   (k) 18 + 42 + 12 = _____
   (l) 12 + 18 + 42 = _____

When adding and subtracting, I always do the addition first.

18 − 24 + 19 = ☆

→ 18 + 19 − 24

→ 37 − 24 = 13

I always bring the number with the minus sign to the end.

2. Complete the following **addition** and **subtraction** questions.
   (a) 32 + 27 − 16 = _____
   (b) 23 − 16 + 18 = _____
   (c) 26 − 34 + 16 = _____
   (d) 52 − 74 + 28 = _____
   (e) 37 − 68 + 43 = _____
   (f) 71 − 97 + 54 = _____
   (g) 37 − 85 + 78 = _____
   (h) 16 − 39 + 73 = _____
   (i) 63 − 84 + 48 = _____
   (j) 48 + 53 − 64 = _____
   (k) 99 − 57 + 65 = _____
   (l) 81 − 57 + 87 = _____

Teacher asked two children to solve 8 × 6 + 2 = ☆

Which child solved the equation correctly?

Nell

8 × 6 + 2 = ☆

→ 48 + 2 = 50

Niall

8 × 6 + 2 = ☆

→ 8 × 8 = 64

Nell did because we must do multiplication before addition or subtraction.

Complete the following. Remember to do the **multiplication** first.

3. (a) 5 × 6 − 7 = _____
   (b) 7 × 5 + 3 = _____
   (c) 4 × 8 − 5 = _____
   (d) 7 × 8 + 4 = _____
   (e) 9 × 7 + 6 = _____
   (f) 8 × 7 − 9 = _____
   (g) 11 + 9 × 6 = _____
   (h) 78 − 9 × 7 = _____
   (i) 6 × 8 − 5 = _____
   (j) 9 × 5 + 4 = _____
   (k) 13 + 8 × 4 = _____
   (l) 65 + 3 × 9 = _____

Find $\frac{4}{5}$ of 30

$\frac{5}{5}$ = 30

$\frac{1}{5}$ = 6

$\frac{4}{5}$ = 24

When asked to find a fraction of a number, I multiply the fraction by the number because **of** really means **multiply**.

Find $\frac{4}{5}$ of 30

→ $\frac{4}{{}_1 5} \times \frac{{}^6 \cancel{30}}{1}$

= 24

4. Complete the following using the **multiplication** method.
   Find:
   (a) $\frac{3}{4}$ of 28
   (b) $\frac{2}{3}$ of 18
   (c) $\frac{5}{8}$ of 56
   (d) $\frac{7}{9}$ of 72
   (e) $\frac{3}{5}$ of 110
   (f) $\frac{7}{8}$ of 216
   (g) $\frac{5}{9}$ of 315
   (h) $\frac{4}{11}$ of 308
   (i) $\frac{3}{8}$ of 184
   (j) $\frac{4}{5}$ of 345
   (k) $\frac{5}{7}$ of 294
   (l) $\frac{11}{12}$ of 144

More rules

1. (a) $(6 \times 4) + 3 = $ _____

(b) $(18 - 7) - 7 = $ _____

(c) $18 - (4 \times 3) = $ _____

(d) $24 + (4 \times 5) = $ _____

(e) $(36 \div 4) - 8 = $ _____

(f) $32 - (48 \div 6) = $ _____

(g) $(72 \div 8) + 7 = $ _____

(h) $(13 + 17) \div 3 = $ _____

(i) $(48 - 30) \div 3 = $ _____

(j) $(7 \times 4) - (8 \times 2) = $ _____

(k) $(64 \div 8) + (48 \div 6) = $ _____

(l) $(9 \times 8) \div (8 + 4) = $ _____

> Remember! You must always do the part inside the **brackets** first.

Teacher asked the children to solve | $40 \div 4 + 1 = $ ☆

Sam

$40 \div 4 + 1 = $ ☆

→ $10 + 1 = 11$

Suna

$40 \div 4 + 1 = $ ☆

→ $40 \div 5 = 8$

Which child solved the equation correctly? Sam did because we **must** do division before addition or subtraction.

---

2. Complete the following. Remember to do the **division** first.

(a) $42 \div 7 + 6 = $ _____

(b) $32 \div 8 - 3 = $ _____

(c) $56 \div 7 + 4 = $ _____

(d) $88 \div 8 - 5 = $ _____

(e) $9 + 48 \div 6 = $ _____

(f) $12 + 36 \div 6 = $ _____

(g) $17 - 54 \div 9 = $ _____

(h) $18 - 72 \div 12 = $ _____

(i) $23 - 96 \div 12 = $ _____

Here is an easy way to remember the order of operations.

> I use the **BOMDAS** rule to remember the order of operations.

Brackets first	B
Of	O
Multiplication and **D**ivision	MD
Addition and **S**ubtraction	AS

> I remember the rule this way. **B**oats **O**ften **M**ay **D**rift **A**t **S**ea.

> When **×** and **÷** appear together in a question, always start with the **operation** that appears **first**.

3. Now try these.

(a) $7 \times (12 + 9)$

(b) $(81 \div 9) \times 6$

(c) $32 + 32 \div 8$

(d) $80 - 72 \div 8$

(e) $38 - 12 \times 2 + 8$

(f) $48 \div 8 + 3 \times 7$

(g) $7 \times 8 - 42 \div 6$

(h) $72 \div 9 + \frac{3}{4}$ of 24

---

4. Complete the following.

(a) $6 \times 7 + 8$

(b) $47 - 45 \div 5$

(c) $42 \div 6 + 53$

(d) $55 - 4 \times 9$

(e) $23 + 54 \div 9$

(f) $36 \cdot 9 \div 3 \times 8$

(g) $7 \times 4 \div 2$

(h) $108 \div 9 \times 8 \div 2$

(i) $7 \times 6 + 3 \cdot 7$

(j) $12 \cdot 7 + 56 \div 8$

(k) $63 \div 9 \times 7$

(l) $25 \times 4 \div 10$

(m) $48 \cdot 6 \div 9 \times 7$

(n) $2 + 7 \times 6 \times 5$

(o) $43 + 12 \div 3 - 4$

(p) $54 \div 6 + 9 - 12$

Insert the correct operation sign (**+, −, × or ÷**) in the following.

5. Conor invested €700 in shares. On Monday his shares showed a loss of €200. On Tuesday their value was double what they were on Monday. What are his shares worth now?

(€700 ◯ €200) ◯ 2 = € _____

6. Noleen invested €680. Its value was $\frac{1}{4}$ less on Monday. She made a further loss of €80 on Tuesday. How much is her investment worth now?

€680 ◯ 4 ◯ 3 ◯ €80 = € _____

Problem-solving

t-shirt €20
shirt €29
jeans €54
dress €36
coat €48

Write an equation for each of the following. Solve.

1. Jacinta had €28 in her bag. She withdrew €150 from the **CREDIT UNION**. She bought two t-shirts. How much money had she then?

2. Liam had €148. He bought two shirts and a pair of jeans. How much had he left?

3. Killian had €125. He lost €40 on the bus. He then bought a pair of jeans and a t-shirt. How much had he left?

4. Seán had €196. He gave €15 to charity. His uncle gave him €20. He bought a coat and shirt. How much had he left?

5. Anne had €148. She spent $\frac{1}{4}$ of it on a lunch for her friends. She then bought a dress. How much had she left?

6. Terri bought two dresses and a coat. If she had €237 originally, how much money has she now?

7. Dad had €460. He bought two coats and three shirts. He gave the rest to charity. How much did he give to charity?

8. Mam had €580. She bought three t-shirts and four dresses. She returned one dress to the shop the next day. How much money had she left?

9. A lady spent €240 buying t-shirts and €180 buying dresses. How many of each of these items did she buy?

10. A man bought eight shirts and seven coats. He gave the salesman a tip of €15. How much change did he get from €600?

11. A coat was sold at a discount of 20% during a sale. What change did Sofia get from €300 if she bought seven of these coats during the sale?

Challenge Laura has €400 invested in shares. On Wednesday the shares show a profit of $12\frac{1}{2}$%. On Thursday they show a loss of $\frac{1}{5}$ on her **original** investment. What are her shares worth now? € _____

A quick look back 8

1. The perimeter of a rectangle is 60cm. If its width is double its length, what is its area?

   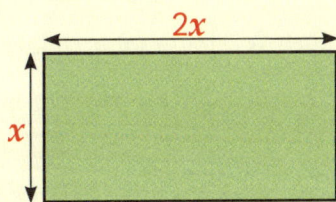

   _____ cm²

2. 0·924 ÷ 0·7 = _____

3. 0·048 × 0·5 = _____

4. By selling a scooter for €72 a dealer made a profit of €20%. How much did the dealer pay for the scooter?

   € _____

5.  A selling price of €36 represents a loss of 25% on the value of the dress. What was the cost price?

   € _____

6. A dealer bought a snowboard for €45 and sold it for €54. What was her percentage profit?

   _____

7. What is the value of the underlined digit?

   2,068,659 _____

8. What is 80% of 3,000? _____

9. A tennis racquet that was normally sold for €40, was reduced in price by $37\frac{1}{2}$%. What was the new price?

   € _____

10.  The temperature in New York was +34°C one day. It was ⁻18°C in Antarctica. By how many degrees was New York warmer than Antarctica? _____

11.  A carton of 6 eggs costs €1·80. How much would two dozen eggs cost?

    € _____

12. A kilogramme of rashers costs €7·00. How much should 800 grammes cost?

    € _____

13. A set of headphones cost €10 plus VAT @ 23%. What was the total cost?

    € _____

14. VAT for hotel bills is charged @ 13%. The hotel bill for a family was €500 before VAT. What was the total cost?

    € _____

15. Bonnie borrowed €600 for a year. She was charged interest at 7% per year. How much did she have to pay back in total?

    € _____

16. A euro is worth US $1·25. How many dollars should a person get for €800.

    US $ _____

17. 8 × 6 − (5 × 4) + 17 = _____

18. 39 ÷ 3 × 5 − 15 = _____

19. $\frac{5}{9} \times \frac{12}{25} = \frac{\Box}{\Box}$ when simplified.

20. A circle has the same shape as a pizza. A pizza was cut into 8 equal slices. How many degrees were in the angle of each slice?

    _____

Chapter 30: Data 3 – Pie charts

Hair Colours

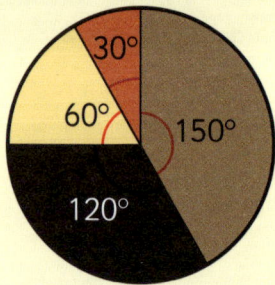

There are 36 children in the class. How many children have brown hair?

Step 1: Work out what fraction of the children have brown hair.

$$\frac{150°}{360°} = \frac{5}{12}$$

Always break it down to its simplest fraction.

Step 2: Calculate $\frac{5}{12}$ of 36 children.

$\frac{1}{12} = 3$ children $\longrightarrow$ $\frac{5}{12} = 15$ children

---

1. Complete this grid.

	colour	degrees	fraction	number of children
(a)	brown	150°	$\frac{5}{12}$	15
(b)	black			
(c)	blonde			
(d)	red			

Now complete the following grids.

2. **78 children** were surveyed about birthdays.

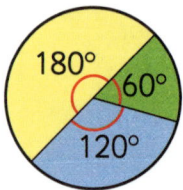

Best thing about birthdays
- ▨ presents
- ▨ cake
- ▨ party

		degrees	fraction	votes
(a)	presents			
(b)	cake			
(c)	party			

3. **104 children** were surveyed about fruit juice.

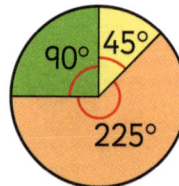

Favourite fruit juice
- ▨ pineapple
- ▨ apple
- ▨ orange

	fruit juice	degrees	fraction	votes
(a)	pineapple			
(b)	orange			
(c)	apple			

4. **120 children** were surveyed about dinners.

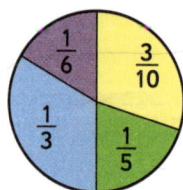

Favourite dinner
- ▨ roast chicken
- ▨ spaghetti bolognese
- ▨ lasagne
- ▨ curry

	dinner	degrees	fraction	votes
(a)	roast chicken			
(b)	spaghetti bolognese			
(c)	lasagne			
(d)	curry			

5. **144 children** were surveyed about family outings.

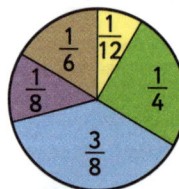

Favourite family outing
- ▨ bowling
- ▨ cinema
- ▨ visiting relatives
- ▨ shopping
- ▨ beach

	activity	degrees	fraction	votes
(a)	bowling			
(b)	shopping			
(c)	cinema			
(d)	beach			
(e)	visting relatives			

STRAND **Data**   STRAND UNIT/ELEMENT *Representing and interpreting data*
LANGUAGE *Fraction, degrees, votes, survey, circle, fraction, total, percentages, calculate, recorded, table, multiple, average, above, below*

Data 3 – Pie charts

Let's look at how we constructed the pie chart for favourite family outings on page 158.

Step 1: We calculated the degrees for each sector.

Step 2: Using a compass, we drew a circle.

Step 3: We drew a radius. This became the starting point for the first angle (sector).

Step 4: We drew each sector using the protractor.

Step 5: We created a colour key.

Step 6: We gave the pie chart a title.

Step 1:

	activity	degrees	fraction	votes
(a)	bowling	30°	$\frac{1}{12}$	12
(b)	shopping	90°	$\frac{1}{4}$	36
(c)	cinema	135°	$\frac{3}{8}$	54
(d)	beach	45°	$\frac{1}{8}$	18
(e)	visiting relatives	60°	$\frac{1}{6}$	24

Steps 2–6:

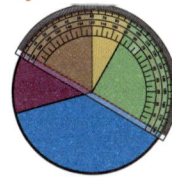

Favourite family outings
- bowling
- shopping
- cinema
- beach
- visiting relatives

1. **80 children** were asked what foreign language they would like to learn in secondary school. The votes are recorded on the table below.

   (a) Copy and complete the table.

   To begin, work out what fraction of 80 each language got. Then calculate the number of degrees!

   s'il vous plait!   Nín hǎo!   au revoir!   merci!   Hola!   Bonjour!

	language	degrees	fraction	votes
(i)	French			16
(ii)	German			24
(iii)	Spanish			32
(iv)	Chinese			8

   (b) Represent the information on a pie chart. Follow the steps carefully.

   (c) What percentage of children voted for each language?

   (d) How many more degrees are there in the largest sector than in the smallest?

Challenge The following grid shows the eye colours of a group of **72 children**.

(i) Copy and complete the information from this grid.

colour	blue	brown	green	hazel	grey
number of children			6		
fraction	$\frac{3}{8}$				$\frac{1}{12}$
degrees		120°		45°	

(ii) Represent the information on a pie chart.

Data 3 – Revision

Two new books went on sale in *Murphy's Bookstore* last Tuesday. The following table shows the sales of each book over the first five days.

	Tues	Wed	Thurs	Fri	Sat
Percy Panda	10	20	15	30	45
Poems for Peace	45	27	18	9	9

1. **(a)** Copy and complete this multiple bar chart in your copybook to represent the above data.

(b) How many copies of
(i) **Percy Panda** and
(ii) **Poems for Peace** were sold?

(c) Calculate the average number of copies of **Percy Panda** sold per day.

(d) On which days were sales of **Percy Panda** above average?

(e) Calculate the average number of **Poems for Peace** books sold per day. Your answer will not be a whole number!

(f) On which days were sales of **Poems for Peace** below average?

(g) Calculate the average number of new books sold on Saturday.

■ Percy Panda
■ Poems for Peace

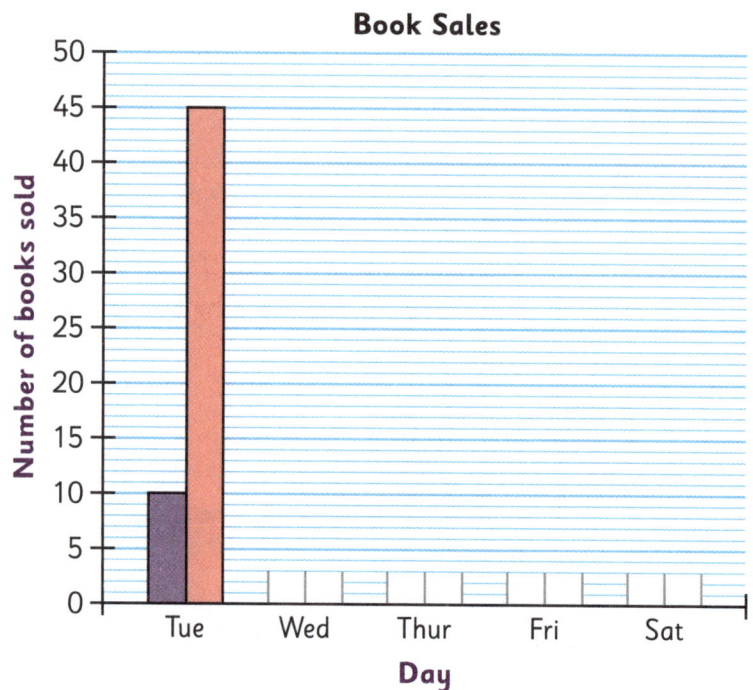

Book Sales

Number of books sold (y-axis: 0, 5, 10, 15, 20, 25, 30, 35, 40, 45, 50)

Day (x-axis: Tue, Wed, Thur, Fri, Sat)

2. **(a)** Copy and complete the tables below for sales of **Percy Panda** and **Poems for Peace**. The degrees are calculated on sectors of a pie chart. Use the figures from the multiple bar chart.

(i) Percy Panda

	Tues	Wed	Thurs	Fri	Sat
fraction					
degrees					
sales	10	20	15	30	45

(ii) Poems for Peace

	Tues	Wed	Thurs	Fri	Sat
fraction					
degrees					
sales	45	27	18	9	9

(b) Draw two separate pie charts to represent this data.

Data 3 – Revision

3. (a) Copy and complete these **trend graphs** to show the sales of both books over the five days.

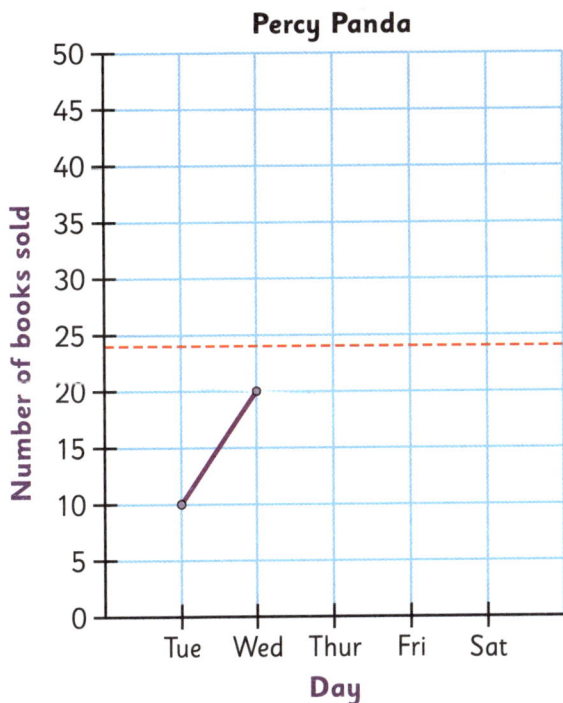

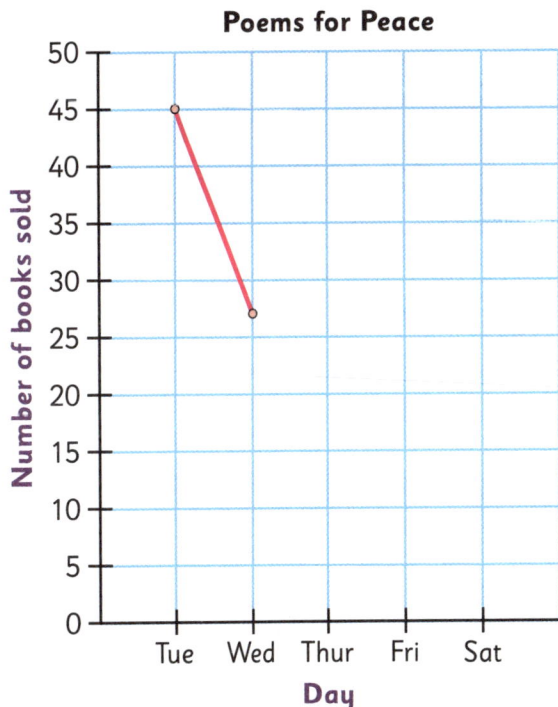

Percy Panda

Number of books sold (y-axis: 0, 5, 10, 15, 20, 25, 30, 35, 40, 45, 50)
Day (x-axis: Tue, Wed, Thur, Fri, Sat)

Poems for Peace

Number of books sold (y-axis: 0, 5, 10, 15, 20, 25, 30, 35, 40, 45, 50)
Day (x-axis: Tue, Wed, Thur, Fri, Sat)

(b) On which days did sales of **Percy Panda** increase over the previous day?

(c) Which day showed a decrease in sales of **Percy Panda**?

(d) On which days did **Poems for Peace** show a decrease over the previous day?

(e) From looking at the trend, is **Poems for Peace** getting more or less popular as the days go on?

(f) On the following Sunday morning, there are 28 copies of **Percy Panda** in stock. Do you think this will be enough to meet demand? Explain.

(g) Look at the dotted line on the **Percy Panda** trend graph. What does it represent? Explain.

(h) Draw a red dotted line on the **Poems for Peace** trend graph to show the average sales. (Round the answer to the nearest whole number).

4.

Percy Panda
cost price = €10·56
selling price = €14·08

POEMS for PEACE
cost price = €6·25
selling price = €7·50

(a) How much profit does the bookshop make on each copy of (i) **Percy Panda** and (ii) **Poems for Peace**?

(b) How much profit did the shop make on sales of **Poems for Peace** over the five days?

(c) How much profit did the shop make on both books on Thursday?

Challenge What percentage profit does the shop make on each copy of

(i) **Percy Panda** [ ] and (ii) **Poems for Peace**? [ ]

Chapter 31: Weight – Using the correct measure

Here are some of the most common weighing instruments we use.

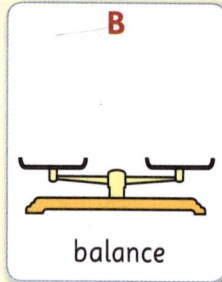

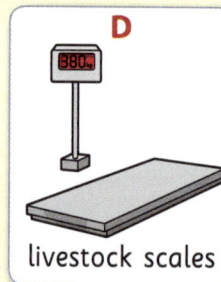

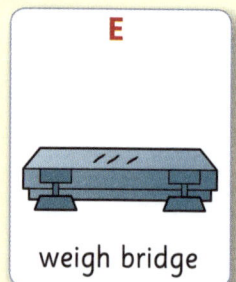

A	B	C	D	E
kitchen scales	balance	spring balance	livestock scales	weigh bridge

1. **Which of the above scales would you use to weigh each of these items?**

   (a) a family suitcase _____

   (b) a turkey _____

   (c) a car transporter _____

   (d) a small truck of logs _____

   (e) a box of crayons _____

   (f) a horse _____

   (g) a bowl of rice _____

   (h) a kitten _____

   (i) a pineapple _____

2. **Write two other items you would measure with each of the above weighing instruments.**

   Each of these items weighs about 1 gramme.

   (a) paperclip

   (b) a pinch of salt

   (c) a €5 note

   Each of these items weighs about 1kg.

   (a) a litre of water

   (b) 6 apples

   (c) $1\frac{1}{2}$ loaves of bread

   Remember:

   $1g = \frac{1}{1000}kg = 0.001kg$

   $1kg = \frac{1}{1000}$ tonnes $= 0.001$ tonnes

   $1,000kg = 1$ tonne (1t)

   $1,600kg = 1.6$ tonnes (1·6t)

   A small family car weighs approximately 1·3 tonnes.

   An adult giraffe weighs about 1·2 tonnes.

3. **Give your best estimate in grammes (g), kilogrammes (kg), or tonnes (t) for each of these.**

   (a) Average newborn baby _____

   (b) An adult whale _____

   (c) Standard concrete block _____

   (d) An average adult _____

   (e) An African elephant _____

   (f) Regular jar of coffee _____

Maths Fact   825 tonnes of coal were used to fire the ship's engines every day the Titanic sailed.

Challenge   The Titanic sank four days into its voyage. How many tonnes of coal would have been used, if it had completed the usual eight-day crossing? _____

STRAND **Measures**   STRAND UNIT/ELEMENT *Weight*

LANGUAGE *Weigh, weight, measure, estimate, scales, balance, gramme (g), kilogramme (kg), litre, recipe, cost, heaviest, lightest, sold, unsold, dozen*

Weight – Rename measures in weight

> Paula is baking and wishes to convert 1,430g to kg.
> 1,430g = 1·430kg

> 1,000g = 1kg
> 1kg = 1,000g

> $1,400g = \frac{1400}{1000}kg = 1·4kg$
> $1,430g = \frac{1430}{1000}kg = 1·43kg$

Write these gramme weights as kilogrammes (kg) using the decimal point.

1. (a) 1,650g = _____ (b) 1,800g = _____ (c) 2,370g = _____ (d) 5,075g = _____ (e) 3,005g = _____

2. (a) 4,450g = _____ (b) 445g = _____ (c) 45g = _____ (d) 5g = _____ (e) 700g = _____

Write these kilogramme weights as grammes.

3. (a) 3kg 625g = _____ (b) 5kg 700g = _____ (c) 1kg 85g _____ (d) 2kg 60g = _____

4. (a) $3\frac{1}{4}kg$ = _____ (b) $6\frac{7}{10}kg$ = _____ (c) $2\frac{3}{100}kg$ = _____ (d) $3\frac{375}{1000}kg$ = _____

> Christy took a delivery of 2,375kg of concrete for a building job. How much is this in tonnes?

> 1,000kg = 1 tonne
> 1 tonne = 1,000kg

> $2,300kg = \frac{2300}{1000}t = 2·3t$
> $2,375kg = \frac{2375}{1000}t = 2·375t$

Convert these weights to tonnes using the decimal point.

5. (a) 1,470kg = _____ t (b) 2,260kg = _____ t (c) 1,700kg = _____ t (d) 3,025kg = _____ t

6. (a) 770kg = _____ t (b) 95kg = _____ t (c) 8kg = _____ t (d) 300kg = _____ t

7. (a) 1t 840kg = _____ t (b) 5t 300kg = _____ t (c) 6t 90kg = _____ t (d) 3t 8kg = _____ t

8. (a) $5\frac{9}{10}t$ = _____ t (b) $3\frac{3}{4}t$ = _____ t (c) $6\frac{3}{5}t$ = _____ t (d) $4\frac{57}{100}t$ = _____ t

> Frances knows that 125g can also be written as a fraction of a kg. Help her write it in its lowest terms.

> $125g = \frac{125}{1000}kg$

> $\frac{125}{1000} \rightarrow \frac{25}{200} \rightarrow \frac{5}{40} = \frac{1}{8}$

Convert these weights to fractions of kilogrammes or tonnes in their lowest terms.

9. (a) 750g = _____ kg (b) 600g = _____ kg (c) 375g = _____ kg (d) 900g = _____ kg

10. (a) 700kg = _____ t (b) 0·4t = _____ t (c) 650kg = _____ t (d) 0·36t = _____ t

11. (a) 6kg = _____ t (b) 50kg = _____ t (c) 0·65t = _____ t (d) 0·15t = _____ t

12. (a) 510kg = _____ t (b) 875kg = _____ t (c) 175kg = _____ t (d) 75kg = _____ t

> **Maths Fact** A blue whale's diet consists of a daily intake of about 3,600kg of krill.

> **Challenge** Convert the Maths Fact figure of 3,600kg to tonnes using (a) the decimal point and (b) as tonnes and a fraction of a tonne in its lowest terms.

Weight – Addition, subtraction, multiplication and division

1. (a) $4 \cdot 937 \text{kg} \times 8$ (b) $7 \cdot 256 \text{kg} \times 17$ (c) $9 \cdot 036 \text{kg} \times 35$ (d) $9 \cdot 608 \text{kg} \times 7 \cdot 3$ (e) $45 \cdot 2 \text{kg} \times 6 \cdot 8$

2. (a) $7 \overline{)3 \cdot 696t}$ (b) $8 \overline{)3 \cdot 08t}$ (c) $16 \overline{)4 \cdot 416t}$ (d) $39 \overline{)6 \cdot 357t}$ (e) $27 \overline{)77 \cdot 49t}$

Do the following. Remember to complete the part inside the brackets first.

3. (a) $(5279g + 3 \cdot 714 \text{kg}) \times 6 = $ _____

    (b) $(7126g - 2 \cdot 338 \text{kg}) \times 7 = $ _____

    (c) $(6\frac{256}{1000}\text{kg} \times 9\frac{1}{4}\text{kg}) \times 8 = $ _____

    (d) $(9 \cdot 03 \text{kg} - 933g) \div 3 = $ _____

    (e) $(83 \cdot 228 \text{kg} - 6\frac{988}{1000}\text{kg}) \div 16 = $ _____

    (f) $(6\frac{1}{4}t + 3 \cdot 098t) \div 38 = $ _____

4. (i) Write each of these groups of weights in order, starting with the **smallest**.

   (ii) Subtract the **smallest** from the **largest** number in each case.

   (a) $5,500 \text{kg}$, $5\frac{2}{5}\text{kg}$, $5 \cdot 273 \text{kg}$

   (b) $1,186g$, $1 \cdot 45 \text{kg}$, $1 \text{kg } 279g$

   (c) $6,003g$, $6 \cdot 03 \text{kg}$, $603g$

   (d) $7\frac{72}{100}\text{kg}$, $7,127g$, $7\frac{3}{8}\text{kg}$

   (e) $876g$, $\frac{3}{4}\text{kg}$, $0 \cdot 867 \text{kg}$

   (f) $4\frac{5}{8}\text{kg}$, $4,650g$, $4\frac{3}{5}\text{kg}$

5. Rachel and Jamie are both using this recipe to make their Christmas puddings.

   (a) Rachel follows the recipe. What will be the total weight of the ingredients she uses?

   (b) Jamie leaves out the cherries but doubles the amount of cinnamon. What total weight of ingredients will he use?

   (c) Rachel makes another pudding with 30g less flour but decides to add another egg. What is the total weight of her ingredients for this pudding?

   (d) Jamie sticks to the recipe and makes 27 puddings for a cake sale. What is the total weight of the ingredients?

   (e) If Jamie made another pudding using $\frac{1}{5}$ less flour but twice as much cherries and eggs, what would be the total weight of his pudding?

   (f) Rachel and Jamie both used the quick Christmas pudding recipe and donated a dozen puddings **each** to charity. What was the total weight of the ingredients that they used?

QUICK CHRISTMAS PUDDING

80g of self-raising flour

13·5g of brown sugar

$\frac{1}{8}$kg of margarine

0·005kg of cinnamon

$\frac{1}{10}$kg of cherries

0·175kg of breadcrumbs

2 eggs (75g each)

Maths Fact A newborn giant panda weighs about 85 grammes. This is about 0·2% of its mother's weight.

Challenge Convert the newborn panda's weight to kg. What should be the weight of 24 newborn pandas? _____ kg

Weight

A local store has opened a new deli section. Study the price list. Work out the cost per kilogramme (kg) for each item.

150g of kidney beans cost 39c

150g = 39c
50g = 13c   ← (39c ÷ 3)
100g = 26c   ← (13c × 2)
1,000g (1kg) = €2·60 ← (26c × 10)

150g Red Kidney Beans in water

DELI PRICE LIST

Kidney beans: 39c for 150g
Jalapeno peppers: €1·25 for 500g
Wild mushrooms: €3·30 for 200g
Green chillies: €3·21 for 300g
Stuffed olives: 60c for 125g
Sun-dried tomatoes: €1·89 for 350g
Red peppers: €3·51 for 450g

1. What is the cost per **kg** of each of the following:

(a) Jalapeno peppers _____
(b) Wild mushrooms _____
(c) Green chillies _____
(d) Stuffed olives _____
(e) Sun-dried tomatoes _____
(f) Red peppers _____

2. Work out the total cost for the produce in each basket.

Item	A	B	C	D	E
Kidney beans	450g		600g	500g	
Jalapeno peppers		700g	900g	$1\frac{1}{2}$kg	
Wild mushrooms	500g	300g			800g
Green chillies		800g	700g	200g	
Stuffed olives	375g			625g	875g
Sun-dried tomatoes		450g			550g
Red peppers	1kg		550g		1·2kg
Total cost	€_____	€_____	€_____	€_____	€_____

3. Write the following **kg** weights as **grammes** (g).

(a) $\frac{1}{8}$kg = _____ g
(b) $1\frac{1}{4}$kg = _____ g
(c) 0·625kg = _____ g
(d) 0·35kg = _____ g
(e) 2·45kg = _____ g
(f) 1·15kg = _____ g

4. (a) $\frac{1}{10}$ of 2kg = _____ g
(b) $\frac{3}{10}$ of 5kg = _____ g
(c) $\frac{1}{5}$ of 4kg = _____ g
(d) $\frac{7}{10}$ of 3kg = _____ g
(e) $\frac{3}{5}$ of 2kg = _____ g
(f) $\frac{7}{8}$ of 4kg = _____ g
(g) $1\frac{3}{8}$ of 6kg = _____ g
(h) $1\frac{1}{8}$ of 12kg = _____ g
(i) $\frac{4}{5}$ of 11kg = _____ g

Maths Fact   10 tonnes of rock are needed to extract 30g of platinum. Platinum is a precious metal rarer than gold.

Challenge   At this rate, how many tonnes of rock would be required to produce 3kg of platinum? ☐

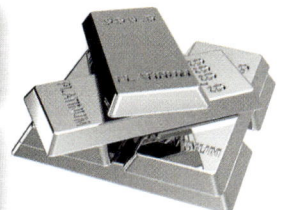

Weight – Weight of Euro coins

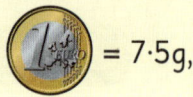

2 = 8·5g,	1 = 7·5g,	50 = 7·8g,	20 = 5·7g,	10 = 4·1g

1. Complete these tables by calculating the **missing weights** for each one.

(a)

	Value	Coin	Weight
(i)	€10	2 × 5	42·5g
(ii)	€10	1 × 10	75g
(iii)	€10	50 × 20	
(iv)	€10	20 × 50	
(v)	€10	10 × 100	410g

(b)

	Value	Coin	Weight
(i)	€50	2 × 25	
(ii)	€40	1 × 40	
(iii)	€20	50 × 40	312g
(iv)	€12	20 × 60	
(v)	€15	10 × 150	615g

(c)

	Value	Coin	Weight
(i)	€100	2 × 50	
(ii)	€73	1 × 73	
(iii)	€39	50 × 78	
(iv)	€6·80	20 × 34	
(v)	€7·40	10 × 74	303·4g

2. These tables show the total weight of the coins used. Find the value of the coins in €.

(a)

	Weight	Coin	Value
(i)	204g	2	
(ii)	484·5g	2	€114
(iii)	561g	2	
(iv)	365·5g	2	
(v)	144·5g	2	

(b)

	Weight	Coin	Value
(i)	202·5g	1	
(ii)	435g	1	
(iii)	1·02kg	1	
(iv)	304·2g	50	
(v)	302·1g	20	

(c)

	Weight	Coin	Value
(i)	561·7g	10	
(ii)	649·8g	20	
(iii)	2·262kg	50	
(iv)	3,135g	20	
(v)	1·476kg	10	

3. Calculate the weight for each of these amounts using the least number of **coins**.

(a) €5·90   (b) €3·60   (c) €2·70   (d) €8·40   (e) €11·30   (f) €17·80

Weight: _____ _____ _____ _____ _____ _____

4. Eoghan went shopping and spent the following amounts in each shop. He used a €20 note as payment in each shop. Calculate the weight of his **change** using the **least number** of coins.

Spent: (a) €18·20   (b) €17·40   (c) €15·50   (d) €17·90   (e) €16·30   (f) €15·70

Change: _____ _____ _____ _____ _____ _____

Weight: _____ _____ _____ _____ _____ _____

Maths Fact 900 grammes is the weight of the heaviest recorded African giant snail. It was 39·3cm long.

Challenge How many of these record snails would it take to weigh 7kg 200g? _____

Weight (and more)

The Ploughing Championships

1. Dad took students, Paul and Niamh, to the ploughing championships. What entry fee did he pay?

2. If he had booked online, he would have received a 10% discount.
   (a) What would he have paid? (b) How much was this discount worth in euro?

3. The cake stall has prepared 6 trays of oatmeal muffins. Each muffin weighs 136g. There are two dozen on each tray. What is the weight per tray in (a) g, and (b) kg?

4. If $1\frac{1}{4}$ trays were unsold, what weight of muffins was sold?

5. How much money was taken in by the stall-holder, if the muffins were sold for 69c each?

6. The average sheep fleece weighs 3·6kg. What would 24 fleeces weigh in grammes?

7. In a demonstration, the shearer can shear a sheep in 2 minutes. At this rate, what weight of sheep fleece was sheared in $1\frac{1}{2}$ hrs?

8. 2·592t was the weight of wool after a record 9 hour shearing session. If each fleece weighed 3·6kg, how many sheep were sheared?

9. A tractor hauled in 27 round bales of hay. If each bale weighed 360kg:
   (a) What was the total weight of hay hauled? (answer in tonnes)
   (b) What is the value of the 27 bales if each bale sells for €34·75?

10. The vintage tractor section has 11 John Deere 60s from 1955. Their total weight is 24·64t.
    (a) What is the average weight in kg of the tractors?
    (b) What would 29 full fuel tanks hold if each tank can hold 77·6lt?

Entrance:
Adult: €20
Student: €15

Maths Fact

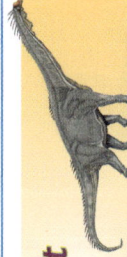

The Brachiosaurus dinosaur could eat about 180kg of plants daily. Luckily it was vegetarian!

Challenge

About how many tonnes of plants would have been eaten by the Brachiosaurus during June, July and August one year?

167

Chapter 32: 3-D shapes – Revision Quiz

How much do you remember about 3-D shapes? Circle each correct answer.

1. 3-D shapes …
- are flat.
- are solid.
- have 3 sides.

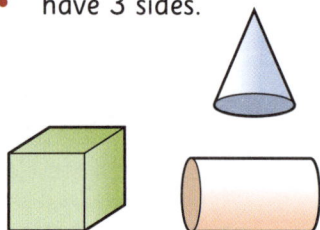

2. The dimensions of a 3-D shape are …
- length, height.
- length, faces, edges.
- length, width, height.

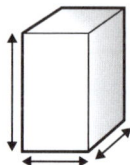

3. A corner of a 3-D shape is called a . . .
- tip.
- vertex.
- edge.

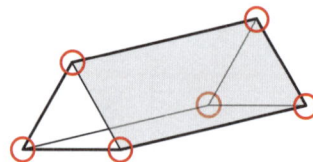

4. The face that a pyramid sits on is called its …
- base.
- seat.
- apex.

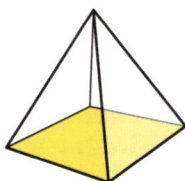

5. The vertex at the top of a pyramid is called its …
- base.
- apex.
- summit.

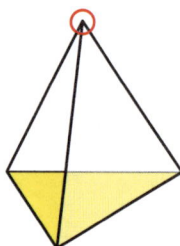

6. Pyramids are named after the …
- shape of their bases.
- person who discovered them.
- shape of their sides.

7. A triangular pyramid is also known as a …
- triangular prism.
- three-sided pyramid.
- tetrahedron.

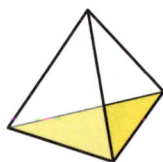

8. Which type of 3-D shape can always be cut into equal slices?
- pyramid
- polyhedron
- prism

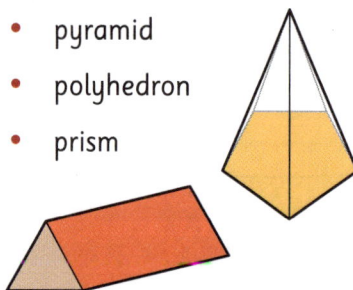

9. Which of the following is **not** a prism?

10. All 3-D shapes with flat faces and straight sides are known as …
- polyhedra.
- polygons.
- solids.

11. A sphere has a curved face, so it is **not** a …
- polyhedron.
- 3-D shape.
- solid.

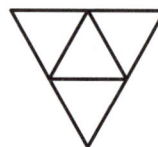

12. This is called a …
- shape skeleton.
- shape drawing.
- shape net.

STRAND Shape and space   **STRAND UNIT/ELEMENT** 3-D shapes
LANGUAGE 3-D, flat, solid, edges, sides, dimensions, length, width, height, vertex, pyramid, cube, cuboid, cylinder, sphere, triangular prism, pentagonal, hexagonal, octagonal, octahedron, dodecahedron, polyhedron, polyhedra, tetrahedron

3-D Shapes – polyhedra

A **polyhedron** is any 3-D shape with flat faces and straight edges.

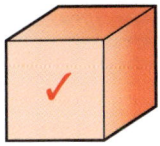

Prisms can be cut into identical slices. They have straight edges only.

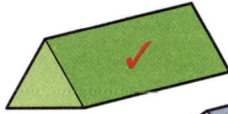

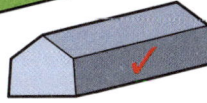

Pyramids are named after the 2-D shape of their bases.

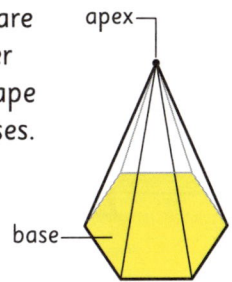

apex

base

1. Copy and complete this grid.

	Shape	Name	Number of ...			How many edges meet at each vertex?
			Faces	Edges	Vertices	
(a)						
(b)						3
(c)		pentagonal prism			10	
(d)						
(e)						
(f)	(i) → (ii) →					(i) _____ (ii) _____

2. Which **3-D shapes** can be made from the following shape **nets**?

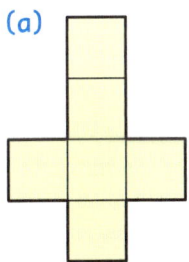

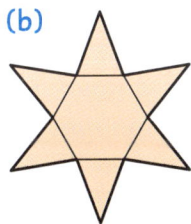

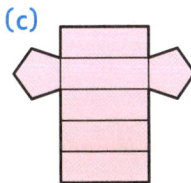

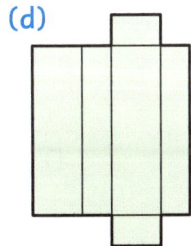

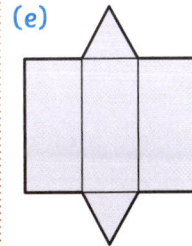

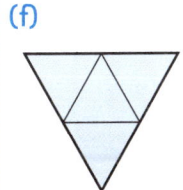

(a)   (b)   (c)   (d)   (e)   (f)

Challenge 1 A prism can be cut into equal slices. Is this cylinder a prism? ____ Explain!

Challenge 2 Name three 3-D shapes that are not polyhedra.

____ ____ ____

3-D shapes – Regular polyhedra

All faces of **regular polyhedra** are equal.

There are only 5 **regular polyhedra** in total.

1. Tetrahedron

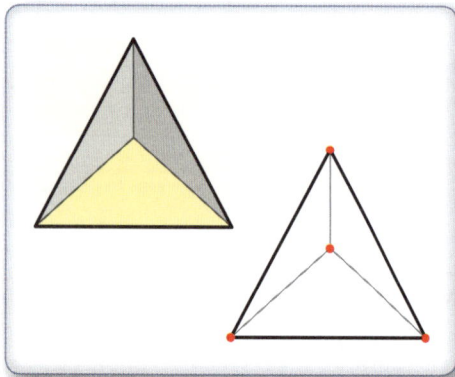

    (a) Also known as a tr_____ py_____.

    (b) Number of edges? _____

    (c) Number of faces? _____

    (d) What 2-D shape is each face? _____

    (e) Number of vertices? _____

2. Cube

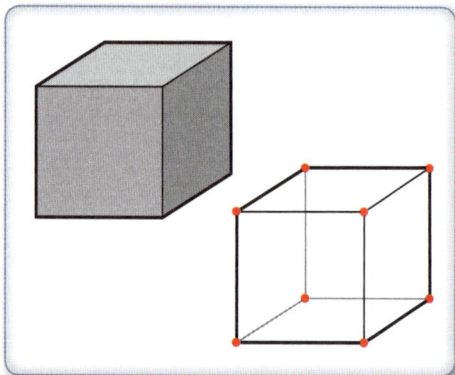

    (a) Number of edges? _____

    (b) Number of faces? _____

    (c) What 2-D shape is each face? _____

    (d) Number of vertices? _____

    (e) A cube is also a (pyramid / prism).

3. Octahedron

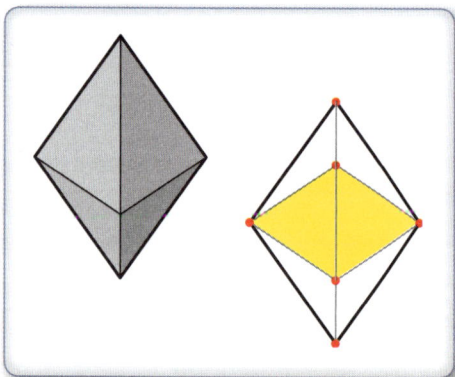

    (a) Number of edges? _____

    (b) Number of faces? _____

    (c) What 2-D shape is each face? _____

    (d) Number of vertices? _____

    (e) It is made by joining two sq_____ py_____ together, base to base.

Challenge   Here are the two remaining regular polyhedra.
Count the number of (i) faces, (ii) edges and (iii) vertices on each.

    (a) dodecahedron

    (b) icosahedron

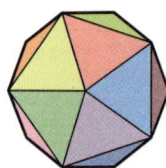

Only half of each shape is shown.

3-D shapes – Perspective

When we view a 3-D solid from different angles, we see a different 2-D shape or outline.

Front	Side	Top

1. Each of these images shows the **side** view. Circle the **2-D shadow** that shows the …

(a) front view.   (b) front view.   (c) top view.   (d) top view.

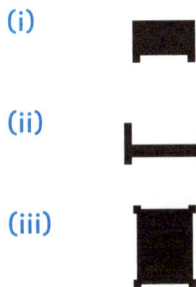      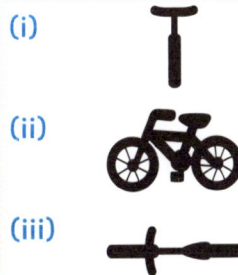   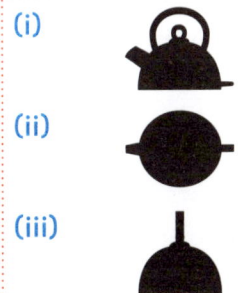

	(a)	(b)	(c)	(d)
(i)				
(ii)				
(iii)				

2. Each of these images shows the **front** view. Identify which view each of the following shadows shows: **front**, **side** and **top**.

(a)    (b)    (c) 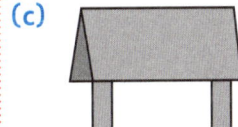   (d)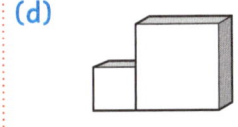

(i)   (ii)   (iii)   (i)   (ii)   (iii)   (i)   (ii)   (iii)   (i)   (ii)   (iii)

   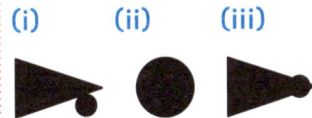   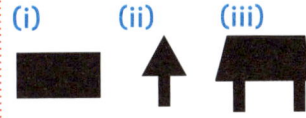   

3. What view of each 3-D shape does the 2-D shape show: **front**, **side** or **top**?

(a) 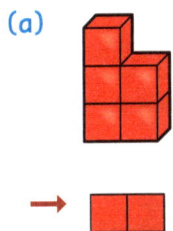   (b) 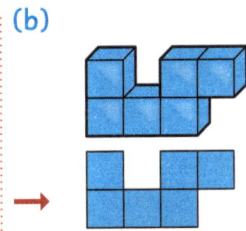   (c) 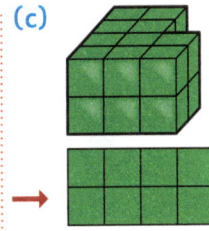   (d)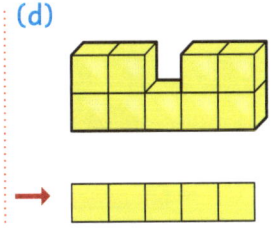

Challenge 1

Draw the **(i)** front, **(ii)** side and **(iii)** top view of each of these shapes: **(a)**   **(b)**

Challenge 2

Draw **(i)** front, **(ii)** side and **(iii)** top views of your:

(a) pencil case.
(b) chair.
(c) lunchbox.

Chapter 33: Capacity – Estimating capacity

Capacity is the amount of liquid a container holds.

A teaspoon holds about 5ml.

An average car fuel tank holds about 60l.

A standard milk carton holds 1l.

A domestic oil tank holds about 1,000l.

We measure capacity in millilitres (ml) and litres (l).

1. Circle your **best estimate** for the capacity of each of these. Discuss.

(a) Fabric conditioner

50ml   1l $4\frac{1}{2}$l

(b)

700ml   250ml   900ml

(c)

5l   50l   15l

(d) Shampoo

300ml   3,000ml   30ml

(e)

800l   20,000l   2,000l

(f)

30ml   2l   280ml

2. Write your **best estimate** for the capacity of each of these. Discuss.

(a) A gardener's watering can

(b) An egg cup

(c) An eye-dropper

_____

_____

_____

(d) A standard kitchen kettle

(e) An oil tanker

(f) A bottle of olive oil

_____

_____

_____

Maths Fact   A 30cm long dinosaur egg found in France had a capacity of 3 litres.

Challenge   Based on this Maths Fact, what would you expect the capacity of 100 of these dinosaur eggs to be?

STRAND Measures   **STRAND UNIT/ELEMENT** Capacity
LANGUAGE Capacity, liquid, containers, estimate, measure, litre (l), millilitre (ml), amounts, decimals, fractions, length, width, height, depth, volume, formula, calculate

Capacity

Remember: 1,000ml = 1l $2\frac{376}{1000}l = 2.376l$ $350ml = \frac{350}{1000}l = 0.35l$

1l = 1,000ml $70ml = \frac{70}{1000}l = 0.07l$ $3ml = \frac{3}{1000}l = 0.003l$

Rewrite the following **millilitres** as **litres** in (i) fraction form and (ii) decimal form.

1. (a) 450ml   (b) 2,452ml   (c) 600ml   (d) 1,782ml   (e) 95ml   (f) 395ml

   (g) 7ml   (h) 700ml   (i) 2,320ml   (j) 80ml   (k) 1,010ml   (l) 67ml

2. How many **millilitres** are there in each of the following?

   (a) $2\frac{1}{2}l$ (b) 0.763l   (c) 1.493l   (d) 0.92l   (e) $3\frac{1}{4}l$ (f) 4.065l

   (g) $5\frac{7}{10}l$ (h) 0.008l   (i) 0.307l   (j) 2.007l   (k) 0.08l   (l) $5\frac{3}{8}l$

   (m) $\frac{2}{5}l$ (n) 6.105l   (o) 2.2l   (p) $1\frac{1}{8}l$ (q) 0.1l   (r) $3\frac{3}{4}l$

3. A horticulturalist in a garden centre feeds her plants in **millilitres** from a 5-litre container. How many **millilitres** does each plant from (a)–(j) get?

   (a) $\frac{1}{2}l =$ _____ ml   (b) $\frac{1}{5}l =$ _____ ml   (c) $\frac{1}{4}l =$ _____ ml   (d) $\frac{1}{10}l =$ _____ ml   (e) $\frac{1}{8}l =$ _____ ml

   (f) $\frac{3}{5}l =$ _____ ml   (g) $\frac{7}{10}l =$ _____ ml   (h) $\frac{5}{8}l =$ _____ ml   (i) $\frac{3}{4}l =$ _____ ml   (j) $\frac{7}{8}l =$ _____ ml

4. The school caretaker must divide a 3.5l bottle of concentrated bleach equally among 7 spray trigger-bottles.

   (a) What fraction of a litre goes into each spray trigger-bottle? _____

   (b) How many **ml** is this? _____

   (c) If he had 10 spray trigger-bottles, how many **ml** of bleach would he put in each? _____

   (d) How many **ml** would have been left over if he had put 450**ml** into each of the 7 spray trigger-bottles? _____

5. *Start* dishwasher rinse aid is sold in bottles, each containing 400ml.

   (a) *Start* rinse aid comes packed in cartons of 12 bottles. In litres, what is the total amount of liquid contained in:

   (i) one carton _____ l?   (ii) six cartons _____ l?   (iii) 15 cartons _____ l?

   (b) What is the value of the cartons in each of the answers in question (a) if a 400ml bottle of *Start rinse aid* sells for €2.79?

   (i) € _____   (ii) € _____   (iii) € _____

   (c) A restaurant used 6.4l of *Start rinse aid* during one month.

   (i) How many of these bottles did the restaurant use? _____

   (ii) How much did it cost the restaurant to buy these bottles? € _____

Maths Fact The hagfish has a unique defence mechanism. It excretes up to 8 litres of slime to clog up the gills of its predators each time it is attacked.

Challenge How many predators did the hagfish fend off, if it excreted 2,976 litres of slime?

Capacity

1. Rewrite these amounts as **millilitres**.

   (a) 3l 628ml   (b) 5l 300ml   (c) 7l 54ml   (d) 6l 150ml   (e) 2l 40ml   (f) 1l 9ml

   (g) $6\frac{3}{10}$ l   (h) $6\frac{3}{20}$ l   (i) $2\frac{9}{20}$ l   (j) $3\frac{72}{1000}$ l   (k) $4\frac{39}{100}$ l   (l) $5\frac{7}{100}$ l

Addition	Subtraction	Multiplication	Division
3·548 l + 2·694 l ——— 6·242 l	7·075 l − 2·698 l ——— 4·377 l	4·739 l × 14 ——— 18 956 47 390 ——— 66·346 l	0·134l 23)3·082l 23 —— 78 69 —— 92 92 —— 0

2. Complete these operations by first rewriting as **litres** using the **decimal point**.

   (a) $5\frac{2}{5}$ l − 2l 638ml

   (b) 4l 44ml + 3,576ml

   (c) 3l 87ml × 7

   (d) $9\frac{17}{20}$ l − 6,886ml

   (e) 6l 60ml + 5l 550ml

   (f) 5l 326ml × 49

   (g) 0·7 × 8l 350ml

   (h) $7\frac{7}{20}$ l − $5\frac{83}{100}$ l

   (i) 5l 236ml ÷ 14

   (j) $3\frac{546}{1000}$ l + $5\frac{86}{100}$ l

   (k) 42l 336ml ÷ 27

   (l) 46l ÷ 16

3. Rewrite these capacities as litres and (i) add the **smallest** to the **largest** and (ii) subtract the **middle** capacity from the **largest**.

   (a) 7,257ml, $7\frac{3}{8}$ l, $7\frac{65}{100}$ l

   (i) _____ (ii) _____

   (b) $9\frac{5}{8}$ l, 9,720ml, 9l 689ml

   (i) _____ (ii) _____

   (c) 8l, 80ml, $8\frac{8}{1000}$ l

   (i) _____ (ii) _____

   (d) $4\frac{11}{20}$ l, 4,498ml, $4\frac{53}{100}$ l

   (i) _____ (ii) _____

4. Fuel was rationed during winter. An oil truck had 9,996 litres on board.
   The driver delivered an equal amount to each of the 28 homes he visited.

   (a) How many litres did each home receive? _____ l

   (b) How much did each have to pay, if fuel was charged at 92c per litre? €_____

5. A $2\frac{1}{2}$ l bottle of orange juice contains 35% pure fruit juice.
   How many millilitres of pure juice is this? _____ ml

6. Ann's mug holds 0·456l. She also has a tablespoon that holds 19ml.
   How many tablespoonfuls would it take to fill the mug? _____

Challenge 1   A car travelled from 10:30 to 13:50 at an average speed of 90km/h.

   (a) How far did the car travel? _____ km

   (b) What was the cost of diesel fuel for the journey if diesel cost
   €1·40 per litre and the car travelled 50km on each litre of diesel? € _____

Challenge 2   A domestic heating oil tank had 1,652l of oil. A household used an
   average of 28l of oil per day. For how many days did the oil last? _____

Capacity – Volume

The amount of space taken up by a solid shape is called its **volume**.
We make use of **cubes** to measure volume.
To measure a cube we multiply: **length × width × height**.
We write it like this: **cm³** (cm cubed): 1cm × 1cm × 1cm = **1cm³**.

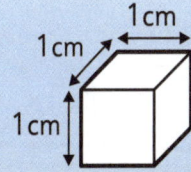

The volume of a centimetre cube is 1cm³.

1. **There are two ways to calculate the volume of each shape.**
   (i) Count the number of cubes.   (ii) Multiply l × w × h.

   Write the answer to each shape in **cm³** and complete the grid.
   Note: each cube represents 1cm³, but these shapes are not exact measurements.

shape	total cubes	l × w × h = cm³
(a)		
(b)		
(c)		
(d)		

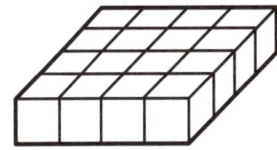

(a) _____

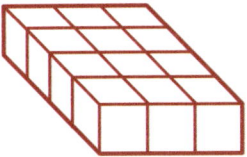

(b) _____

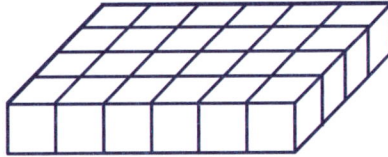

(c) _____

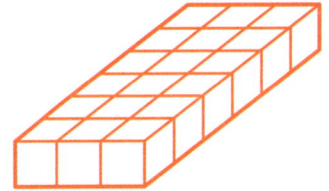

(d) _____

2. **The volume of this cuboid is 24cm³.**

   (a) How do we calculate this? Discuss with a partner.

   (b) Now find the volume of this cuboid.

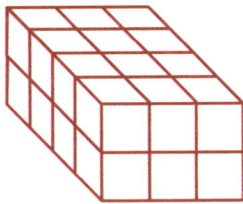

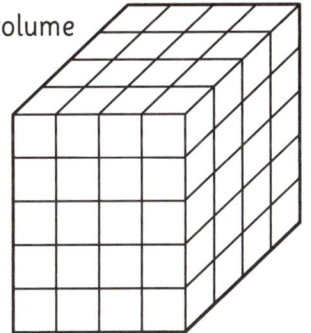

_____ cm³

3. **Use your findings to calculate the volume of these shapes in cm³.**

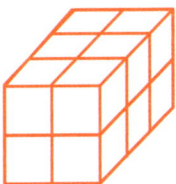

(a) _____

(b) _____

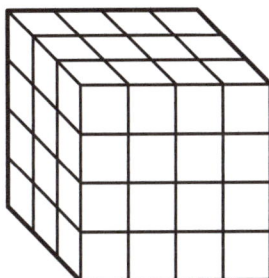

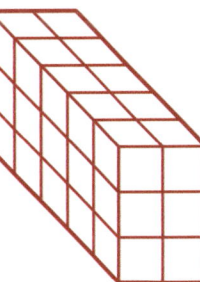

(c) _____

(d) _____

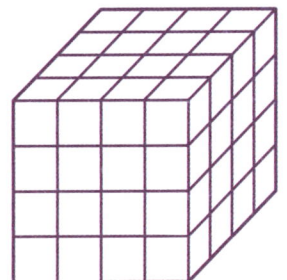

Capacity – Volume

We measure larger volumes and capacities using **cubic metres (m³)**.

length	×	**w**idth	×	**h**eight	=	volume
5m	×	4m	×	3m	=	60m³

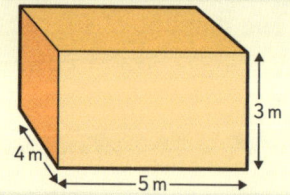

1. Use the formula to calculate the number of **cubic metres (m³)** needed to fill your classroom. Round the length, width and height to the nearest metre.

   Volume of classroom ➜ **l** _____ m × **w** _____ m × **h** _____ m = _____ m³

2. Use these models to calculate the **volume** of each in m³.

   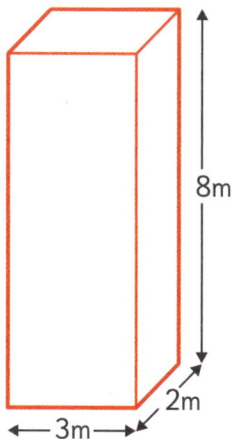

   (a) _____

   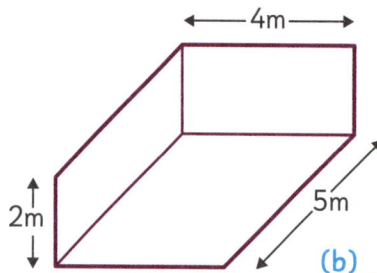

   (b) _____

   > Cuboids of different shapes may have the same volume.

   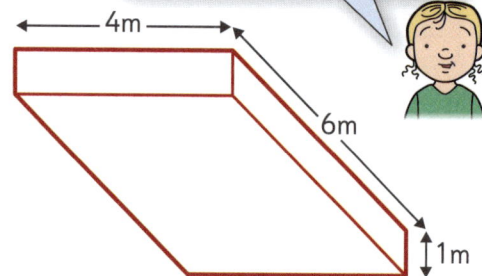

   (c) _____

3. Concrete is usually delivered in m³. How much concrete is required to fill each of these cavities?

   (a)
l	w	h	Volume
7m	5m	2m	= _____

   (b)
l	w	h	Volume
4m	4m	3m	= _____

   (c)
l	w	h	Volume
6m	3m	4m	= _____

   (d)
l	w	h	Volume
6m	$3\frac{1}{2}$m	12m	= _____

   (e)
l	w	h	Volume
7·2m	4·5m	5m	= _____

   (f)
l	w	h	Volume
$8\frac{7}{10}$m	6m	3m	= _____

4. An aquarium has ordered a new tank to display its range of tropical fish. It will be 5·4m long, have a width of 2·6m and be 1·5m tall.

   (a) What will be the volume of this tank in cubic metres (m³)?

   (b) One day it was only $\frac{1}{2}$ full of water. What volume of water was that?

   (c) How many cubic metres of water would be needed to fill 16 such aquariums?

5. A school was planning to build a new P.E. hall. It will be 96m long, 48m wide and have a height of 16m.

   (a) What will be the volume of this hall in m³? _____ m³

   (b) If the dimensions of the hall were reduced by 25%, what would be the volume then? _____ m³

Maths Fact   1 cubic metre (m³) of water has the same volume as 1,000*l* of water.

Challenge   How many cubic metres of water would equal 17,000*l* of water? [____]

Capacity

Organic Shopping

1. Ann buys 3l of milk, 250ml of cream, and an 8 × 100ml pack of yoghurts.
   (a) What quantity of foodstuffs did she buy in litres? _____
   (b) How much did it cost her? _____

2. Pat bought $1\frac{1}{2}$l of orange juice. Mark bought three 500ml cartons of orange juice.
   (a) How much did each pay per litre? _____
   (b) Who got the better value? _____

3. Tom and Charlie both bought $3\frac{1}{2}$l of orange juice, but Tom bought only 350ml bottles while Charlie bought only 500ml bottles.
   (a) How many bottles did each buy? Tom: _____ Charlie: _____
   (b) How much did each pay for their $3\frac{1}{2}$l of orange juice? Tom: _____ Charlie: _____

4. On Saturday the store sold 19 bottles of goat's milk.
   (a) How many litres of goat's milk were sold? _____
   (b) What was the value of this sale? € _____

5. The store received a delivery of 12l of each size of apple juice drinks.
   (a) How many cartons of each did the store receive? 400ml: _____ 800ml: _____
   (b) What was the total sale value of these drinks, if all of them were sold? _____

6. Smoothies are sold in two sizes. What is the cost per litre for each? (a) _____ (b) _____

7. Gráinne bought one of the **largest** carton sizes of cranberry juice, orange & mango juice and cream.
   (a) How many litres altogether did she buy? _____ (b) How much did she pay? _____

8. Barry bought one of the **smallest** carton sizes of cranberry juice, apple juice and orange juice.
   (a) How many litres altogether did he buy? _____ (b) How much did he pay? _____

9. Lara and Emma each made 15l of organic yoghurt. (a) Lara fills only 300ml pots while Emma fills only 600ml pots. How many pots will each fill? (a) _____ (b) _____

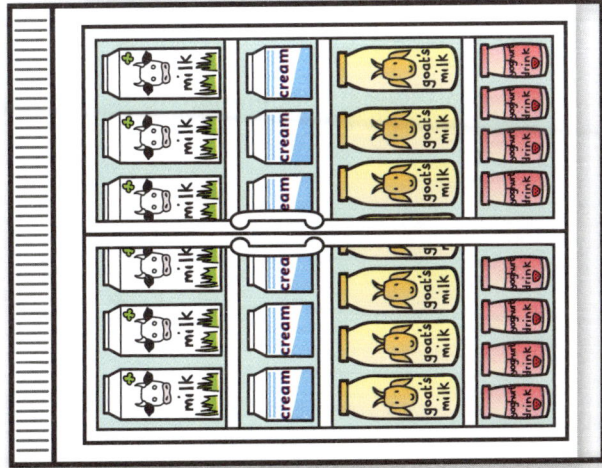

Price

Milk
1l = €1·30
2l = €2·45/3l = €3·60

Cream
250ml = €1·80
500ml = €3·40
750ml = €5·10

Goat's milk
850ml = €2·35

Yoghurt drinks
300ml = €2·40
700ml = €5·50
(8 × 100ml) = €4·70

Price

Orange juice
350ml = €1·70
500ml = €2·60
$1\frac{1}{2}$l = €5·85

Apple juice
400ml = €1·95
800ml = €3·65

Cranberry juice
300ml = €0·75
600ml = €1·35

Orange & mango
275ml = €2·60
550ml = €5·10

Smoothies
200ml = €2·55
(4 × 200ml) = €4·20

Chapter 34: Chance – The language of chance

impossible	possible	certain

1. Use one of the above words to predict the **chance** of the following happening.

   (a) The principal will come into the classroom today. _____

   (b) Your friend will have a birthday next month. _____

   (c) Your friend will have a birthday next year. _____

   (d) There will be no advertisements on television tonight. _____

   (e) The moon and sun will swap positions. _____

   (f) The grass on the football pitch will grow a blue colour. _____

   (g) A giraffe will teach in this school next year. _____

   (h) The traffic light will turn green after red. _____

Even chance

When there are two possible outcomes and both are **equally** likely to happen, this is called an **even chance** or a 50/50 chance.

Ariana has an even chance of picking the green cube.

2. Which of the following has an **even chance** of happening?

   (a)

   When I turn this playing card over it is a red card.

   (b)

   I will choose a green cube.

   (c)

   Liam will catch the ball.

   (d)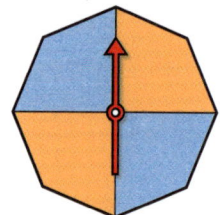

   The arrow will stop on orange.

---

impossible	possible	certain	even chance

3. Use one of the above words to predict the **chance** of the following happening.

   (a) We will win our next camogie match. _____

   (b) It will rain next week. _____

   (c) Barcelona will be renamed Madrid. _____

   (d) The next baby born in Ireland will be a girl. _____

   (e) The River Lee will continue to flow through Cork City. _____

   (f) If I throw a die, I will throw an even number. _____

STRAND Data **STRAND UNIT/ELEMENT** Chance

LANGUAGE Even chance, impossible, possible, certain, probability, possible outcomes, fractions, decimals, percentages

Chance – Probability

What is the chance of tossing a 'tail'?

- There are two possible outcomes – 'heads' or 'tails'.
- Both outcomes have an equal or even chance.
- There is a **one in two chance**.
  → 1:2 or $\frac{1}{2}$ or 50/50

What is the chance of throwing a 3?

- There are six possible outcomes
  1 2 3 4 5 or 6.
- All outcomes have an equal chance.
- There is a **one in six chance**.
  → 1:6 or $\frac{1}{6}$

1. If you throw a regular 6-sided die, what is the **chance** of:

(a) throwing a 2? ____ : ____ or ▢/▢

(b) throwing a 5? ____ : ____ or ▢/▢

(c) throwing a 4? ____ : ____ or ▢/▢

(d) throwing a 0? ____ : ____ or ▢/▢

(e) throwing an odd number? ____ : ____ or ▢/▢

(f) throwing a 9? ____ : ____ or ▢/▢

(g) throwing a multiple of 3? ____ : ____ or ▢/▢

(h) throwing a multiple of 2? ____ : ____ or ▢/▢

We measure the chance of something happening by using **probability**. We can place events on a probability line to illustrate this.

| impossible | even chance | certain |

As we move from left to right on this line, there is a greater likelihood of an event happening.

2. Place the following statements on the appropriate part of the **probability lines**.

(a) The sun will set tonight.

impossible   even chance   certain

(b) Fuel prices will rise next year.

impossible   even chance   certain

(c) A crocodile will escape from the zoo.

impossible   even chance   certain

(d) School will close for a week in February.

impossible   even chance   certain

(e) It will snow in Donegal in December.

impossible   even chance   certain

(f) I will win a race against my friend.

impossible   even chance   certain

Chance

1. Aaron's uncle has promised to do **one** special activity with him next Saturday. He has suggested the following activities from which Aaron must choose. Aaron's uncle placed the activity names in a box. Aaron then had to choose an activity from the box while blindfolded.

| swimming | bowling | tennis | archery | football |

(a) There is a _____ in _____ chance they will go swimming.

(b) Write the probability of them going swimming as a fraction. $\frac{\square}{\square}$

(c) What is the probability of one of their activities involving a ball? _____ in _____

(d) Write this probability as a fraction. $\frac{\square}{\square}$

(e) Imagine you were given the same five choices. Copy the following probability line into your copybook and place the activities on it in order, according to your preference.

uninterested   **interested**

2. Six friends were arguing over how to spend their Saturday afternoon. They decided to each write their preference on a card. The cards were then placed in a jar. They all agreed that they would take part in the first activity to be chosen **at random** from the jar!

(a) The chance of them going to the shopping centre is _____ in _____ .

(b) Write this probability as a fraction. $\frac{\square}{\square}$

(c) There is a _____ in _____ chance that the friends will go to the cinema.

(d) Express this probability as a fraction. $\frac{\square}{\square}$

(e) What is the probability that all these activities will be free of charge? _____ in _____

(f) What is the probability that they will **not** go to the cinema? _____ in _____

(g) What is the probability that they will go ice-skating? _____ in _____

3. Write the probability of picking a yellow cube from the following jars while blindfolded.

(a)   (b)   (c)   (d)

_____ : _____ or $\frac{\square}{\square}$ _____ : _____ or $\frac{\square}{\square}$ _____ : _____ or $\frac{\square}{\square}$ _____ : _____ or $\frac{\square}{\square}$

Chance

Here is a good experiment with which to explore probability with a partner.

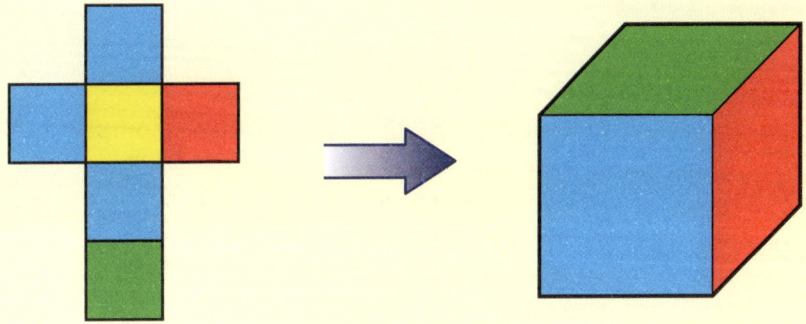

Step 1: Make a die.

(i) Cut out a cube net.

(ii) Colour:
- 3 sides blue
- 1 side red
- 1 side yellow
- 1 side green

Step 2:

(i) Throw the die 12 times.

(ii) Use a tally to record which colour is facing up after each throw.

(iii) Express each final result as a fraction of the number of throws.

(iv) Repeat the experiment 2 more times. Record the results on these separate result charts.

> To make it interesting, use coloured unifix cubes to predict the outcome before conducting each experiment.

Experiment 1				
Tally				
Fraction				

Experiment 2				
Tally				
Fraction				

Experiment 3				
Tally				
Fraction				

Step 3: Record your results on these pie charts which are already divided into twelfths.

Experiment 1	Experiment 2	Experiment 3

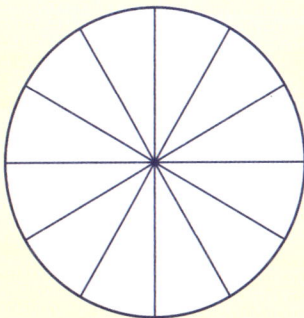
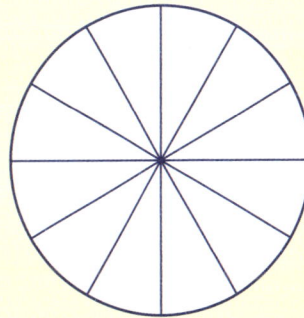
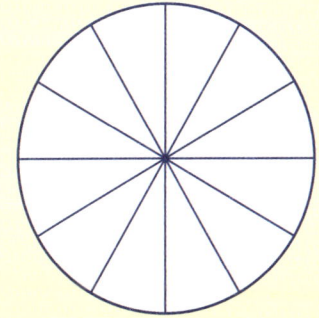

Think and discuss.
- Did all three experiments give the same results?
- Were your predictions close or accurate?
- Can we rely on chance always going in our favour?

Chance – Using fractions, decimals and percentages

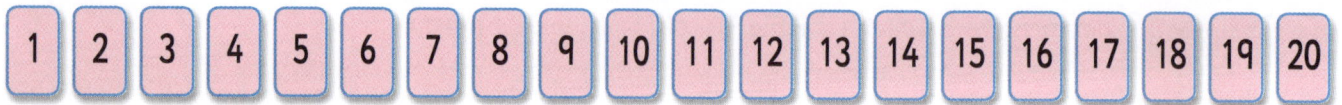

| 1 | 2 | 3 | 4 | 5 | 6 | 7 | 8 | 9 | 10 | 11 | 12 | 13 | 14 | 15 | 16 | 17 | 18 | 19 | 20 |

1. These digit cards (1–20) are placed in a box.
   You are asked to pick a card while blindfolded. Complete the grid.

What are the chances of picking:	Chance	Fraction	Decimal	Percentage
The digit card 6?	1 in 20	$\frac{1}{20}$	0·05	5%
The digit card 15?	☐ in ☐			
An even number?	☐ in ☐			
An odd number?	☐ in ☐			
A digit that is a multiple of 5?	☐ in ☐			
A digit that is a multiple of 6?	☐ in ☐			
A digit that is a multiple of 7?	☐ in ☐			
A digit that is a multiple of 2?	☐ in ☐			
A digit that is a multiple of 9?	☐ in ☐			
Digit cards 7, 9, or 13?	☐ in ☐			
Digit cards 6, 10, 14, or 17?	☐ in ☐			
Digit cards 19 or a multiple of 4?	☐ in ☐			

2. These coloured marbles are placed into a bag. You are asked to pick a marble while blindfolded. Complete the grid.

What are the chances of picking:	Chance	Fraction	Decimal	Percentage
A **green** marble?	5 in 25	$\frac{1}{5}$	0·2	20%
A **red** marble?	☐ in ☐			
A **black** marble?	☐ in ☐			
A **blue** marble?	☐ in ☐			
A **yellow** marble?	☐ in ☐			
A **pink** marble?	☐ in ☐			
A **blue** or **red** marble?	☐ in ☐			
A **pink** or **green** marble?	☐ in ☐			
A **yellow** or black marble?	☐ in ☐			

A quick look back 9

1. Write the name for this part of a circle.

   _____

2. 3·14 × 6 = _____

3. If the diameter of a circle is 10cm. What is the **approximate** length of its circumference?

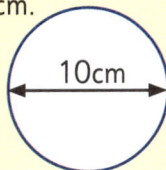

   10cm

   _____

4. Write the missing operation sign.

   (8 ◯ 3) – 2 × 9 = 6

   Remember the BOMDAS rule.

5. Write the answer to complete this equation. (Remember the BOMDAS rule.)

   (23 – 7) + 9 × 4 ÷ 6 = _____

6. 45°

   This pie chart represents 120 bananas. The coloured section represents the number of green ones. How many green bananas are there?

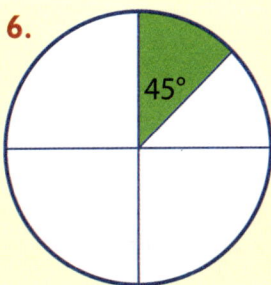

   _____

7. What fraction of this pie chart is coloured?

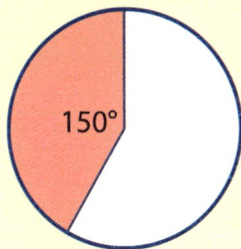

   150°

   ▢/▢

8. How many grammes are there in 2·65kg?

   _____ g

9. How many kilogrammes are there in $\frac{3}{4}$ of a tonne?

   _____ kg

10. There were $6\frac{1}{4}$ tonnes of grain in a conical-shaped storage unit. How many kg was that?

    _____ kg

11. Hay costs €40·50 per bale. How much should 8 bales cost? € _____

12. Write the name of this shape.

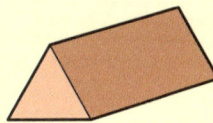

    _____
    _____

13. How many vertices has a cuboid?

    _____

14. How many millilitres of water are there in a litre bottle if it is only $\frac{3}{4}$ full?

    _____ ml

15. Write $5\frac{38}{1000}$ litres as litres in decimal form.

    _____ l

16. A container of liquid plant food holds 4·5l. How many times can amounts of 50ml be poured from the container?

    _____

17. A square is drawn around a circle of diameter 6cm. What is the **approximate** area of the circle?

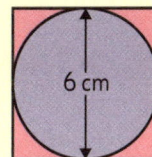

    6 cm

    _____ cm²

18. In a table quiz, one member said he was 75% sure his answer was correct. Write his chance of being correct as a ratio.

    ___ : ___

19. One golfer had a score of ⁺7 on a golf course. Her partner had a ⁻4 score (4 under par). By how many shots was one score better than the other?

    _____

20. If I throw a 6-sided die, what are the chances of me throwing an even number?

    _____ in _____

Maths trail –

Walt Disney World!

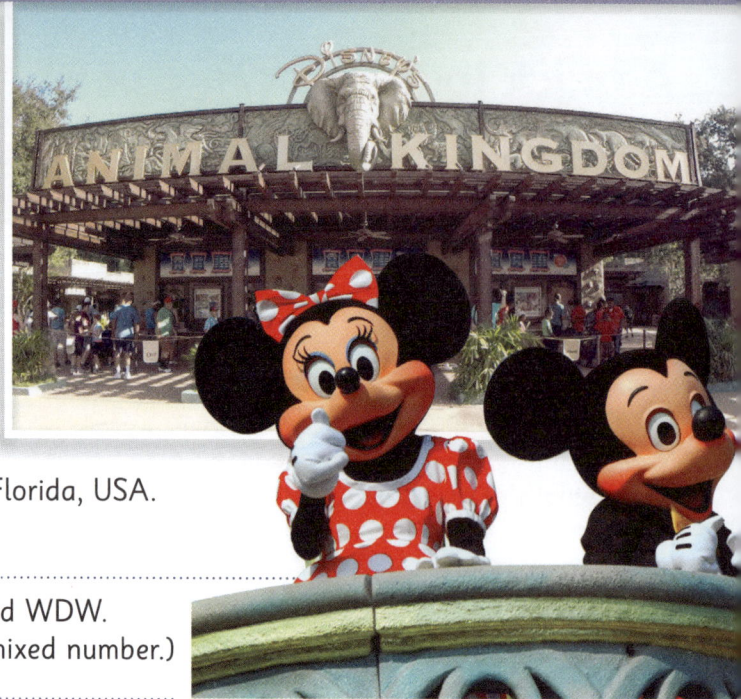

1. Walt Disney World (WDW) opened in 1971, in Florida, USA. How many years have passed since then?

2. 52 months of construction time was need to build WDW. How many years was this? (Write answer as a mixed number.)

3. Originally the park occupied about 12,350 hectares. The Animal Kingdom occupies about 200 hectares. About how many Animal Kingdoms could be made in the whole park? (round to the nearest 10).

4. In 1971, WDW employed about 5,500 'cast members'. Today it employs more than 60,000. Write the ratio of 1971 employees to today's number as a (i) fraction, (ii) decimal and (iii) percentage (2 decimal places).

5. On opening day, 7 tickets for the rollercoaster cost $4·75.

   (a) How much would it have cost a family of 6 to buy 7 tickets for each member. $ _____

   (b) It cost $ _____ for a group of 14 to buy 11 tickets for each person.

6. Mickey Mouse has a total of 175 different outfits. Minnie Mouse has 200 different outfits.

   (a) Express Mickey Mouse's number as a (i) fraction, (ii) decimal and (iii) percentage of Minnie's outfits.

   (b) If 20% of Mickey's outfits and 26% of Minnie's were in the laundry, how many would each have left to choose from?

7. During Christmas, 8 million lights are used in total on the 1,600 trees in WDW.

   (a) What is the average number of lights on a tree?

   (b) How many lights would be needed for (i) 95 trees and (ii) 99 trees?

8. The 30th anniversary of the opening of WDW was celebrated in 2001. In what year will WDW celebrate its (i) 60th anniversary and (ii) 75th anniversary?

9. 13,000 roses decorate WDW and many varieties are used. If $\frac{1}{5}$ of them are red, $37\frac{1}{2}$% are pink and 0·19 are white:

   (a) How many of each of these colours are there?

   (b) What percentage of the roses are none of these colours?

10. There is a total of 7,242km of beach line in the Seven Seas Lagoon and Bay Lake. How many metres is this?

11. One day, 0·15 of the beach line was closed for refurbishment. How many km were still available to patrons?

12. 263 buses service WDW. Each bus can take an average of 35 passengers. How many passengers can all of the buses take when full?

13. Ten of the twelve trains are stored in the maintenance shop. Two trains are parked outside the gates of Magic Kingdom each night.

   (a) What (i) fraction (ii) decimal and (iii) percentage of them are outside?

   (b) What (i) fraction (ii) decimal and (iii) percentage of them are in the maintenance shop?

14. 210 adults can be seated on the trams. 5 can sit in each row.

   (a) How many rows are there in a tram?

   (b) On one journey only 21 rows were full. What (i) fraction, (ii) decimal (iii) and percentage of the tram was full?

15. A water slide called Blizzard Beach's Summit Plummet is 110 metres long and travels at speeds of up to 100km/h. At 80 km/h, a person travels 22m per second. How long would it take to complete the slide at an average speed of 80km/h?

16. Disney's Animal Kingdom lodge has 1,307 rooms. If each room costs $89 per night (room rate) and all the rooms are booked, how many dollars would the hotel earn (on room bookings) in (i) a night? (ii) a week?

17. It takes 20 mins to fill Splash Mountain and 5 mins to drain it. It was filled and drained 8 times one day.

   (a) How long altogether did this take in minutes?

   (b) Express the length of time it takes to drain as a ratio of the filling time.

   It was filled and drained 27 times on another day.

   (c) How long did this take altogether in minutes?

   (d) Express the time it took to drain in hours and minutes.

18. An Irish family spent $8,500 on a trip to WDW. How much was this in euro if the exchange rate was €1 = $1·25?

A quick look back 10

1. By how much is 2,538,796 greater than 2,138,796?

   _____

2. A prize of €200 was shared among 3 winners in the ratio 4:9:7. What was the value of the smallest share?

   € _____

3. What is the average of 20, 50, 70 and 40?

   _____

4. What is the value of 20 × 4 × 6? _____

5. How many degrees are there in $\frac{3}{4}$ of a full turn?

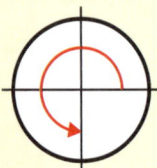

   _____

6. Arrange these fractions in order of size starting with the smallest.

   $\frac{1}{8}, \frac{1}{9}, \frac{1}{12}, \frac{1}{11}$ _____

7. What is the size in degrees of the 3rd angle?

   _____ degrees

   55°   65°

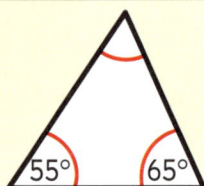

8. $2\frac{1}{6} + 3\frac{5}{12} = \square \dfrac{\square}{\square}$

9. $7\frac{5}{6} - 4\frac{2}{3} = \square \dfrac{\square}{\square}$

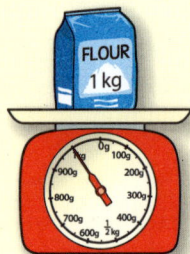

10. Frank needs $\frac{2}{5}$ of a kg of flour to make some scones. How many grammes of flour should he pour on to the kitchen scales?

    FLOUR 1 kg

    _____ g

11. Round 13·674 to the nearest tenth.

    _____

12. What is the value of 12^2. _____

13. Rewrite $6\frac{49}{1000}$ l as millilitres.

    _____ ml

14.
    ←— 12 cm —→

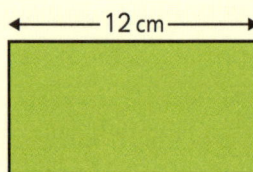

    A rectangle has an area of 108cm². If one of its sides measures 12cm, what is the length of its perimeter?

    _____

15. The perimeter of a square is 44cm. What is the area of the square?

    _____

16. Sydney's time is 10 hours ahead of London's. When it is 4pm on Monday in Sydney, what time is it in London (in digital form)?

    [__ : __]

17. Increase €320 by $37\frac{1}{2}$%. € _____

18. Janice borrowed €4,000 to buy a car. She was charged 8% interest for a year. How much interest did she pay for the year?

    € _____

19. A selling price of €120 represents a loss of 20% on a coat. What was the cost price?

    € _____

20. A man was born in 1973 AD. In what year will he be 89-years-old?

    _____